# ORGANIZATIONS AND CLIENTS
*Essays in the Sociology of Service*

# The Merrill Sociology Series

*Under the General Editorship of*

## Richard L. Simpson

*University of North Carolina*
*Chapel Hill*

# ORGANIZATIONS AND CLIENTS

*Essays in the Sociology of Service*

edited by

## WILLIAM R. ROSENGREN

*University of Rhode Island*

## MARK LEFTON

*Case Western Reserve University*

with essays by

**Charles E. Bidwell**

**Eliot Freidson**

**Mark Lefton**

**Eugene Litwak**

**Jack Rothman**

**Norton E. Long**

**Talcott Parsons**

**Charles Perrow**

**William R. Rosengren**

Charles E. Merrill Publishing Company

*A Bell & Howell Company*

Columbus, Ohio

International Standard Book Number
  0–675–09313–9   Clothbound
  0–675–09314–7   Paperbound

Library of Congress Catalog Card Number   72–122308

1 2 3 4 5 6 7 8—75 74 73 72 71 70

Printed in the United States of America

# INTRODUCTION

THE CHAPTERS IN THIS BOOK DEAL WITH CLIENT MEMBERSHIP IN ORGAN-
izations. The aim of these introductory remarks is to indicate in broad
outline how this matter is addressed in the following chapters.

Professor Parsons begins by pointing out that the concept of membership relates directly to the joint issues of the division of labor on the one
hand and problems of solidarity on the other. His analysis proceeds from
the perspective of an economic model, in terms of which the primary distinction between staff members and clients has to do with those whose
primary responsibility is to produce services and those who are to consume those services. The economic analog is only partial, however, inas-
much as the consumer in service organizations has to take a more or less
active part in the production of the very services he will ultimately be expected to consume. From a perspective such as this, membership status
may be bestowed upon persons because the organization regards them as
possessing some input vital to the organization. And the less willing the
person is to surrender his critical input, the more full the membership
offered to him is likely to be. This peculiarity of service organizations, as
Parsons explicates, leads to a series of tensions and strains within and
across the client-staff sectors, one element of which involves how much
of the whole man shall enter into the membership role.

In the second chapter, Mark Lefton addresses the membership question directly at the point of first contact between the in-coming client and
the receiving organization. Here we see the beginning of a determination
concerning what the client's membership status shall be initially. And it

is also at this point that the client—by design or not—attempts to carry into the organization more or less of his self than the organization is prepared to accept. In this connection, a central dilemma faced by organizations is the fact that while usually they neither want, nor can control, the whole person, in-coming members do arrive at organizations as whole persons, often with identities and motives quite contrary to the functions of the organization. This means that the organization offers to the client *new* identities and *new* motives, while attempting to extinguish the old ones. The success with which the desired new clienthood is imprinted may be a rough measure of what Freidson calls the dominance of the organization and its professional cadre.

The two chapters which follow—the first by Charles E. Bidwell and the second by Eliot Freidson—deal with two organizational spheres which, while different, have similar membership problems. The first discusses the element of trust in the relationship between students and schools; the second sets forth a new conception of professionalization by emphasizing the drift toward dominance in the relation of professionals to clients and its profound impact when it occurs in bureaucracies.

Bidwell points out that schools are peculiar in that students do not normally pay for the services rendered to them. They enter schools in batches and move through in cohorts; and they are there involuntarily. These oddities are reflected in the difficulties schools encounter in establishing and sustaining attitudes of trust on the part of the pupils, a problem complicated by the fact that schools engage in both moral and technical socialization. Partially as a result of this, the student is both consumer and neophyte, and the teacher is at once the provider of a service and a role model. The whole student may be taken into school, but *only* insofar as while acquiring full membership he exhibits the proper evidence of his growing trust in the organization as personified by the teacher.

An additional force in the relation between clients and organization is highlighted by Freidson, and this has to do with the tendency of persons to maximize control over the conditions of their work. Using the medical profession as the archetype, Freidson points to the paradox that large organizations run by professionals seem to be more rigid, controlling, and generally more bureaucratic than others are. The reason seems to be that handling patients in any other way would reduce the doctor's control over his work. The corrolary would also hold then: as membership is bestowed upon the client, the worker's control over his work condition would be weakened. As a result, the concept of trust seems somewhat less relevant to professional *organizations,* at least in the sense that it is so critical in places such as schools. This of course does not mean that in organizations such as hospitals solidarity is not an issue. An additional way of putting the matter is that workers with technical expertise attend to some specific aspect of the client; a disease in the case of medicine. This aspect's entanglement with a living person may appear to be little more than an awkward encumberance to be dealt with through strategies of professional dominance.

Perrow moves away from organizations in which there is a more or less clear-cut distinction between producer and consumers. He focuses on voluntary organizations where the division of labor is more complex because organizational values are produced and consumed by the same people. Hence, the organizational officialdom is its own client and its own resource.

Perrow contends that these organizations tend to mobilize more resources than are expended for the avowed purposes of the organization; thus surpluses accumulate which can be turned to other purposes. These "derived goals" have the character of residual power and, as Perrow argues, "power is always contested for." One result of this competition for free-floating power is the constant confrontation between democracy and oligarchy in voluntary organizations. Since members carry resources to and from organizations, they also carry resources among and between many different organizations. This chapter, therefore, serves as a link to the second theme of this book—organizations as partial members of *other* organizations.

In the next chapter Rosengren maintains that organizations follow distinctive careers over time, which importantly influence the kinds of contacts which are likely to develop *between* organizations, as well as the manner in which clients are handled. The argument is that organizations tend to begin their careers with a broad scope but short term interest in clients. As they are, they tend to drift towards a specific but long term interest in the persons served. Organizations seem to be propelled through such a career line by both internal and external forces, including the search for a clientele and a patronage, and for membership in existing organizational sets. The success with which the last is acheived can be taken as a crude measure of potential interorganizational membership.

The chapter by Litwak addresses this question in depth by exploring the division of labor among welfare organizations at the local community level. A key point in this paper—and analogous to the earlier discussion of the problematic nature of membership and solidarity—is that an organization must maintain distance from other organizations, while at the same time engaging in coordinate activities—sometimes cooperative and sometimes competetive. An important distinction made is between "sequential" and "homogenous" coordination. In the first, high interdependence may exist in the absence of interorganizational awareness of that fact. In the second—wherein multiple organizations perform similar functions—awareness of similarity may actually impede the development of working interdependence. Hence, just like persons, organizations may be "members" of other organizations without ever knowing it.

Norton Long's chapter begins with the assumption that there are parallels between the way in which classically conceived laissez-faire economic systems are supposed to operate, and the way in which social and political organizations are thought to function. Long finds it paradoxical that even though it is widely acknowledged that laissez-faire economics seldom produced socially desirable allocations of wealth, we stubbornly refuse to intervene in the "natural" relations between service-producing organizations so as to render a more just distribution of services to clients.

Finally, the last chapter by Rosengren represents an attempt to draw together some of the points made in the preceding chapters by framing the relations between clients and organizations in an economic language. Here, the two parties to solidarity—client and organization—are regarded as economies engaged in the exchange of values with one another. The fact that the exchange relationship is often asymmetrical is testimony to the great power organizations—and the division of labor—have over clients, even where full membership is held by the consumer.

But however all this might be, full membership must always remain partial and illusory, and complete solidarity must always be something of a will-o-the-wisp, if only for the reason that while man *creates* divisions of labor and concepts of solidarity, these creations are not *man*.

For in speaking of the separateness of man from social organization, Clark Moustakas has written:

> . . . loneliness is a condition of human life, an experience of being human which enables the individual to sustain, extend, and deepen his humanity. Man is ultimately and forever lonely whether his loneliness is the exquisite pain of the individual living in isolation or illness, the sense of absence caused by a loved one's death, or the piercing joy experienced in triumphant creation . . . man is alone, terribly, utterly alone.

The chapters in this book fix attention on this matter.

# ACKNOWLEDGEMENTS

WE THANK FIRST THE CONTRIBUTING AUTHORS WHOSE CHAPTERS WERE originally developed for presentation at a symposium on "Clients and Organizations," held at the University of Rhode Island in June 1968. All worked assiduously on their papers for many months before and after the symposium.

Also, we gratefully acknowledge the Division of Community Health Services of the U.S. Public Health Service for its part in helping to defray the costs of the symposium in Kingston. Many of the ideas set down in the chapters by the editors were developed out of Grant No. CH-00289 from the Division of Community Health Services. Thanks are due also to the Departments of Sociology at the University of Rhode Island and at Case Western Reserve University for their support.

Warm gratitude is extended to Robert V. Gardner of the University of Rhode Island, and to Harold W. Pfautz and Basil G. Zimmer of Brown University for their willing and skillful service as chairmen at the meetings.

The rumored disadvantages of "editing" a book of newly authored chapters are legend. These tales need not be re-told here because in the present case they are purely fictional. Quite the contrary, there was a distinct advantage in editing this book that ought to be mentioned. The editors of such a book are freed from the customary constraint that inhibits the single author from saying anything good about the book he alone has written. Having thus freed ourselves from any charges of self-aggrandizement, we can now say that we believe the contributing authors

*Acknowledgement*

have produced a set of papers that is valuable in both a conceptual and practical sense. It *does* address an issue of contemporary importance, and its individual parts illuminate aspects of relations between clients and organizations in ways which retain the special idiom, problem focii, and theoretical persuasions of their authors.

If the book is under-edited, it is because its contributed parts were written so well separately. We know it was not over-edited, and if that should prove a defect it is our fault. The quality of our own contributions are of course our own responsibility.

Therefore, we thank again our contributors; this book is quite truly a collaborative effort.

**Mark Lefton**
**William R. Rosengren**

# CONTENTS

# ORGANIZATIONS AND CLIENTS
*Essays in the Sociology of Service*

# I HOW ARE CLIENTS INTEGRATED IN SERVICE ORGANIZATIONS?

*Talcott Parsons*

## INTRODUCTION

THE PURPOSE OF THIS CHAPTER IS TO INTRODUCE AN ANALYTICAL FRAME of reference for integrating the very rich contributions of the substantive chapters which follow. I shall also attempt a few very tentative critical generalizations.

Though there is a good deal of concern with both intra- and inter-organizational problems throughout this symposium, particularly in Chapter 7, it seems fair to say that the main stress is on the organization-client relationship. We can therefore start with the commonplace observation that such a relationship comes to be problematic through extensions of the division of labor—I use division of labor not only in the narrow sense of a strictly economic differentiation, but also in the sense of so-called political pluralism and Durkheim's conception of organic solidarity. It can be said in this context that the type of organization which Mr. Perrow attempts to delineate under the heading of the voluntary association is a limiting type if his principal criterion is accepted, namely that the members of the association are overwhelmingly the consumers of its output. However, in such typical examples as the producing firm, the professional organization, various kinds of service groups and the like, the case is quite other than this.

# THE ECONOMIC MARKET MODEL AND THE CONCEPT OF CLIENT MEMBERSHIP

Seen in terms of the history of thought, the prototypical model of the division of labor seems to be that of the economic market, with the analytical distinction between the producing and consuming units and the nexus of relations among them. To my mind, one of the major merits of this symposium is Mr. Long's attempt to use a special modification of this paradigm in a specifically constructive way. I feel that there has been too much of a hiatus between the interests of economists and sociologists in this respect, and an attempt to link those interests the way Mr. Long does is most welcome. Economists, it is perhaps fair to say, have at least until relatively recently been somewhat obsessed with pure competition as an idea, and Mr. Long gives an excellent demonstration of the possible merits of deliberately planned deviations from the competitive model.

In another direction, there has been a tendency to use the economic market as a kind of ideal type for the conditions under which services other than the purveying of commodities in the economic sense are involved. An old prototype of this, of course, is the professional-client relationship in a sense of what may be called the individual "fee-for-service" relationship. Mr. Bidwell takes this as his point of departure and tends to feel that any considerable modification of this pattern in a collectivistic direction raises serious functional problems. Having worked with this model for a considerable period, I am inclined to be skeptical of Bidwell's point of view in a rather general way. I started [1] with the conception of the market for professional services (specifically the medical case) in this fee-for-service context and attempted to introduce, on the basis of special characteristics of the service, a series of modifications of the typical commercial market structure, notably the sliding scale and the objection to "shopping around." Only very gradually did it dawn on me that a theoretically more fruitful approach, one capable of greatly simplified generalization, would be to treat the agency providing service and the recipients of service as fellow members of a collectivity.[2] As Bidwell cogently points out, the school, and secondarily

---

[1] See my *Social System* (New York, The Free Press, 1951), Chapter X.
Sociology" in Talcott Parsons, *Social Structure and Personality* (New York, The
[2] See my paper "Some Theoretical Considerations Bearing on the Field of Medical Sociology" in Talcott Parsons, *Social Structure and Personality* (New York, The Free Press, 1964), Chapter 12, especially pp. 337ff. As discussed in this paper, the individual practice relation may be a limiting case of the collectivity conception.

the hospital, are type cases of the inclusion of the client in the organization providing the service. Theoretically speaking, this shift of position is fully in accord with the Durkheimian tradition, and this point may serve as a transition to a consideration of solidarity as a major theme which pervades the symposium as a whole.

If I am correct that Bidwell is at least somewhat biased in stressing the "normality" of the individual professional practice relationship, then this seems to me to hold certain important implications. One is that, if in a sense common collectivity membership is a keynote for defining the professional-client relationship, then where a plurality of clients is involved, it creates a presumption that some kind of more or less formal membership in the service organization is at least a serious possibility.[3] Secondly, however, common collectivity membership, formalized or not, *strongly* suggests reciprocal relationships. These, of course, are generally highly asymmetrical, but it is important to search explicitly for all the principal components in both directions in the interchange. There are certain egalitarian strains in associational collectivities which in some ways can mitigate the asymmetry.

This stands in some contrast to the ideal type of the market-consumer role which is generally treated as almost wholly "one-way"; that is, a product is offered on the market and the consumer either takes it or leaves it, or at most bargains over terms. At this ideal type level, anything resembling membership is of course meaningless.[4] There are,

---

[3] Bidwell is, it seems to me, wrong in stressing that a physican—in private practice—deals with "one" patient. There is a kind of isolation of each patient from the others, but having many patients is surely a defining characteristic of being "in practice." The physician must, of course, balance his obligation to his various patients. This is of course different from the teacher of a class, where all the pupils in the class meet together with him (or her), but it is also very different from a monogamous marriage where a husband, in the nature of the case, has only one wife (at a time).

[4] A conforming case should be called to attention, namely what we may now call "broadcasting" of information and symbolic content. I should very definitely include publishing in this category. The criterion is parallel to the market, that the producer does not have specific bonds to particular consumers of the output. Neither the author nor the publisher of a book knows specifically into whose hands it may come and what kind of reaction may be expected from it. Of course, the development of recent mass media, especially radio and television, have vastly extended the range of this kind of relationship.

An interesting modification is the case of "official journals" of disciplinary and other associations. Sometimes subscriptions to these are given *ipso facto* with membership, but even if this is not the case, one must "buy" a package of articles, book reviews, and so on. One cannot say, "I would like John Jones's article, but I very definitely don't want the others which appear in the same issue." There is, however, sometimes the same order of option to accept or reject the output.

however, relatively established "clienteles" of old customers who can expect special treatment, and hence occupy a *kind* of membership status. An important recent development concerns durable goods which require servicing and hence lead to the establishment of relatively continuing relationships between producer and consumer.

Whatever the case may be with borderline situations, when we deal with membership categories we need a typology of, first, the kinds of collectivities involved, second, the basis of the solidarity of the collectivities, and third, the components of outputs received by members from their participation as well as of inputs or contributions they make to the collectivity.

## TYPOLOGY OF RELEVANT DIMENSIONS: KINDS OF ORGANIZATIONS, COMPETENCE, AND AUTHORITY

The aspects of organizations mentioned in the title of this section will be discussed with reference to the contributions contained in this volume. First let me note that the concept of client membership brings all "service" organizations to which it applies close to Mr. Perrow's principal criterion of the voluntary association, or at least to one of its boundaries. The main respect in which it does not hold, of course, is that resources and control are inputs often not provided by the clients— thus certainly children neither pay for nor control the public schools they attend, though there are some possibilities for this on part of their parents. This circumstance makes me skeptical of the adequacy of the internal consumption criterion in general.

Some of the difficulties in this field arise from the facts of plural collectivity membership, one of the most salient features of a highly differentiated modern society. From the point of view of the participants, many of the voluntary associations Perrow deals with are highly "segmental" even though in some cases, like the American Medical Association, this status is closely related to the occupational roles of members. The same is true of many service orgnizations. Thus, being a patient, or the client of a lawyer is in most cases far from being a full time job, though in the case of a severe acute illness it can be even more than that for a time. Hence, the client's inputs from and outputs to the membership role must be intricately balanced with his other roles, and may not loom very large.

It is at this point that the problem of scope of membership and intensity of involvement arises. It is one aspect of this problem which Mr. Lefton and Mr. Rosengren call "laterality." Scope in this sense, however, is a matter not only of a given cross sectional moment, but also of duration. One of the most critical cases of limited duration is that of student or pupil, since one more or less automatically graduates from such a status by the mere fact of filling out a stated period of participation. Similarly, most illnesses are of limited duration, and of course the problem of care of the chronically ill is very different from that of the acutely and temporarily ill. Even prisoners are generally "in" for limited terms.

One of the principal sources of asymmetry, then, lies in the fact that most of the purveyors of service are performing full-time occupational roles. In some sense they are committed in principle to careers in these roles, hence their participation is of long duration, and at any given time the role is a primary focus of interest and obligation. This is compounded by the fact that each agent of service deals with many recipients, as described by "teaching load," "case load," etc.

As Mr. Freidson particularly emphasizes, the service organization is itself internally stratified. A school's function centers on the teachers and the principal but there are also secretaries and janitors. In the much more complex case of the hospital there is the "dominant" corps of physicians, but also nurses, orderlies, technicians, maids, janitors, etc.

The gap between client-member status and that of staff, and the related but not identical gap between the status of "subordinate" personnel and the "higher" echelons, both rest on special competence and administrative authority. These two primary functions, with respect to which superiority (and hence inequality) is institutionalized, are in part exercised by the same person. The teacher not only instructs, but is also responsible for classroom discipline, which is partly an exercise of authority. In more macroscopic terms, however, these two functions tend to differentiate out at the level of roles, of suborganizations, and of types of organization, though always with some interpenetration.

For a great many sociological purposes it is highly important to distinguish these two factors—competence and authority—in superiority. Very broadly one can say that superior competence tends to be institutionalized in the associational direction whereas administrative authority leads in the bureaucratic-hierarchical direction. Mr. Freidson, however, makes an important contribution in showing that, in the medical case and the organizational setting of the large hospital, a "dominant profession," as he calls it, may generate alienative attitudes which bear a striking resemblance to those commonly associated with large, impersonal bureaucracies. Freidson, however, is not very clear in specifying the conditions under which these consequences of a dominant profession materialize. It seems to me that much further research is needed to establish these conditions. Yet, staying on the more general level, I may suggest that these alienative influences operate particularly on the client role, due to restricted active participation by the client, as well as organizational shortcomings of overloading, understaffing, and the like. There must, however, be immense differences in the "morale" of the clientele of different organizations, both in the same general category, such as hospitals, and in different categories as well.

A certain caution does, however, need to be observed in attributing these phenomena to organizational shortcomings as Freidson tends to do—though he of course recognizes the society-wide status of the medical profession. I will illustrate with a case on which I have been working. The spokesmen of student protest, which in some respects is touched upon by Bidwell, often use very similar features of the university as a target of attack, e.g., impersonality, bureaucracy, authoritarianism and the like. It may indeed be argued that the academic profession, organized as it is in faculties similar in ways to medical staffs in hospitals, is a "dominant profession" in Freidson's sense and hence subject to similar social pathologies.

A colleague and I, however, have argued that there is more to it than that.[5] Specifically, I may mention two other factors. The first is the enormous recent and current expansion of the system of higher education, with the consequence both of great increase of scale and of drawing in large elements of the age cohort who, even one short generation ago, would not have gone to college, and whose parents for the most part in fact did not.

Secondly, we have presented evidence that the college phase, which we treat as *post* adolescent and call "studentry," involves a process of socialization which in some ways is analogous to the oedipal phase in the family. Here the relevant point is that, just as there is no family sufficiently "good" altogether to eliminate emotional disturbance in the oedipal phases for its children, so it is unreasonable to expect a college

---

[5] Cf. Talcott Parsons and Gerald M. Platt, "Considerations on the American Academic System," *Minerva*, Vol. VI, No. 4 (1968), pp. 497–523.

or university not to generate *any* disturbance on the part of its students. It is a technical and difficult matter to disentangle the factors of organizational deficiency on the one hand, and on the other of disturbance attendant on its effective functioning. Perhaps the greatest paradigm of this problem is the process of psychotherapy, especially in its intensive psychoanalytic version, where negative transference is routinely to be expected. This factor, plus the "growing pains" engendered by very rapid expansion, may account for a good deal, though of course by no means everything.

As compared to Mr. Perrow's ideal type voluntary association, the implementation of the functions of professional levels of expertise tends to occur in a context of associational organization which I like to call "collegial." In some respects the academic faculty and academic department are type cases. The basic difference from a standard voluntary association, of course, lies in the fact that the client's type of membership role cannot presume to be equal in terms of professional competence to the professional role. In addition to this there is naturally some concentration of authority clearly centering on the "nonclient" parts of the organization.

## THE BASIS OF SOLIDARITY OF COLLECTIVITIES AND THE ROLE INFLUENCE

If the kinds of alienation which Freidson and several other contributors to this book imply, notably Rosengren in his concluding chapter, are to be minimized—granting that they probably cannot be eliminated altogether—there must be solidarity which extends *across* these lines of inequality, as is the case with the generation difference within the family. Where such solidarity does and can exist, it must be created and sustained by some kind of interchange of inputs and outputs between the professional and the client components of the organization. There is, of course, the obvious factor of self-interest in the sense parallel to the classical analysis of market exchange—the patient has an interest in recovery, the student in acquiring knowledge, etc., and in a somewhat different sense physicians have self interest in curing patients, teachers in effectively imparting knowledge to their students.

Though clearly this rational self interest factor is not enough, its importance should not be overlooked, as Mr. Long's paper emphasizes in particular. But if it *were* adequate, there would be no *raison d'etre* for this volume. A good approach to generalizing one particularly vital class of other components is through Mr. Bidwell's stress on the problem of trust which I will follow even though I disagree a good deal with his views. Trust should be seen as a necessary input to the solidarity system by the client. The question then turns to the conditions which motivate adequate trust to in turn accept risks and burdens, including especially the superiority involved in the competence and authority of the professional and organizational elements.

The more complex the system, the genesis of trust operates in the sense of structural differentiation, through the mechanism I have been calling *influence,* in a technical sense,[6] as a generalized medium of societal interchange. The code component of an influence system I call *prestige.* Influence and prestige are here analytically to be sharply distinguished from power and authority. They are parts of a system of persuasion, not of binding decision-making backed by coercive sanctions.

The state of a collective system which tends to maximize the amount of influence in "circulation" is *solidarity* in Durkheim's sense. We may think of trust as the member unit's primary contribution to the solidarity of the system, seen vis-a-vis other member units, whereas "loyalty" may be thought of as the member unit's trust in the collective system as a whole. Influence, grounded in prestige, is exchangeable for both the "consumers'" outputs of the system and for factors necessary for the generation of its solidarity.

The groundwork of such solidarity lies in the institutionalization of a relevant set of "rights," essentially in the sense of "civil" rights which, as specifications of the more general value system, should ideally be recognized as legitimate by all participants. These specifications relate to the function or functions of the system in the larger society, e.g., promotion of the health of patients for a hospital, or the education of the oncoming generation for a school or college. Then, a therapeutic system requires a component more competent than the general public in health care, and an educational system requires a component especially competent in the transmission of knowledge, values, etc.[7] Client membership is grounded in rights to the primary output of the system;

---

[6] Talcott Parsons, "On the Concept of Influence," *Public Opinion Quarterly,* 17 (1963), pp. 37–62. For comments and rejoinder on this paper, see same issue, pp. 63–92. See also Talcott Parsons, "Social Stratification Revisited," *Sociological Inquiry,* Special Issue on Stratification, E. Laumann (ed.), forthcoming.

[7] Cf. Robert Dreeben, *On What Is Learned in School* (Reading, Mass., Addison Wesley, 1968).

"staff" membership is grounded in functional contributions to bringing about that output.

Influence in this sense I conceive to be an integrative mechanism. It operates, when successful, to integrate on the one hand the "interests" of the various and differentiated member units, but also to integrate the collective system which is constituted by their participation. The persuasiveness of influence is, from this point of view, grounded in a capacity to *justify* recommended courses of action, not only to the "objects" of such recommendations, but to all member units which are interested, as being both in the interest of the unit and that of the collectivity. The basis of justification is probable contribution to the implementation of one or more of the rights which in turn justify client membership. The other main context of justification is that of securing and combining the factors necessary to produce the relevant output.

Here we encounter what is often a source of confusion: a double functional reference. Most functionally specialized organizations are agencies for the production of outputs *other* than the enhancement of their own solidarity, e.g., the education of children. At the same time, they have the problem of maintaining their own solidarity. The latter may necessitate a different set of factors than the former,[8] though the solidarity of the producing agency is of course *one* of the factors in its effectiveness. Our concern here is with the factors of solidarity, not of effective agency function.

As contrasted with the ideal type of commercial market, the significance of client membership lies in the possibility and/or necessity of client contribution to the solidarity of the service system. So far, we mentioned trust and a sense of loyalty, or "obligation," as tentative designations of such contributions. Trust in this context we may consider as the readiness to *be* influenced or persuaded. It is particularly important that trust in this sense, like influence, should be *generalized*. This is a principal basis on which I differ from Bidwell about the superior virtues he attributes to "individual" practice. If the basis of trust really is limited to the individual practitioner whom the client "knows," then the basis of integration of wider systems is severely limited. My suggestion is that the development of the influence medium counteracts the particularistic limitations of trust which Bidwell so strongly emphasizes.

---

[8] An especially interesting paper in this respect is Edward Gross, "Universities as Organizations: A Research Approach," *American Sociological Review*, Vol. 33, No. 4 (1968), pp. 518–544.

# ANALYSIS OF INPUT-OUTPUT DIMENSIONS

What, then, are the "ingredients" of trust and trustworthiness? They can, I think, be succinctly stated in four categories. The first is value-commitment to the relevant sector of the rights complex, e.g., health or education. The second is commitment to the appropriate forms of association, i.e., the collective organization which can be expected, to the best of its ability, to implement these rights.[9] This is the basis of a claim to loyalty, which should be reciprocated by trust. Here it should be remembered that not merely the authenticity of the commitments of both sorts is at stake, but also the pull of competing loyalties in other settings to which all persons in such situations are subject. Thus, physicians may be subject to such pulls from research interests which compete with their obligations to patients. Or a mother may neglect her own health because it is difficult to reconcile the demands of hospital or clinic with her loyalty to her children.

The third category is commitment to collective performance. Commitments to actual and effective participation in a sense "validate" claims to loyalty. Similarly, trust is a function of the extent to which the organization can be expected to "deliver" in the sense of making binding operative decisions which contribute to the solution of real problems. Where, as so generally, the client does not have the power to control such decisions himself, the focus of trust must be in the level of responsibility of the organization to carry them out. Since, typically, the client is relatively low on power, this means the superordinated components of the organization must act in a *leadership* capacity to ensure this. The focus of trust then must be in the genuine responsibility of this leadership.

Finally, collective performance and unit contributions to it require claims to mobile resources and justifications of those claims. The time and attention of the professional component is of course crucial, but so is the willingness of the client to do his part. A deficit with respect to this late category of input on the part of the client may of course be motivated by mistrust, while unconscious processes may also operate so that he is unaware of his noncooperation.[10]

---

[9] Cf. Talcott Parsons, "The Academic System: A Sociologist's View," *The Public Interest,* No. 13 (1968), pp. 173–197.

[10] A striking case of this is the situation lying back of the statement to me by the head of a hospital pediatric service that in his opinion fully half of their therapeutic failures were attributable to patients—including of course parents—failing to

It can be seen that two of these four ingredients are of a "moral" or value commitment character. The value component, that is, enters at two different levels. The first of these defines the function through a general commitment to the implementation of basic rights in the social system. The second level then specifies the commitment to the level of the concrete organization, what I have called "valued association." Even though one has a right to adequate medical care it can be implemented in general only through concrete agencies. Similarly, with education a young person must attend a particular school or college. These concrete agencies must then, as noted, deliver the "goods" through making and implementing decisions, and they must command the necessary resources, at the level of money funds, personnel, equipment and the like, including —as noted—in all four of these categories the inputs from clients as well as service personnel.

These factors, of course, have to be balanced in the actions of all the significant units in the system. The influence mechanism is, with respect to solidarity as distinguished from efficiency, the principal regulator of this balancing through justifying to participants in the organization, and often to elements in the outside social environment, the many plans and acts which are continually being generated or are occurring.

Here a particularly crucial aspect of the use of influence is the assumption of what I have called leadership responsibility. This is the point at which the inequalities inherent in professional competence on the one hand, concentration of organizational authority on the other, come to focus. A particularly important aspect of trust is involved here.

One primary axis of the problem of trust concerns what is sometimes called "accountability." This is the question of the grounds for confidence that a trust will not be betrayed. Obviously a very important part of the problem of enhancing the need of trust is the element of risk and uncertainty in so many human activities, so that failures will often occur for which the agents of the function cannot reasonably be held responsible. Trustworthiness, in this sense, has been held to be guaranteed by three kinds of mechanisms which cannot be adequate here. These are first, the "discipline of the market" by which, it is said, untrustworthy sellers will

---

carry out instructions properly, rather than lack of adequate technical therapeutic resources. With regard to the allocation of resources, there are vast differences even within a profession, with differing justifying claims. See the investigation of Ronald L. Akers and Richard Quinney, "Differential Organization of Health Professions: A Comparative Analysis," *American Sociological Review*, Vol. 33, No. 1 (1968), pp. 104–121.

lose out to their competitors; second, the accountability of the elected official, governmental or private, to his constituents with the punishment of electoral defeat for betrayal of trust; third, the administrative enforcement of directly imposing penalties for non-compliance.

By contrast to all of these, the responsibility of leadership in the present must be *fiduciary*. It must rest on a sharing of values and the expectation that superior competence and authority will be used to implement those values within the limits of organizational and personal capacity. In this critically important sector of society there is no substitute for this trust in the fiduciary integrity of leadership since all the devices for ensuring accountability without involving it are altogether inappropriate, or fall short of filling the gaps of competence and organizational authority.

In a highly differentiated solidarity system all of the units are interdependent with each other, with respect to all the elements of input and output. Thus the door is open to vicious circle types of disturbance where, for example, mistrust on the part of clients directly generates deficits of important outputs in the functioning of the professional elements and, of course, vice-versa.[11] These disturbances are of a general character comparable to those of inflation and deflation of economic systems. Such instabilities, which of course vary enormously in character and intensity, suggest in systems of the type we are concerned with the presence of pervasive modes of structured tension.

## SOURCES OF TENSION IN THE CONTEXT OF SOLIDARITY

### Persuasion and Voluntarism

In the light of the previous analysis, I should like to discuss briefly three dilemmas which figure prominently in several of the chapters of the symposium.

---

[11] This process is a case of Merton's concept of self-fulfilling prophecy, in which the role of trust is obvious. Cf. Robert Merton, *Social Theory and Social Structure* (New York, The Free Press, 1957), pp. 421–436. On the interaction level, the role of trust in this context is nicely illustrated by N. Cameron, "The Paranoid Pseudo-Community," *American Journal of Sociology*, Vol. 49 (1941), pp. 32–38.

First, solidarity being so highly dependent on the influence mechanism and this being a generalized medium of persuasion, it is almost obvious that there should be a strong presumption in favor of the voluntary principle. This is particularly true because, with the development of modern society, there has been so much weakening of the older ascriptive solidarities that, over a very wide area, there is an alternative between voluntariness and some kind of compulsion—as Bidwell emphasizes for the case of public education. The voluntary principle is of course very widely institutionalized with respect to employment, however serious realistic limitations to freedom of choice of job may be. Our main concern here is with the relevance of voluntariness to the client membership role.

Among the factors of trust, the bearing of the voluntary principle is especially strong in securing commitments to particular associations and the associated claims to loyalty. This principle operates, however, at many levels, being perhaps most feasible at the point of assuming the membership role. Bidwell points out that in many service organizations the client cannot be given *throughout* the free choice of particular personnel—e.g., one's "own" chosen physician in a large clinic. Moreover, sometimes particular organizations are so overwhelmingly convenient that alternatives are not very realistic, and sometimes disproportionately costly. Finally, once in the membership role there are many limitations on the feasibility of giving "voluntary informed consent" to every procedure to which the client is subject, at every step.[12] The most important generalization perhaps is that limitations on voluntariness create a need for other factors of trust such as reputation for high quality service, and confidence in the fiduciary responsibility of the leadership elements. This problem is clearly a source of tension. One consequence is that limitations on voluntariness constitute a convenient target for displacement of disaffection factors which may originate in other contexts.

---

[12] Bidwell repeats many times a phrasing which seems to me pejorative, namely with respect to the pupil or student "submitting" to the authority of the teacher or school. By and large the professional-client relationship is, though as I have emphasized, unequal, not *mainly* one of dominance-submission.

On two other points, as a member of the Harvard University faculty, there are many advantages, including financial, for me to utilize the University Health Service, but of course I am free to seek other agencies of medical care. So long as the indicated one has a reputation for high quality, one is inclined to trust it and thus choose it.

## The Scope of Involvement

The second focus of tension is over the scope of involvement of the client in his role in the organization. In my own theoretical jargon, I have called this the pattern-variable of "specificity-diffuseness." I find especially interesting, in this connection, Mr. Rosengren's discussion of the tendency for organizations to start out with more diffuse scope and to move over time toward greater specificity. One may conclude that diffuseness of scope is a source of organizational tensions which can be mitigated by a narrowing of scope. On the other hand, too much narrowing of scope may generate other tensions. Thus, much of the complaint about the modern organization in such terms as impersonality seems to relate to feelings that scope is unduly narrow.

In some respects it is easier for responsible leadership groups to justify their roles within a narrow scope—e.g., for physicians to define their expertise in health matters relatively strictly. A very important problem area here which pervades the whole world of professional function is that of the importance of privacy and its protection.[13] On the one side, a person's privacy concerns his "interests" in areas of his life other than the particular relations of interaction of reference. Claims to his loyalty can be more easily justified if it can be made clear that his membership will not jeopardize such other interests. This consideration combines with the basing of the claims of leadership on competence, which is a function of degrees of specialization. The other side concerns the positive importance of the "laterality" which Mr. Lefton discusses so illuminatingly, with special reference to hospital patients. A particularly important and complicated case is that of the student role, which in some aspects goes especially far in encompassing, while it lasts, the "whole man." Even through high school the typical pupil-student lives at home with his family. Colleges, however, have tended to become increasingly residential so that not only his studies but most of the "private life" of the student is part of the academic community. There are strong pressures to make this complex *as a whole* "meaningful" and yet to do so in ways in which the administration and the faculty respect the privacy of students, and yet somehow facilitate a "full" life for them and not a narrowly academic one. This seems to be one of the primary sources of tension in the academic world, and it is clear from several of the chapters in this book that

---

A particularly interesting context in which the problem of voluntariness has figured prominently in recent years is that of experimentation with human subjects, e.g., in medical research. Cf. Talcott Parsons, "Research with Human Subjects and the Professional Complex," *Daedalus*, Spring 1969, pp. 325–357.

[13] See my paper on research with human subjects, referenced in footnote 10.

it is one which is greatly generalized. It may also be remarked that the Perrow criterion of internal consumption of outputs is relevant roughly in proportion as the laterality scope of the organization is wide for the typical participant. The further question here is how far the client role is merged with that of the "service" component as compared to how far they remain distinct.

## Types of Orientation

This point leads directly to the third dilemma of tension which is particularly emphasized by Mr. Rosengren in his final chapter. He speaks of the importance of a "humane" orientation of organizations. Although this may not be all that he has in mind, I should like to try to relate it to the contrast I have worked with between "instrumental" and "expressive" orientations. This seems to resemble the specificity-diffuseness axis, but it is different. A prison is, in Goffman's terms, a prototype of a "total" institution, but it is surely not primarily expressive in function.

It seems to be in the nature of the division of labor that "service" organizations should make a clear distinction between the providers and the recipients of service. This "fact of life" was the primary point of departure of my paper, and permeates the entire book. This means that every such organization is justified by providing something which is valuable, but not provided for in the otherwise life-circumstances of the beneficiaries—something for their futures, whether it be recovery from illness, improvement of the educational level, reconciliation with "the law," and so on. The question then is how these interests, on both sides of the differentiation, can be reconciled with the needs of the participants to live in the here and now, and somehow maintain their equilibrium. For instance, we are frequently told these days that the new generation will have none of deferred gratification but insist that every aspect of their current mode of life should be intrinsically gratifying, as of the here and now.

This is so exaggerated as to be a caricature, yet this is well known to be one of the great age-old dilemmas of human life, and commitments to the relevantly specified common values are particularly crucial to this point. They cannot be successfully implemented, specifically at the level of the motivation of the individual, without the latter's participation in the appropriate solidary systems. Education, for example, is never only instruction but always in a sense socialization, i.e., inclusion in solidarity collectivities and thereby internalization of their values. Or

15

to take the case of health, even where the "pathology" is overwhelmingly "somatic," recovery is never wholly a function of manipulation of the physiological and biochemical conditions, but of recovery—through social reintegration—of the will to be active and functionally effective, to renounce the "secondary gains" of illness.

The theme of the nature and importance of solidarity, across the service-client line, of service-rendering organizations—which I take to be the main theme of this book—thus seems to me to be one of the most important with which social scientists who care about the future of their society can concern themselves.

# II

# CLIENT CHARACTERISTICS AND STRUCTURAL OUTCOMES: TOWARD THE SPECIFICATION OF LINKAGES

*Mark Lefton*

LATERALITY AND LONGITUDINALITY REFER TO TWO DISTINCT ASPECTS of organizational orientations toward clients. *Laterality* represents an interest in the client's biographical space, ranging from a focus upon a limited aspect of the client (typically found in the hospital emergency room) to a broad interest in who the client is as a person.

*Longitudinality* is a time dimension. Organizational interest may range from a truncated span of time (again, as the emergency room) to an almost indeterminate span of time (as in chronic illness hospitals).[1] The argument is that these interests may vary independently of one another and the four logically different kinds of arrangement which emerge will have significantly different impacts upon the internal structures, inter-personal processes, and external relationships of organizations.[2] This conception of client-serving organizations points to the behavior of clients as just as vital in the determination of organizational structure as is that of officials and operatives. To the extent that behavior informs structural outcomes, the analyst cannot ignore the actual

---

[1] M. Lefton and W. R. Rosengren, "Organizations and Clients: Lateral and Longitudinal Dimensions," *American Sociological Review,* 31 (December, 1966), pp. 802–810.

[2] This theme is more fully developed in W. R. Rosengren, "Organizational Age, Structure, and Orientations Toward Clients," *Social Forces,* 47 (September, 1968), pp. 1–11, and in W. R. Rosengren and M. Lefton, *Hospitals and Patients: A Theory of Clients and Organizations,* Atherton Press, New York, 1969.

behavior of any person defined as belonging to the organization, however great the effort to formally predetermine that behavior.

Central to this thesis is the concept of *social role*. While the notion of structure deals with behavioral events, the concept of role focuses on *official expectations* for persons occupying specific positions within the organization. Such expectations are expressed in prescribed activity which constitutes the "formal" organization: "a formalized *role-system,* then, is one in which the rules defining the expected interdependent behavior of incumbents of system positions are explicitly formulated and sanctions employed to enforce the rule." [3] Hence, the objective of formally constituted role systems is to govern behavior by standardized expectations rather than allow it to be guided by personal and idosyncratic determinants.

When we move to a social-psychological level of analysis attention shifts from prescribed performances to actual behavior. Thus, the psychological view of social roles implies that only segments of personalities are involved in system functioning. As Katz and Kahn say, "The organization neither requires nor wants the whole person. . . . The organizational role stipulates behaviors which imply only a 'psychological slice' of the person, yet people are not recruited to organizations on this basis; willy-nilly the organization brings within its boundaries the entire person." [4]

These ideas have added significance for service organizations which introduce the social role of "client." "Human beings as objects of a change process require different organizational processes than materials transformed in a manufacturing plant . . . human beings are reactive, participating objects in any molding process, and their cooperation to enter many organizations must first be secured. Moreover, their cooperation in an educational or even a therapeutic procedure is essential to its successful outcome." [5]

Congruent with these ideas, Kahn and Katz cite Parsons' description of the educational process: [6]

> The school class is a social system with an important degree of integration between teacher and pupils. Teaching cannot be effective if

---

[3] D. Katz, and R. L. Kahn, *The Social Psychology of Organizations* (New York, John Wiley and Sons, Inc., 1966), p. 49.

[4] *Ibid.,* p. 50.

[5] *Ibid.,* p. 116.

[6] Talcott Parsons, *Structure and Process in Modern Societies* (New York, The Free Press, 1960), pp. 72–73; cited in Katz and Kahn, *ibid.,* p. 116.

the pupil is simply a 'customer' to whom the 'commodity' of educa-tion is 'turned over' without any further relation to its purveyor than is required for the settlement of the terms of the transfer—as in the case of the typical commercial transaction. . . . There must be a long-standing relation between a pupil and a succession of teachers. . . . This difference between the processes of physical production and various types of 'service' has much to do with the fact that the *products* of physical technology in our society tend to be disposed of through the process of commercial marketing, while services—with many variations, of course—are much more frequently pur-veyed within different kinds of nonprofit contexts.

Organizations processing social objects—clients—are different from those processing physical objects in two basic ways. *First,* the internal procedures and forms of such organizations must be able to attract and then motivate temporary members or clients to be served. As Katz and Kahn put it, "The reactive nature of subjects or patients requires reciprocal spontaneity on the part of the staff." [7]

*Second,* the transactions of service organizations traditionally are not determined by the requirements of the "market place" in any direct sense. Almost always schools, hospitals, etc., are economically dependent on the larger community whether through public subsidy or private endowment. Therefore, client-serving institutions are generally assumed to be concerned more with social goals and less with profit and loss. Parsons puts it this way: "This insulation from immediate external pressures, at least those of the market place, justifies and intensifies the insistence of the public that people-molding organizations such as hospitals and schools be guided by norms of somewhat gentler, more individually oriented nature than might be imposed on an economic, object-molding organization." [8]

These two features of people-processing organizations are largely embodied in the central constructs of the client model—laterality and longitudinality. The construct *plus-laterality* expresses the extent to which a client-serving organization takes the "whole" person into account in its efforts to effect given social, psychological or physical

---

[7] *Ibid.,* p. 116.

[8] *Ibid.,* p. 116–117. Similar issues are raised and discussed by Charles Perrow, Orville G. Brim, Jr., and Stanton Wheeler. See for example, Perrow's chapter, "Hos-pitals: Technology, Structure and Goals," in J. G. March (ed.), *Handbook of Or-ganizations* (Chicago, Rand McNally and Co., 1965), pp. 910–971; see also Brim and Wheeler's, *Socialization After Childhood: Two Essays* (New York, John Wiley and Sons, Inc., 1966).

changes. Its converse, *minus-laterality,* describes a purposively restricted focus on specific or segmented features of clients. Clearly, an emphasis on the reaction potential of clients and on the social-humanitarian goals of service organizations would seem to indicate a leaning toward plus-laterality. Indeed it is often suggested that a prolific source of organizational problems lies precisely in the neglect of human considerations which may be regarded as irrelevant to specific organizational aims. The claim that hospitals, for example, tend to de-personalize individuals illustrates one major outcome of minus-laterality.

To recapitulate: organizations involved in "people-processing" confront several problems of structure and function which are less at issue in organizations processing non-human products. As organizations, however, they share the problems common to all formal efforts to rationalize decision-making, authority, and division of labor. But additional problems arise which are peculiar to the capacity of the "product" to react and to interact with those persons who are instruments of organizational goals. A viewpoint totally committed to rational, standardized procedures overlooks the capability of clients—trainees, students, or patients—to interpret and to behave in ways contrary to organizational expectations, making for malintegration of the client role within the organization.

The constructs, laterality-longitudinality, previously shown to be intricately linked to a series of structural aspects of service organizations, may also be useful when viewed from the perspectives of the client. It seems reasonable, for instance, to define laterality alternatively according to the client's view of the relevance of his personal and social life to the tasks of particular organizations from which he seeks a service. Plus-laterality then may be deemed appropriate from the client's vantage point when he considers that the organization ought to understand his total situation in order to meet his service expectations. Similarly, minus-laterality may be prescribed wherever the client perceives the organization's legitimate interest in him as limited—where a broad intervention may be seen as unwarranted and perhaps even illegal (as in overemphasis on race, religion or morality, etc.).

Longitudinality may also be viewed either from the client's perspective or that of the organization. The value of both constructs inheres in the fact that they can serve in this dual capacity, and thus point up areas of mutual, or conflicting interests between them. For example, there are many instances in which clients as patients, students, or welfare recipients object to the stance organizations take towards them. While the obvious and currently popular instances illustrate client resentment of the "de-humanizing" propensities of organizations such as state universities, hospitals, government bureaucracies, etc., difficulties may also derive from the reverse circumstance in which the organization is considered "too interested" in just "who" the client is.

Similarly, the organization-client relationship may suffer from difference in perceptions of appropriate longitudinality. It should be noted, however, that while an analytic distinction can be made between biographical time and space, these dimensions are generally experienced as inseparable features of one's own life. For a client, long term commitment to an organization necessarily involves his total personality however segmented the interest of the organization. Conversely, in other circumstances, a too quick discharge to an unready environment may seem to reveal the organization's total indifference to the client as a person. Again, longitudinality *per se,* may have lateral implications not evident to the client.

The analytically important fact about laterality and longitudinality is that these dual sets of interests may vary independently of one another. Further, their applicability to both the organization and the person makes them serviceable as a way of tracing the dynamic connections between the organization and its clientele. In short, laterality-longitudinality permits a ready shift from a purely sociological level to the social psychological level. Given that such attempts are worthwhile, the fact remains that there is "still a good deal of uncertainty as to which aspects of personality are most relevant for, and how they enter into, the functioning of institutions." [9]

Laterality, then, refers to the extent to which an organization is responsive to the reaction-potential of its clients in determining formal procedures. Plus-laterality, thus, indicates a high degree of organizational responsiveness to client reactions, demonstrated in official operations. Minus-lateral organizations, conversely, make little or no effort to permit client reactions to influence formal operations.

These definitions may seem merely to call attention to the fact that some organizations adhere to rigid bureaucratic methods, while others are more flexible and adapt to changing pressures. The concern here is not with discussing alternative ways of defining bureaucratic types of organization. The interest here is in the explanation of *why* it is that

---

[9] A. Inkeles and D. J. Levinson, "The Personal System and the Sociocultural System in Large Scale Organizations," *Sociometry,* 26 (1963), p. 217.

organizations, especially hospitals, do differ in responsiveness to client reactivity. In this paper we are inquiring into the logic of certain organizational structures for specific service activities, and the factors which seem to sustain, negate, or otherwise affect such structures.[10]

By pointing to the involvement of client characteristics in the determination of formal structures, whether a hospital will be more or less lateral, emerges as quite problematic. The issue before us concerns those client characteristics which have a bearing on laterality as an organizational outcome rather than as a departure point.


## PERSONS AS CONTINGENCIES IN ORGANIZATIONAL LATERALITY

### Characteristics of the Patient as a Person

Pine and Levinson say: "The patient's illness, in the sense of a delimited pathology, is only a part of what he brings with him to hospitalization." [11] He also brings his "personal system," a configuration of psychophysical and psychosocial attributes, his ideational system, and his personality. The person in the world of the hospital is a patient. For him there is a prescribed role to assume, but into this he injects his own style, strengths and weaknesses, and his own complicating potential.

As a "role occupant" the patient is automatically assigned a position in an existing role set by criteria largely beyond his control. He may or may not be prepared, or able, to accept all implications of this role. Each person, for example, occupies a general status in the wider society which accompanies him to the hospital. This fact implies a degree of particularism in the categorization of patients, consistent, of course, with general cultural values and criteria of evaluation. At the same time the strain toward universalistic standards is also manifest. For example,

---

[10] R. W. Hetherington arrives at a simular formulation as he raises the question of who is to be viewed as a "member" of a given organizational type (in this case, Medical Insurance Organizations) which may have varying perspectives as to the exact nature of the services rendered, their determinants and limits. See his paper, "Organization Theory and the Field of Health Insurance," report of an investigation supported by Public Health Service Research Grant Ch0012 from the Division of Community Health Services, Bureau of State Services, mimeographed, Fall, 1966.

[11] F. Pine, and D. J. Levinson, "A Sociopsychological Conception of Patienthood," *The International Journal of Social Psychiatry*, 7 (1961), p. 106.

essential medical procedures are not supposed to be denied anyone for financial or status reasons. Still, subtle distinctions with far reaching consequences are made. Thus, there is both overt and covert particularism affecting the patient's perception of his assigned role when in hospital, and the organization's perception of its patients and, hence, the kinds of categories which result. In a word, the patient role is not equally perceived by all categories of patients, nor is it assigned to them entirely without bias.[12]

From the perspective of the patient as a person, the analytic problem involves specifying the consequences *for* the individual—his personal system—as he attempts to accomodate to the personal qualities required or rejected by the patient role. It is equally apparent, however, that this goodness of fit is not *only* a problem for the patient, it is an organization problem as well.

## Characteristics of the Person as Patient

From a medical point of view: [13]

> The hospitalized patient has been conceived of as a 'case' of a given type of illness treated by the doctor within a supporting hospital facility. In this conception the crucial features of the patient are his 'signs and symptoms' and their origins in a central *pathological process;* the crucial feature of his hospital environment is the *definitive treatment* (shock, drugs, psychotherapy, or the like) it gives the patient; and the crucial features of his response is his *clinical course* toward (or away from) elimination of pathology.

This is a true but narrow perspective. Even more important is the fact that such a conception not only depersonalizes the patient, it also oversimplifies the influence of variables not always relevant to diagnosis and

---

[12] These themes have been explored extensively in the area of mental hospitalization; see for example, A. B. Hollingshead and F. C. Redlich, *Social Class and Mental Illness: A Community Study* (New York, John Wiley and Sons, 1958), see also, N. H. Siegel, R. L. Kahn, M. Pollack, and M. Fink, "Social Class, Diagnosis, and Treatment in Three Psychiatric Hospitals," *Social Problems,* 10 (1962), pp. 191–196. More recently, R. S. Duff and A. B. Hollingshead have examined patient perceptions and differential medical attitudes toward patients in non-mental hospital settings—see their work, *Sickness and Society* (New York, Harper and Row, 1968), especially chapters 8, "Patients and Physicians," 13, "Reactions to Hospitalization," and 14, "The Patient Views his Illness."

[13] Pine and Levinson, *op. cit.,* p. 106.

treatment. I have in mind here questions of staffing and specialized facilities, questions of professional expertise and experience, financial arrangements, control mechanisms, and the nature of the "exchange" network of which the hospital is a part.

In the context of these comments, laterality takes on added meaning. The attempt to analyze organizational responsiveness to salient client characteristics demands consideration of variables and factors other than those which are officially designated. At the same time, the issue of salience is as much a matter of organizational requirements as it is a concern for clients.

Three major types of characteristics relate to illness as warranting hospitalization and effect the dynamic interplay between hospital and patient.

## Qualifying (Primary) Characteristics

These are specific patient properties thought to be necessary and sufficient grounds for admission to hospital, i.e., explicit diagnostic and symptomatic categories stemming from defined causal roots.

## Related (Secondary) Characteristics

These refer to properties of patients which are related to a qualifying category in such a way as to affect the course and outcome of treatment, e.g., age, sex, previous illnesses. These are generally treated on an equal basis with Qualifying factors. Their impact exacerbates the Primary condition or limits treatment options. But they are normally perceived as crucial to primary goal attainment and as such are a source of increased laterality at least on a physiological level.

## Extraneous or Extra-Disease Characteristics

These affect the capacity of the patient to utilize hospital services because of ignorance, cultural traditions, psychological predispositions or other impediments. These may block or delay admission, retard or inhibit cooperation while in hospital, or vitiate the benefits of hospitalization later. But while these characteristics may be objectively quite relevant they are often not so treated for various reasons.

In the first place, lack of knowledge may lead to unsatisfactory outcomes, just as it was once considered "irrelevant" to surgery whether or not the surgeon had clean hands. Lack of knowledge may also be a factor in the inability to deal with an important problem, just as in the case of pain in surgery before anesthesia was available. In the case of socio-psychological and socio-economic factors more than simple ignorance may be involved. For example, there is a lingering cultural predisposition to view medical problems as basically the responsibility of individuals. Thus, the failure to use available services is often regarded as a form of deviance rather than evidence of psychological or social pathology.[14]

It is important to note that not all hospitals allocate given patient characteristics to the same categories. Our interest here is in just how the definition of functional goals affects the perceptual distribution of client characteristics among the categories. More concretely, the problem for laterality lies in the allocation of certain kinds of characteristics to either Qualifying or Related categories rather than to the Extra-Disease category. The allocation is obviously interpreted here as less dependent on the existence of given client characteristics than on the organization's perceptions of their nature and their relation to the hospitals' goals.

It is to be noted, however, that any particular goal orientation is *not* considered to be an independent variable here, but only one in a chain of connected and interacting variables, constant at the moment in time only in an analytic sense. Therefore, organizational goal orientation is viewed here as an intervening variable which influences organizational perceptions, interests, and definitions of patient characteristics.

In the following section an attempt is made to more fully explicate these ideas in relation to a concrete organization, the tuberculosis hospital. This institution is uniquely appropriate because it demonstrates both the utility of the ideas set forth above in explaining what happens as compared to what is supposed to happen in such hospitals.

---

[14] Parsons' classic discussion of the dimensions of the "sick role" is most relevant to this point; see Talcott Parsons, *The Social System* (Glencoe, Illinois, The Free Press, 1951), pp. 428–479. It is to be noted however, that whereas Parsons' concern is with "sickness" in its most general form, the question of defining "deviance" as distinct from psychopathology is a major one confronting mental health professionals. See for example Thomas Szasz, "The Myth of Mental Illness," *American Psychologist,* 15 (1960), pp. 113–118; David P. Ausabel, "Personality Disorder As Disease," *American Psychologist,* 16 (1961), pp. 69–74; and Shirley S. Angrist, "Mental Illness and Deviant Behavior," *The Sociological Quarterly,* 7 (Fall, 1960), pp. 436–448.

It also points to several lines of innovation that are suggestive for structural arrangements and experimental designs that would be safe and manageable for hospitals of this kind.

## THE CASE OF THE TUBERCULOSIS PATIENT

Modern chemotherapy has drastically cut the length of hospital stay required for most cases of tuberculosis, while at the same time creating new problems in overall control.[15] Discharged patients may be permitted to return to normal occupations relatively soon, but it is mandatory that they continue taking prescribed drugs regularly for some years thereafter. Neglect will result in relapse and renewed infectiousness. But that is not all, because an intermittent schedule of drug administration tends to cause resistance to the drug so that subsequent treatment is much more difficult and costly. On considering the seriousness of this situation, one observer has noted that, "outpatient management is becoming increasingly important . . . known difficulties in persuading patients to follow their medical programs is increasing the responsibilities and work loads of health departments and public health nurses."[16] The suggested remedies include practical measures for improving follow-up and the efficiency of outpatient supervision with some highly ingenious suggestions for tracking down patients who have disappeared. In fact, one is struck by the complex and cumbersome maneuvers required to repair the damages the patient inflicts upon himself, compared with the relatively simple task of repairing the damage of the disease process.

Moulding's comments may be interpreted, in our terms, as indicating that the tuberculosis hospital is indeed a minus-lateral institution. There *is* a limited and specific goal, defined in terms of remission of symptoms and control of the disease process. The problem of human failings which interfere with programmed therapeutic measures (drugs) are defined as not in the hospital's sphere of concern because they occur after the point of discharge. While the follow-up is still a medical problem (i.e., not extra-disease), it is thought to be extraneous to the hospital's

[15] Mary E. Blake, *Profile of 38 Oregon Tuberculosis Relapse Patients,* The League Exchange, 75, published by the National League for Nursing, (1965).
[16] Thomas Moulding, "New Responsibilities for Health Departments and Public Health Nurses in Tuberculosis: Keeping the Outpatient Therapy," *American Journal of Public Health,* 56 (1966), p. 417.

defined limits as a primary treatment institution. Thus, the minus-lateral stance forces a conception of the patient in terms of narrowly defined restoration of physiological capacities. His personal and social problems, his psychological capacity to continue treatment on his own, are not included as part of the hospital's responsibility for diagnosis and therapy.

The discussion of the problem stated above assumes that the root cause of treatment neglect lies in such "human failings" as forgetfulness, carelessness, etc. But the rubric "human failing" may cover manifestations of a more subtle psychological or social nature such as denial of illness, refusal to "play" the sick role, a general incapacity to accept normal role responsibilities, or an inadequate assessment by the patient of the seriousness of his condition. To classify a diverse array of personal system variables as instances of a general category results in failure to plan for the task appropriately belonging to the hospital as a treatment agent. This failure to broaden diagnostic and treatment goals to include the total array of factors logically and intimately connected with overall goal attainment, leads to artificial definitions of success. Failure to consider these kinds of personal factors vitiates the apparent success of the first stage of treatment. Because responsibility for treatment management is to be relegated to the patient for an extended period of time, his active participation is a necessary ingredient for a truly successful treatment program. To secure this participation is as important as to ensure that the drugs required will be available. What is seen as socially necessary but personally lacking, must somehow be provided socially.[17]

Viewed in this perspective, the problem of treating tuberculosis can only be defined as infinitely more complex than merely controlling the

---

[17] In support of this argument, see the striking results obtained by application of such principles in tuberculosis follow-up described in F. J. Curry, "A New Approach for Improving Attendance at Tuberculosis Clinics," *American Journal of Public Health*, 58, 5 (May 1968), 877–881. Parallel issues are raised in the contexts of mental hospitals and schools, indicating that much of what is applicable in the context of hospital organization may well be relevant generally to professional service organizations. See for example George H. Wolkon and Arden E. Meltzer, "Disease or Deviance: Effects on the Treatment Continuum," in M. Lefton, J. K. Skipper, and C. H. McCaghy (eds.), *Approaches to Deviance: Theories, Concepts and Research Findings* (New York: Appleton-Century-Crofts, 1968), pp. 339–348; and also Richard O. Carlson, "Environmental Constraints and Organizational Consequences: The Public School and Its Clients," in Daniel E. Griffiths (ed.), *Behavioral Science and Educational Administration Yearbook*, Part II, National Society for the Study of Education, (Chicago: University of Chicago Press, 1964), pp. 262–276.

bacillus. It must expand to include the treatment of the person who has the illness, rather than merely the illness the person has. Thus, complications caused by social and psychological factors are drawn within the range of Related Characteristics exactly as are physical complications which are also separate from the bacillus itself. This does not mean that the hospital will perceive this extension of its function as mandatory. The lateral mechanisms which hospitals might use to offset malevolent psycho-social interference with treatment goals tend to be neglected for many reasons. First, these strategies are often not well developed procedurely and show up poorly in comparison with outcome documentation which is characteristic of physiological treatment modalities. Second, such processes that *have* been shown to be successful in treating psycho-social problems are usually expensive and difficult to man. For example, additions to hospital programs such as group therapy, detailed social and psychological histories taken on admission, and differential and careful referrals for follow-up all present monumental demands for resources in contrast to the relatively inexpensive procedure of "dumping" all discharges into general public health programs for follow-up.

Specific to tuberculosis, and perhaps to all long term treatment facilities, the cooperation of the patient in the treatment process is another important consideration. Certainly, in the case of tuberculosis, it is clear that patient participation should be encouraged from the outset. The active "membership" of the patient in the treatment team would seem desirable if not from the beginning of the program, certainly as recovery begins. A process of patient socialization is wanted which is quite different from that which usually occurs. Traditional treatment modes foster a highly docile patient role and there is much evidence that this attitude persists.[18] Compliancy and regimentation are considered essential to the economics of the operation.

Hence, even with the means at hand to eradicate this destructive and costly disease from society, its control remains problematic.[19] But as expensive as it may be to staff and organize for more genuinely effective tuberculosis control programs, it may be a far smaller cost in

---

[18] See Julius A. Roth, "Information and the Control of Treatment in Tuberculosis Hospitals," in Eliot Freidson (ed.), *The Hospital in Modern Society* (Glencoe, The Free Press, 1963), pp. 293–318.

[19] See *Morbidity and Mortality,* National Communicable Disease Center of the U.S. Dept. of Health, Education and Welfare, Public Health Service, Vol. 18 (1), Weekly Report for the week ending Jan. 4, 1969.

the long run than that which will otherwise be exacted from society. The point to be emphasized is that the basic problem in tuberculosis control extends beyond the bacillus which causes it and into the dimly lit areas of personality and social circumstances. It is therefore logical that discharge should depend as much on evaluation and control of the predictable complications from that direction as from any other.

It should be noted that there may be an attempt to offer posthospital services to discharged tuberculosis patients which takes very seriously the psycho-social problems involved in staying well. The social interest is unequivocally perceived, but it is perceived as separate from treatment of the disease *per se*. As a consequence, it is a generalized follow-up which seeks to find, define and treat the problem after it develops. There is a considerable waste of personnel and effort in such a program, because it reduces the number of personnel available for those cases which turn out to be recalcitrant and likely to relapse. Intensive plus-laterality is expensive, demanding, and difficult. Furthermore, it may be resented where it is deemed unnecessary. And in many cases, it may not be necessary, because fewer *do* relapse than stay well.

Thus the necessity of good selective referral to other agencies places the onus for a more adequate lateral diagnosis squarely on the hospital. This is the ideal place to observe the patient day-to-day in relation to his illness. Here is the place to determine exactly *who* needs intensive follow-up service (beyond what he may be counted on to provide for himself) and to prepare each patient accordingly. Patients socialized to such a membership role can be expected not only to behave more responsibly after discharge, but to accept reciprocal membership from the follow-up agent in the post-hospital treatment course. It seems as dangerous and reprehensible to release an irresponsible patient to self-management as it is to release a virile case of active disease, because with only a temporal difference in consequences, they amount to the same thing.[20]

I am suggesting that an orientation which places lateral emphasis only and precisely where it belongs is required of the organization. For the hospital, laterality implies not only differential diagnosis but the specification of procedures to handle problems tangential to the disease entity but profound in producing deleterious results. The very anticipation

---

[20] See for example J. S. Kennedy and H. Bakst, "Influence of Emotions on the Outcome of Cardiac Surgery: A Predictive Study," *Bulletin of the New York Academy of Medicine,* 42 (Oct. 1966), 811–845.

that the patient is capable of positively or negatively influencing the therapeutic process ought to be reflected in organizational mechanisms capable of reacting to this influence.

This description of the tuberculosis hospital is extreme. It is intended to highlight the importance not only of lateral interests in the patient but also the crucial significance of the medical perspective in the determination of the conditions under which lateral interests may become influential in hospital structure and functioning. Tuberculosis hospitals have for many years provided long term treatment for many thousands of patients. Tuberculosis is a virulent and infectious disease and isolation is a mandatory public measure because contact virtually implies contamination. Hence, hospitals must and do make serious efforts to educate and socialize their patients. Where these efforts fail, prolonged hospital tenure is called for. The point at issue is *how* they socialize, and whether towards ends which are sufficiently comprehensive.

Raised here is a central question in regard to the degree of "membership" in the organization that properly belongs to the patient. We have suggested that the crucial fact is that the long term treatment inherent in the therapeutic process, and its extension beyond hospitalization, assigns ultimate treatment responsibility to the patient himself. No agency can offer or enforce day and night supervision, such as is theoretically possible in the hospital.[21]

Here, then, is a clear case of organizational goals in conflict with those of the patient, and perhaps with those of society at large. Because a longitudinal dimension approaching the indefinite cannot be effectively controlled externally, socialization of the patient to his new role is crucial from the point of diagnosis on. The patient is the first resource to be exploited for his capacity for supervising his own program, utilizing the public health nurse, physicians and out-patient departments essentially as "consultants." If by age, circumstance, or personality, the patient is unable to achieve sufficient independence to be "in charge," then his family or other community resources may have to be mobilized on his behalf. While family and community have a

---

[21] In fact the desirability can be questioned on several counts, both theoretical and practical. When much more extended tenure was the role for tuberculosis, there appears to have developed in sanitoria a dual culture with staff and patient groups opposed, each seeming vigorously devoted to subverting the goals of the other. Through the eyes of a participant-observer on both "sides" of the fence, at different times, Roth gives a perceptive description of what appears to be a macabre "gamesmanship" and he indicates many of the causal links between motivations, existing structural exigencies, and the dysfunctional outcomes. (See Roth, *op. cit.*)

legitimate stake in the patient's continuing health, it is the importance of the other side of the coin which has been less well appreciated. External compulsion is far less effective than are internal controls and this sets limits for manipulative treatment interference.[22]

## THEORETICAL IMPLICATIONS

Highlighting concerns such as hospital orientation to posthospital therapeutic continuity, leads to the proposition that lateral interest in the patient becomes relevant in the hospital context as a primary medical criteria for admission. Several considerations are involved in this proposition: *first* is the fact that hospitals can, and do, select certain patients and exclude others. Admission criteria simply and obviously serve to distinguish among different types of medical problems—e.g., acute, chronic, infectious, surgical, medical, psychiatric, among others. *Second* is the fact that medical problems differ in the degree to which they are life-threatening conditions—hospitalization is indicated for the schizophrenic as well as for ruptured appendix. *Third,* hospital intervention in the course of an illness varies with the capacity to diagnose and/or control the disabling illness—e.g., the availability of particular types of diagnostic tools, therapeutic instruments, knowledgeable experts, care facilities, etc. *Fourth,* hospitals are geared to specifiable procedures. Hence, failure to specify the linkage to the focal disease or the exact corrective means, may cause defining an extra-disease factor as "irrelevant;" e.g., physiotherapy and occupational therapy as post-surgical and pre-discharge requirements, where considerable function has been lost.

These considerations underscore the following point: lateral interests are not automatically nor identically relevant in all instances of

---

[22] Much experimentation in limited patient wards will be needed to specify exact processes, staff requirements, etc., that would effectively counter these malignant tendencies and still be organizationally realistic. However, these theoretical ideas are not in themselves new; in slightly different form they may be found in considerable contemporary writing; see for example, *Nursing and the Task Force Report to the Surgeon General and Keys to Improved Patient Care,* Presentations at Nursing Sessions N.T.A., 1965 Annual Meeting, Chicago, National League for Nursing, Columbus Circle, N.Y., and also Blake, *op. cit.* In fact, the first group therapy in this country appears to have involved the problem of motivating tuberculosis patients; see Joseph E. Garland, *An Experiment in Medicine: The First Twenty Years of the Pratt Clinic and the New England Center Hospital of Boston* (Cambridge, The Riverside Press, 1960).

hospitalization. Furthermore, hospitals, by virtue of their admission policies, strongly influence the types of extra-disease factors which may be seen as relevant.

The capability of the hospital to control and differentiate admission, and the relevance of extra-disease factors, both suggest two opposing organizational forces. On the one hand, hospitals tend to perpetuate existing structure and procedural arrangements. On the other hand, their own admission policies may subtly but significantly alter existing structural patterns.[23] In the context of laterality, this means that hospitals vary in the extent to which their own policies and treatment aims contribute to either minus or plus laterality.

It is important once more to indicate the central ingredient of *laterality*—extent to which a given hospital is responsive to the reactions or reaction potential of its clientele, and the effects on hospital procedures and structural outcomes. Laterality, therefore, is to be viewed in terms of the *perceptual* linkages between patients and hospitals. It is important to note that though the concept is defined so as to point to those characteristics of patients which may be relevant to the organization, this does not mean that personal factors are not important. Whether a patient has a family, whether he has a personal physician, whether he resides in the community served by the hospital, are all significant biographical facts which affect the outcome of individual cases.

"Particularism" with respect to patients, however, is a special form of lateral interest. Acute general hospitals, for example, may employ social workers, psychologists and other specialists to provide non-medical services. But these are generally outside the mainstream of hospital decision-making and its major task objectives. For acute hospitals, ancillary services are invariably secondary to the primary aims of controlling the acute, and often life-threatening condition which prompts admission. The existence of social and other services, in addition to purely "medical" ones, somewhat counters the often presumed "coldness" and "de-personalization" of acute general hospitals. It seems that the "de-personalized" nature of such institutions has to do not so much with the absence of extra-medical services but more with the fact that they are "hidden" and optional. They are of less organizational importance than the ancillary services more obviously related to medical functions, such as nurses and dieticians. In other words, such services

---

[23] Carlson, *op. cit.*

deal with individual patients' problems only when they are forced to the attention of the hospital. But in normal circumstances their importance as significant organizational components is quite minimal.[24]

In order for lateral interests in patients to become organizationally relevant and to influence structure and functioning of hospitals, they must have "universalistic" qualities rather than being seen as peculiar attributes of certain patients. *Categories* of extra-disease factors must be recognized and understood as pertinent *in general*. For example, the use of psychological counseling services is usually ancillary and optional in general hospitals, depending on requirements of individual patients, and even more on the interest of individual physicians. The same service becomes "universalistic" when it is assumed that certain groups of admitted patients, of specified description or diagnosis, all require psychological counseling or screening. This universalistic usage is most commonly found in the chronic illness-rehabilitation institution. Similar distinctions can apply to social service, vocational rehabilitation, and others.

We have already noted that the universal application of ancillary services depends on the type of hospital under consideration and its admission criteria. Extra-illness factors may be involved in the determination of admission as in the chronic illness institution. This very often implies a nearly universal social service consideration. Medical considerations notwithstanding, it is my contention that lateral interests in patients will significantly influence the organizational patterns of a given hospital when these are assumed to be potentially relevant to patients at admission rather than being emergent conditions turning up during the course of an illness and its treatment. In other words, of special interest in understanding hospital dynamics is whether patient exigencies are "cooled out" [25] in the sense of being managed without being allowed to affect ongoing structure, or are viewed as an intrinsic

---

[24] It is obvious that patients themselves are usually less likely to worry about the apparent "coldness" of hospitals during the critical period of illness than during convalescence, and one possible explanation of the fact may be overlooked. The patient, during the "sickest" period tends to be focused as narrowly on immediate and urgent physiological problems as is the attending staff. There is high congruity, therefore, of attitude. As symptoms recede and immediate danger is surmounted, other concerns intrude upon the patient's consciousness, probably at the same time as the medical staff feels free to be in less constant attendance. The new concerns may well be not so much less important from the patient's view as from that of the medical staff. Here divergence of focus and consequent patient discontent may be understood.

part of the medical problem, so that these factors become intricately interwoven with the structural apparatus of the hospital.

A "universalistic" as opposed to a "particularistic" stance regarding extra-disease factors implies [26] that they are intrinsic to the medical problem at the point of admission. It means also that the organizational apparatus designated to provide the relevant services shall be commensurate with the magnitude and scope of its task, in terms of adequate staff, equipment and space, and appropriate status and decision-making influence. Implied also is that the operations of such "departments" are considered to be functionally effective and professionally competent by virtue of specialized training and shall be permitted to apply the standards and criteria intrinsic to the discipline involved. These implications lead to another which is of critical importance for laterality in terms of its postulated utility in focusing on the reciprocal relation between the patient and the hospital. That is, the capability of extra-disease considerations or personal attributes of the patient to force an organizational response is directly related to the degree to which such factors are permitted expression through specific structural mechanisms characterized by "universalism" and functional autonomy.

In more general terms, the suggestion here is that laterality is structurally conditioned in that the organizational arrangements of the hospital are designed to anticipate extra-disease contingencies. Of special importance is that patient characteristics are differentially evaluated at the point of admission. The extent to which they operate as feed-back variables into the larger system depends *not* on their intrinsic significance but on organizational readiness to accept their relevance by expanding problem definitions and in providing structural means for their expression and management. The choice of the general categories among which degrees of laterality are differentiated might be expected to vary from one hospital to another and to have far-reaching and distinctive implications for the organization in such basic matters as staffing patterns, ranking of positions, and the nature of interorganizational linkages.

---

[25] Burton Clark, "The Cooling-Out Function in Higher Education," *American Journal of Sociology*, Vol. 65 (1956), pp. 569–576.

[26] The terms "universalism" and "particularism" are of course taken from Parsons' system of pattern variables. For a concise discussion of this system, see M. Black (ed.), *The Social Theories of Talcott Parsons* (Englewood Cliffs, N.J., Prentice-Hall, Inc., 1961), pp. 38–44.

## SUMMARY AND CONCLUSIONS

The departure point for this paper was an earlier work attempting to emphasize the saliency of organizational interest in clients for selected features of organizational structure and functioning. This paper has explored the notion that although client characteristics may be regarded as critical for understanding organizational operations, the issue of *which* particular characteristics are relevant is problematic and becomes a vital empirical question. It was suggested that a first step toward a clarification of the focal concepts is the explication of precisely what their implications are for organizations. Here, the emphasis was on organizations as social psychological systems of interaction. Such an orientation paved the way for an operational definition of laterality as "the extent to which an organization is responsive to the reaction potential of its clients in the determination of functional procedures or structural outcomes." Such a definition underscores three things. First, it prompts a consideration of clients as vital participants in service-oriented organizations. Second, it forces attention upon the "client as a person." Third, it emphasizes the need to more carefully consider the varieties of factors that produce given structural forms as well as variations in modes of operation.

The utility of these ideas was examined in the context of the "client" as a "patient," with reference to the case of the tuberculosis patient. That discussion was intended to show the dynamic and often problematic relations between the "patient as person" on the one hand, and the medical establishment on the other. The point was made that even though specific non-medical client characteristics are clearly relevant to the course of illness, these may be ruled as irrelevant by virtue of powerful medical considerations, especially new drug therapies and concomitant leanings toward medically appropriate in-hospital care and treatment policies. In other words, even though it is quite obvious that certain client characteristics *are* critically related to the service sought or received (and acknowledged by client and agents alike) unless and until appropriate structural mechanisms are made available by which to express the saliency of these factors, they are "cooled out" or perceived as extraneous rather than potentially manageable complications.

The importance of these arguments for the client-organizational relationship inheres in the following conclusion: the capability of extra-disease considerations and attributes of the "patient as person" to command organizational responsiveness is related to the degree to which such interests are permitted expression through *already* existing structural mechanisms characterized by "universalism" and functional autonomy. Such a conclusion suggests that if organizations differ in their responsiveness to client characteristics, not only do they differ in terms of their perception of clients and their intentions toward them, but they do so because they differ significantly in terms of existing structural arrangements.

At the same time, the dynamics of structural change include forces which derive from social perceptions external to, but impinging on the hospital. These, in turn, derive from changes in both objective client characteristics and perceptions of these characteristics. So that while the existing structures may accurately be said to select the relevant patient characteristics, these existing structures are also partly a consequence of those characteristics as they have been defined and recognized.*

---

* The author wishes to acknowledge his indebtedness to Mrs. Gloria Sterin for her indefatigable editorial assistance and for her insights regarding several major substantive ideas.

# III STUDENTS AND SCHOOLS: SOME OBSERVATIONS ON CLIENT TRUST IN CLIENT-SERVING ORGANIZATIONS

*Charles E. Bidwell*

THIS CHAPTER CENTERS ON A QUESTION NEGLECTED BY MOST SOCIOLO-gists of education: the conditions under which students enter schools and the consequences of these conditions for students and for schools. Students become members of the schools they enter, so that schools are shaped as much by the characteristics, aggregate and structural, of the student body as the students are by their exposure to the school. The incorporation of students as full-fledged members of schools imposes distinctive problems of organizational control, while breaking down the barriers of distance and privacy that are imposed, say, between a commercial enterprise and its customers. How teachers conduct their work and how students respond to instruction cannot be understood apart from their relations to one another as two orders in the membership of schools.

In the following pages, I shall outline a few key variables that define the membership status of students and some of the consequences of these variables for the ways schooling is conducted and organized. I shall assume that students as the direct recipients of education are the prime clientele of schools, although schools have major responsibilities to parents and various publics.[1] Nonetheless, the relation of students

---

[1] In colleges and universities, to be sure, the issue of the clientele is complicated by the multi-functional character of these "higher" schools. Nonetheless, instruction appears to be the ultimate justification of their existence. To abandon teaching is to transform the organizational character: from school to research institute or consultant agency.

and schools in several ways differs from the classic bond between professionals and clients. Three of these ways especially merit our attention as they set the terms on which students become client-members of schools.

The classic professional-client relation is voluntary, dyadic, and centered on the exchange of service and fees.[2] The relation of student and teacher, in the usual case, is involuntary—the result of the official status of students and teachers in school organizations, and collective—one teacher, but many students. Moreover, while students may reward teachers with esteem or responsiveness (as may the clients of any professional), they seldom pay fees. Since education in modern societies is a welfare good, payment (except for unusual forms of schooling) is a generalized public burden. These differences, I shall argue, affect the conduct and organization of schooling as they constrain the formation of student-teacher trust. To make these effects clear, I shall first review the ideal-typical professional-client relation and then examine the divergence from this pattern, generally in client-serving organizations and more specifically in schools.

## PROFESSIONAL AND CLIENT: THE IDEAL TYPE

In the ideal case, because the client is more or less ignorant of the professional's esoteric knowledge and inept in his specialist skills, the client must trust the professional. He places himself openly and freely in the professional's hands, confident that skilled and effective help will be forthcoming. At the beginning of the relationship, the client is ready to trust the professional on the basis generally of his professional role and more specifically his reputation (his record of past success, insofar as it is known to the lay public). Prospective client trust thus rests on the assumption that the professional will act responsibly (that is, that there is effective social control of the profession, by the state

---

[2] Fee-payment is less critical to the professional-client relation than voluntarism and the dyadic exchange. Fees at times are paid by friends, family, or public agencies without disrupting the relation. Nonetheless, when client and professional directly exchange fees for service, the bond between them is strengthened. This discussion leaves aside the problem of clients who are minors and therefore usually neither voluntary clients nor fee-payers. I shall return to this problem in the specific discussion of schools. Teaching is the only profession in which adult clients are the exception.

and the professional guild) and on the availability of information about the reputations of individual professional workers.

Once the professional goes to work, he must maintain the client's trust, not only by virtue of the technical quality of his performance (of which the client is not a competent judge), but in part because of his ability to inspire confidence—in the absence of concrete evidence of quality—and in part because of periodic signs that the client is being helped (e.g., he feels better, or no worse, or finally recovers; his case in law is going well or at least better than it might, or finally is won).

As Friedson reminds us, the free professional need not always, in the absence of technical evidence, persuade his client that he is trustworthy. The authority of his position may suffice.[3] That is to say, confidence is inspired as much by the professional's status as by his personality. The general principle follows that the more eminent the profession, the fewer the failures of client trust for any reason (from malpractice to trivial anomalies of the professional's appearance or behavioral style). But in contrast to the professional employee of a client-serving organization (e.g., the social worker or teacher), his authority does *not* inhere formally in an office.

Thus the relation between professional and client is a moral relation and an asymmetrical one—the client submits to the authority of the professional not because he is coerced or paid to do so but in the expectation, however inchoate, of responsible and effective performance. Having once submitted to this authority, he has little control over events. If they go badly, he thinks, he may become recalcitrant; but foot-dragging only impedes the performance of a competent and ethical professional, although it may protect the client from an incompetent or unethical one. Ultimately, if the client does not like what he is getting, he can go elsewhere.

For the professional, trust, as the sole basis of his moral authority, is essential for effective performance. Unless he enjoys his client's confidence, he may be denied access to the client's person, or to the full range of necessary but often covert information about the client while the client may not follow the professional's directives or counsel. Hence the professional cannot fulfill his responsibilities to the client or to his peers for the client's welfare, unless the client trusts him. Thus

---

[3] Eliot Freidson, "The Impurity of Professional Authority," Howard S. Becker *et al.* (eds.), *Institutions and the Person* (Chicago, Aldine Publishing Co., 1968), pp. 25–34.

the responsible professional must reject the client who will not trust him.

But in actual professional service, even that provided by the old-fashioned free professional, trust is a relative matter. Although at times the professional might prefer absolute trust, feeling harassed by a querulous or suspicious clientele, absolute trust is neither functional nor desirable for the client or the society. As I have suggested, it is the tentative quality of trust—its ultimate grounding in the controls of a responsible profession and its more immediate dependence on earned reputation and on performance (however imperfectly demonstrated)—that is at once the client's means of safeguarding his own well-being and in the aggregate a major bulwark of collective professional self-control.

Although the level of client trust seems basically to rest upon the popular prestige of the profession, the professional's public reputation, and his subsequent ability to inspire his client's confidence, two additional factors also induce important variation in the level of client trust. These factors are the client's technical familiarity with the professional service (his access to purportedly esoteric knowledge and ability to assess the skillfulness of performance) and the client's need for professional service (how critical his situation and keen his sense of helplessness).

The less knowledgeable the client, the more absolute must be his trust. The teacher and lawyer, more often than not, are less able than the minister or physician to command an immediate, full grant of moral authority from clients.[4] If, with time, clienteles become more knowledgeable, and more confident of their knowledge, professional authority may tend toward a rational, technique-centered base and away from the moral mystique of the secret. Perhaps, then, the relation of professional and client will become more an instrumental collaboration between equals—a matter of the convenience of a specialist division of labor among members of a knowledgeable community—and less that of trusting subordination to the esoteric.

As a general rule, it would appear that the more the client thinks he needs professional assistance, the greater his willingness to give up control over his own fate and turn to any reasonable source of as-

---

[4] On knowledge and control in modern societies, see Robert Lane, "The Decline of Politics and Ideology in a Knowledgeable Society," *American Sociological Review*, 31 (1966), 649–66.

sistance, not hesitating over fine distinctions of competence, ability, or personal charm. The client's trust then will be more absolute, and his control over the professional correspondingly weaker. To the extent that the prestige of a profession directly affects the tendency of prospective clients to define their needs for professional service as personal crises, this effect will be reinforced.

The level of trust is one major problem that clients must solve; another is what shall be taken in trust.[5] In the ideal-typical relation of client and free professional, what is to be taken by the client in trust is a function of the professional mandate. The relationship is segmental and specialized; the professional can demand of the client only those items of information or action that will further their joint aim of setting right some specific disorder in the client's life or of preventing potential disorder or loss. The doctor, repairing a fracture, may require his patient to wear a cast but not divorce his wife; the lawyer, writing a will, may ask about his client's investments and property, but not about his sexual habits.

Nonetheless, the boundaries of the purportedly specific professional task are almost always uncertain. Some aspects of a professional's demands on his clients are fixed by tradition or are obviously intrinsic to the professional technique; for example, the items of a medical history or a client's appearance at the sessions of his trial. Others, however, may become matters of contention between the professional and his client, subject to their differing conceptions of the scope of the professional mandate, or of the necessity for certain information to be given, orders to be followed, or advice to be taken for effective professional help. The physician, having decided, say, that a skin rash is of psychosomatic origin, may probe into the patient's relations with his wife, or boss, while the patient, seeking only physical treatment for physical symptoms, may regard his doctor as a meddling busybody and seek another who will prescribe a salve and stay out of personal affairs that are "none of his business."

More often we think of the client as on the defensive in these disagreements, but the professional may also find it necessary to deflect client demands that are, according to his own conception of his mandate, embarrassing, irrelevant, or beyond his competence. These efforts most often center on boundary definitions of the professional specialties,

---

[5] Cf. Georg Simmel, *The Sociology of Georg Simmel*, K. Wolff (trans.) (Glencoe, Illinois: The Free Press, 1950), pp. 317–29, 361–76.

but not always. The physician who treats only physical ailments may send a neurotic patient to a psychiatrist, but, to reverse our earlier example, may tell a patient with a rash, who begins to pour out marital woes, to confine himself to the details of the presenting symptoms.

I have suggested that the problem of the scope of trust—what is and is not to be entrusted to the professional—is mainly a matter of variant professional and client conceptions of the professional mandate. These jurisdictional definitions in turn arise from ideas about both the relevance of items in the technical repertoire of the profession to solution of the client's problem (e.g., that following a low-fat diet will in fact lessen the danger of heart attack) and the scope of the professional's moral authority (e.g., that, though diet has little apparent connection with heart trouble, the doctor "knows best").

In general, it would appear that client willingness to honor a broad professional mandate is a function of the same variables that govern the level of client trust. Reputation of the professional, the prestige of his profession, the severity of the client's need, and the client's sophistication, all affect not only the degree but also the scope of trust. The more the client stands in awe of the professional, the greater his tendency to accede to any demand made upon him for revelations or compliance to professional direction. The more he needs help, the more likely he is not only to comply willingly with the professional's requests or orders, but also to do anything that he is told to do. And the sophisticated client, while more likely than the ignorant or naïve to do whatever is demanded once he has decided the demand is legitimate, is at the same time also more likely to reserve the right to make this decision. Thus a sophisticated client is especially likely to differ with a professional on the issue of what is to be taken in trust—educated laymen indeed may be in advance of the professions in their conceptions of professional help, demanding of the internist attention to emotional problems, of the clergyman social relevance, or of the lawyer a conscience.

## CLIENT-SERVING ORGANIZATIONS AND CLIENT-MEMBERSHIP

Professional service, of course, need not be offered in the classical manner of the free professions. In fact, in modern societies free professional service is undergoing bureaucratization, as the individual practitioner yields before the client-serving organization.

Client-serving organizations are of two principal kinds. One admits its clients to organizational membership, the other does not. The former, among which hospitals and schools are the clearest cases, provide sustained professional services—services that require the constant presence of the client within the immediate purview of the organization's staff. These services involve more or less continuous staff intervention, corrected by equally continuous monitoring of the client's progress. The latter, of which law firms, medical clinics, and social service agencies are examples, provide episodic professional services—each episode requires only a brief encounter of the client with one of the professional staff, although these episodes may stretch out in a long series. A few minutes in the office or the client's home, or a few hours in court, are all that an episode requires.

If we take as the defining attribute of organizational membership generalized subordination to the authority structure *of the organization* (in contrast to subordination to one or more of the organization's staff, individually), then the clients of the first variety of client-serving organization are client-members. The decision to accept the organization's services involves payment to the organization, not to the professionals whom it employs (the payment, however, may be made either by or for the client), immersion of the self into a client-member "mass," and a commitment to accept, within the scope of the organization's service jurisdiction, direction from any of the professional staff.

There are, of course, further jurisdictional definitions within the organization that govern staff prerogatives to serve and control categories of client-members—in the school, the classroom; in the hospital, the service. But allocation of client-members among these jurisdictions is ultimately not a matter of client-member judgment, although organizations with responsible and sophisticated client-memberships may permit some freedom of client-member choice (e.g., graduate students who select their dissertation advisers, courses, and specialized fields of study). And once assigned to a jurisdiction, the client-member must defer to any of its professional staff (e.g., the house physicians on the hospital service of one's own doctor, the faculty of one's own university department).

The fact that client-members and professionals share, in these organizations, a common (though stratified) membership radically changes the conditions under which professionals help clients and client trust is nurtured. But this fact does not diminish the importance of trust.

If client-membership is voluntary, it is entered chiefly according to the generalized prestige of the service organization, its more specific reputation for providing some particular kind of service (e.g., the prospective graduate student who chooses a mediocre over a first-rate university because it has nonetheless an outstanding offering in his own field), and some information, more or less flawed, about the organization's facilities and staff.

The reputations of certain of the professional staff may be of great importance in choosing the organization (e.g., one's choice of a physician may fix one's choice of hospital, and, as I have suggested, the eminent department or even one outstanding professor may determine graduate school selection). The more eminent the organization, the more likely it is that any of the staff will be taken on faith by the client-members and the more apparently trustworthy (and often the better known) will be individuals on its professional staff. Nonetheless, having entered the organization, the client-member encounters an array of professional staff about whom he knows nothing but to whom he is subordinated because they, along with (at times, instead of) their better-known colleagues are responsible for the client-member's welfare. Moreover, many client-membership organizations are better known than any of their staff or are chosen by clients *faute de mieux*. The question of level of trust, therefore, is complicated by the necessity of repeated client-member decisions about whom to trust at all, let alone how much.

Confronted by unknown professional staff whom the client-member must trust for the simple reason that they have official jurisdictions over him, the first question that he must answer is whether to submit or resist. Here we have the familiar example of the hospital patient surprised to find himself prodded and poked by a stranger identified as a doctor only by his white coat and authoritative manner. In contrast to the ideal-typical professional-client relation, in which prospective client trust is earned indirectly through the professional's reputation, the client-membership organization is not an automatic guarantee that any of the staff is worthy of trust.

Thus the fact of client-membership makes client trust markedly more problematic and indeterminate than it is in the ideal-typical professional-client dyad. There the question of how much to trust is resolved minimally when the client selects the professional. The upper bound of trust may remain to be determined, but the relation itself is severed whenever the client refuses to trust at all. Instead, in client-member organizations, specific client-member staff relations are subject to organizational determination. They are a matter of official jurisdictions; hospital services, university departments and subject specialists, and the like. Although both client-members and staff may be given some latitude for choice (as in elective systems or the right of professors to select students whose theses they will direct), this freedom is usually constrained by formal rules or by conventions that safeguard staff reputations and work loads. Failures of trust more often are to be endured, and perhaps remedied by the staff and client-members involved, than escaped.

The question of what to take in trust also is complicated by client-membership, for it brings the clientele into the organization as total personalities and as a client collectivity—whether for a substantial series of client "work days" as in the day school or commuter college or around the clock as in the hospital or residential school. In either case, the broad scope of the client-member role makes it more difficult to maintain a functionally specific client-serving relation than in episodic professional service. In the latter, whether provided by a free professional or client-serving organization, clients are seen seriatim as individuals and in situations narrowly defined by the information-collecting or treatment-giving requirements of the professional technique.

For one thing, the simple exigencies of administering a client-membership require rules and procedures that are only indirectly related to the organization's professional task. Patients and boarding students must be fed and housed, their movement from place to place regulated, and use of scarce staff time and facilities scheduled, so as to be present in sufficient amounts and kinds where clients happen to be in time and space. Since none of these logistical necessities can, without chaos, be left to a free market of client-member choice, the client-members find themselves hemmed in by organizational constraints on what they may regard as their private lives—what they can eat and when, what and how many visitors they may receive and at what hours, whether they can enter and leave the premises and at what times, the location and conditions of residence, and so on.

Moreover, the fact that a client-membership is a collectivity means that organizational requirements for order extend into relations among the client-membership. Some of these regulations prevent client-members from getting in each other's way (e.g., hours at which radios are to be played), while others may be more central to the professional task. In schools and therapeutic communities, for example, service is given to groups of clients. If the client-member group is simply an aggregation of client-members brought together for economical staff use, as in college lecture courses, these rules will define the conditions of order necessary for staff interventions or client-member use of organizational facilities. In schools such regulations would be those governing class-room behavior or library circulation.

If social bonds among client-members are themselves to be tools of professional service, these rules may constrain the formation of such bonds. Examples of such limitations are the assignment of client-members to a "work group," team, or residential unit; or the differential assignment of responsibilities for client-member leadership according to some criterion of "progress" or seniority (of which the perfect system in the English Public Schools is a well-known instance). Finally, client-members tend to form client societies that may center on resistance to organizational demands, whether peripheral or central to the service function. Because these societies may organize collective distrust of the organization or its staff, arrangements are necessary to coopt client-member leaders and siphon off client-member unrest. The elaborate arrangements typical of high schools and colleges for "student government," "due process" hearings on disciplinary cases, and student representation to the school's administration (all of which antedate, in however ineffective a form, current student activism) are mechanisms of this kind.

Some or all of these regulations may be rejected by client-members as unwarranted (i.e., professionally irrelevant) intrusions. When this is true, the less willing or certain was entry into client membership, the less eminent is the organization or trustworthy its staff, and the less critical is the client-member's need for the organization's services. When client-members decide that the organization's motives in these matters are not to be trusted (viewed, perhaps, as prurient, "bureaucratic," or imperialist), the organization may find it hard to maintain order or coordinate central activities, as the client-members oppose "intrusive" organizational claims. This opposition will be especially disruptive if it emerges as collective client-member resistance—in which case the organization's mechanisms for the controlled release of client-member hostility are likely to be chief among the objects of scorn.

The staff of client-membership organizations, aware that such resistance is always possible, may seize upon the rhetoric of responsibility to justify to the client-members the apparatus of client-member control. This rhetoric may appeal to external legal requirements (e.g., fire laws), to external constituencies (e.g., *in loco parentis* arrangements or observance of community moral standards), or directly to the client-member's own welfare (e.g., balanced meals or, in the case of college parietals, the defense of female chastity). Generally, however, this rhetoric is more effective if professional responsibility can be invoked, so that the regulation exemplifies legitimate professional concern for client-member welfare.

Apart from rhetorical considerations, the broad scope of the client-member role is an inducement to the staff to use the resources thereby provided to surround the client-member with salutory environments, whether of their fellows, of physical amenities, or of encompassing forms of staff-given treatment (e.g., the dormitory that becomes the Oxbridge-style "college," provisions for bed rest, or intensive nursing care). And, of course, many client-member organizations are founded with the idea of the total professional relevance of the client-member role originally in view.

This thrust toward a professionally inclusive setting may help to justify organizational intrusiveness and broaden client-member trust in organizational policies restricting client-members' self-determination, and therefore in all sorts of staff interventions. If these policies have been associated traditionally with the organization's service, wide-ranging client-member trust will be easier to attain than otherwise, while the same factors that promote high levels of trust also tend to broaden its scope: client-member need, organizational eminence, and a convincing or charismatic staff.

But the absence of one or more of these factors, or a change in the social status of the population elements from which the client-membership is drawn that strengthens their claims to autonomy, will tend to narrow client-member trust, at the same time making any form of trust more tenuous. As a result, unless the client-membership can find immediate justification in the organization's professional technology for restriction of the right to do as they please, trust will come to be focused on specific service activities of a direct instrumental value to the client-members and, in the more extreme case, trust will be weak or absent even there. In the latter instance one may find not only client-member disorder and confrontations with the staff, centered on the regulations immediately at issue, but more pervasive client-member disaffection. This disaffection may occur at several levels of intensity from general distrust of the motives or competence of the staff demonstrated through resistance to staff direction of all kinds, to efforts to elevate the organizational position of the client-membership by gaining the right to affect or set "peripheral" regulations, or even influence central professional policies.

Thus the current wave of American college and university student protest has accompanied both increased latitude for sub-cultural and behavioral independence on the part of adolescents, and, for more and more males, labor market entry deferred for advanced training. At the same time, to the extent that it has focused on conditions in the colleges and universities, this protest has tended to generalize from student claims for viable self-government—of residence, student discipline, and political involvement—into demands for student participation in making curricular policy and faculty appointments. This tendency suggests that the rights claimed by colleges and universities for more or less "total" control of the conditions of student life—never very secure in the United States—have come increasingly into question with changes in the age composition of their student bodies and the social definition of adolescence. As a result student trust in these schools and the faculties and administrators has declined generally.

Hospitals provide an only apparently far-fetched contrast. The traditional right of the hospital to regulate closely the lives of the sick, the more apparent linkages between diet, rest, nursing, and medical treatment, the critical needs of the sick, and the authoritative position of the physician as a guardian of esoteric therapeutic techniques all safeguard the hospital from patient uprisings. "Patient activism" is not likely soon to be a pressing social problem, although physicians may find patient trust eroding on other grounds: rising levels of lay sophistication about medicine and, perhaps, a consequent tendency for laymen to take a more instrumental stance toward medical help. The recurrent restiveness of mental hospital patients, where the technical base of treatment procedures and arrangements for patient life are less apparent and less secure, the status of hospital personnel less exalted, and the patient's frequent uncertainties or recalcitrance about commitment and subsequent treatment, also should be noted.[6]

## SCHOOLS AND STUDENTS

Schools share with other client-membership organizations these problems of winning and keeping client-member trust. But trust is especially tenuous in schools—the result of a typically involuntary clientele, of the batch processing of students, and of the affectivity-based techniques

---

[6] See for example William Caudill, *The Psychiatric Hospital as a Small Society* (Cambridge, Mass.: Harvard University Press, 1958).

and limited reputations of teachers. The remainder of this chapter considers how these qualities of schools bear upon student trust and the relations between schools and teachers and their students. Since schools, especially by level, vary in the degree of student voluntarism, "batching," and faculty eminence, differing effects of these factors for student trust at the several levels of the educational system also will be examined. I shall discuss first trust in teachers as individuals, centering on the question of the level of trust. Then I shall turn to aspects of student trust in schools as organizations, a topic which involves questions of both level and scope of trust.

a) Faculty reputation and technique. Although a few college and university teachers have national and international reputations as teachers, and others local reputations soon discovered by freshmen, most are simply unknown as to their teaching styles or competence until the student enters their classrooms. This is even more likely in lower schools, though certain teachers again may have very potent local reputations. More often teachers' reputations, favorable or unfavorable, have little to do with teaching skill, especially in the universities and better colleges, where the fusion of instructive, scholarly, and service functions in a single faculty means that a professor may be a well-publicized adviser to governments or a Nobel prize-winner, but still an unknown in the classroom.

But even when a teacher's reputation as a teacher is negative, students more often than not can do little to avoid him. In lower schools, students are assigned to teachers. In colleges or universities, assignment of students to teachers is less common; even so he may be the only man offering a course that is needed or required. All the student can do is prepare for the worst, his motivation declining the more precipitously the less the intrinsic or instrumental value he places on the subject matter. And once the course is under way, the student typically is stuck with the man who proves a poor teacher—only in the college or university is there escape by the dropped course (if one's program permits this) or infrequent attendance. Otherwise students escape by inattention or more active resistance—devices that presumably lower teaching effectiveness.

In short, schools at times on grounds of rationality—staff utilization, equitable teaching loads, or the need to spread or balance faculty competence, for example—at other times on grounds of tradition—tend to be indifferent to student preferences among teachers thus making students exceedingly cautious about whom and how much to trust. As a result teachers find themselves living down reputations or, at the least, preoccupied with the problem how to earn the trust of each new crop of students. They are as constrained by school policy as are their students. Typically, neither can reject the other, and failures of trust must be lived with, whatever their impact on what and how much is learned. So, while the responsible fee-earning doctor rejects the patient who will not trust him, the responsible teacher redoubles his efforts to "reach" the recalcitrant. (Or, he may choose professional irresponsibility, only keeping order in a custodial classroom.) To put the point somewhat differently, school policy constraints on teachers' and students' freedom to choose or reject one another, coupled with widespread anticipatory student ignorance of the qualities of their teachers, remove from all but a few schools the self-selective mechanisms, found in the relations of clients and free professionals, by which prospective trust is maximized and failures of trust dealt with, ultimately, by withdrawal by either client or professional.

At the same time, teachers' use of the authority of office—insistence on student compliance with directives without regard for trust—generates little in the way of learning. Whether the teacher seeks to modify students' beliefs, understanding, or motor skills, what is learned is expected to persist beyond the classroom—to carry over into situations in which teacher sanctions are no longer present. Consequently student trust in teachers is of the greatest importance in teaching as it generates those affective bonds between teachers and students—whether between the "mothering" teacher and her brood in the elementary school classroom or between the respected scholar and his disciples in the university laboratory or professor's study—that generate in students motivation to learn (whatever the content to be learned) independently of teacher demands for compliance. That teachers redouble their efforts with reluctant or indifferent students is, therefore, a joint function of the necessity to raise student motives and of the assignment of students to teachers.

It should be clearer now why the less responsible teacher tends to become a custodian—or in higher institutions, a time-server. The teacher's responsibility is three-fold. He is accountable to his employing school, to his colleagues (given the relatively undeveloped quality of teaching as an organized profession at any of the levels of the educational system, this is for the most part the immediate colleague group of the school), and to a set of publics, some of which may have fairly clear expectations about the outcomes of schooling (especially parents and future employers of the student "product"), others of which have only relatively unformed notions of what the schools should do (e.g., general public stress on the "importance of good schools").

But the specific mechanisms through which the teacher is held accountable tend to insulate the teacher, and to only a lesser extent the school or school system, from external control, unless local constituencies in the still exceptional case are mobilized for political action on school issues. As a result, in the day-to-day operation of schools (I am not considering constraints on the long range formation of school policies or forces affecting change in forms of school organization), students, to whom teachers are not directly accountable but whose trust they must win, are a major controlling force. What, then, accounts for the short-run autonomy of the school and school class? How do teachers' attempts at building student trust differ in various sorts of schools, and to what effect?

In modern societies, education is a welfare good, entailing mandatory, universal school attendance up to some specified school-leaving age. Education, moreover, becomes increasingly a public enterprise—through direct government operation, or some form of government subvention or inspection of privately-run schools. Although in the latter, parental wishes are of direct concern to the school and its staff, because the parents pay the fees, in the former the most direct form of teacher accountability is bureaucratic—as a state official he serves students and, most immediately among the school's publics, a parent clientele who can bring their wishes to bear primarily through organizational channels and whose range of choice among schools is severely limited. Other of the school's publics tend to have little interest in its daily work, with a greater interest in employable graduates, low taxes or the appearance of conventionally acceptable facilities, curricula, and teachers. Although schools are, in fact, constrained by parental wishes—more so in decentralized systems like those of the United States than in ministry-dominated systems like those of France—both the reality and the rhetoric of uniform school policies and curricula severely limit the impact of parental demands on what teachers do in class. And although more knowledgeable and well-fixed parents may make effective indirect choices for their children among public schools as they decide where to live, nonetheless, in comparison with the services of free professionals, the supply of qualitatively different forms of public schooling is restricted and freedom of client (i.e., parent) choice limited by the costs of residential mobility.

The public school system, of the various school types in the United

States, is the most clearly insulated from parental preference. Thus responsibility for effective teaching and for student welfare has become principally a matter of internal, organizational accountability. For the teacher, for the individual school, and for school systems, it is a question of political accountability through formal governmental channels. Given the internal structure of public school systems—the virtual isolation of the teacher in her classroom, the thinness of teacher collegiality, the weakness of colleague controls, and the fitful quality of inter-school coordination in school systems—how this responsibility is exercised becomes largely a matter of individual teacher judgment, as Durkheim noted some years ago.[7] Perhaps its exercise is constrained by the general framework of a required curriculum or course of study (in the American case usually not very detailed and not very closely enforced) and occasional "controls by results" (e.g., standard achievement tests, to which relatively little systematic attention is given by the teacher's superiors).

The teacher's relative isolation, physical and social, in the company of his students, may lead to the excesses of autocracy that Durkheim feared, but may also result in a partial cooptation of the teacher by his pupils.[8] This outcome is made even more probable if one considers that teachers, even in the secondary grades, look more to their students than to colleagues, superiors, parents, or the intrinsic content of the curriculum, for the rewards of teaching.[9]

The teachers' stance toward his students obviously varies with school and grade level, that is, with the age-grades and consequent normative orientations and peer affiliations (in school and out) of the school's student body. In the early elementary grades, where peer affiliations and norms are rudimentary, the teacher's position is relatively powerful, and her own preferences with respect to the conduct of the class are especially decisive. Here the isolation of the teacher in the classroom is especially marked, while her pupils, although not yet having learned to be students or to evaluate teacher competence, are moved primarily by what Robert Dreeben calls "goodwill." [10] Goodwill is not contingent on

---

[7] Emile Durkheim, *Moral Education,* E. K. Wilson and H. Schnurer (trans.) (New York: The Free Press, 1961).

[8] Cf. C. Wayne Gordon, *The Social System of the High School* (Glencoe, Illinois: The Free Press, 1957).

[9] Dan C. Lortie, "Authority and Control in Teaching," Amitai Etzioni (ed.), *The Semi-Professions* (forthcoming).

[10] Robert Dreeben, *On What Is Learned in School* (Reading, Mass.: Addison Wesley Press, 1963), pp. 33–37.

given items of student performance, but comprises "those forms of gratuitous pleasure not tied to specific acts in a relationship of exchange"—an analog to the affective climate of the family.[11]

In these classrooms, the teacher may terrorize or brow-beat her students, and Jules Henry has given us rather frightening descriptions of the irresponsible use by elementary school teachers of their diffuse, affective power.[12] But such cases are probably not common, a tribute less to a responsible professional community of teachers than to the benevolent impulses of the larger number of elementary school teachers and to the durability and force of the conventional wisdom that informs so much of the teacher's work. In classrooms of this kind, controls on the teacher's actions are in fact essentially those of personal commitments.

In the upper elementary and high school grades, students will have developed more or less solidarity peer societies within their schools and classrooms. These provide students with the collective organization for standing off or partially coopting teachers, while past experience of classroom life has equipped them with shared understandings about what good teaching is and what the limits of legitimate teacher authority are. Depending on the social origins of the students, their abilities and emergent interests, and the nature of their earlier experience with school, these understandings will dispose students more or less favorably toward a new teacher and toward high levels of academic effort and competitiveness. That is, by the time students have been in schools awhile, trust becomes a group concern, determined by collective student solutions to the problems of studentship (e.g., how hard to work, what to learn and to ignore, how far to push the teacher's patience).[13] At the same time, the student group, like the teacher, remains constrained by legal and administrative requirements. No matter how frequent or how blatant the teacher's violations of group-defined student trust, students cannot escape the teacher's classroom unless a parent decides to move or the students become so unruly that the principal must intervene. They can, however, fail to perform and can seduce the teacher into accepting student definitions of performance standards in exchange for classroom order and, perhaps, willing effort.

The teacher's situation in a private school is rather different. First,

---

[11] *Ibid.,* p. 37.

[12] Jules Henry, "Attitude Organization in Elementary School Classrooms," *American Journal of Orthopsychiatry,* 27 (1957), 117–133.

[13] Cf. Howard S. Becker, *et al., Making the Grade* (New York: John Wiley and Sons, 1968).

the student body is more or less selected, although selection on parental ability to foot the bill may confront the teacher with a very recalcitrant student group. When ability also is an admissions criterion, the private school teacher is more favored, although as the result of school policy and position in the student market, not of a mutually voluntary student-teacher bond.

More important, parents are a visible surrogate clientele. But their power to influence the teacher's actions differs with the school's reputation. When, for every student admitted, several of equal promise are turned away, the parent-clients may serve for the school and its teachers as a buffer against failures of student trust. By choosing the school, one's parents have chosen what it stands for—in academic program, religious training, or social standing—and the faculty, by doing what it thinks is best for its students, also does what the parents presumably want. The student whose failures of trust lead to unsatisfactory performance can be expelled safely. Control over the work of these schools comes from the colleges to which they send their graduates, from tradition, from the background and training of their faculties, and from a sense of what the market will bear (what will maintain the substance and appearance of eminence), rather than from either student resistance or parental demand.

On the other hand, as the eminence of the school declines, and the competition for students correspondingly grows, the parent clientele may be enormously powerful—through direct intervention and faculty anticipation of what parents will demand. This may reinforce the influence of students over teachers—as when parents wish simply to be rid of their children—or of teachers over students—as when the parents demand a specific form of moral or religious upbringing. But whatever the balance of power, we find that both members of the student-teacher pair are constrained as in public schools; the student being unable to bring legitimate controls to bear on the teacher, the teacher being unable to reject untrusting students.

In higher institutions, the nature of the teacher-student relation is not much changed. Although a college student may enjoy somewhat greater latitude than before for teacher choice in the first year or two of college, by the junior and senior years, the range of choice narrows as the specialist requirements of his "major" involve him in more or less set sequence of courses for each of which there is but one instructor. If the college class presents less evidence of student-teacher strain than high-school classrooms, it is mainly because the student population is self-selected and, in the more eminent colleges, screened upon admission. Indeed, there is some evidence that "open-door" colleges are, in this as in other respects, not very different from high schools.[14]

College teachers may feel less compelled to "reach" or "motivate" all of their students, perhaps selecting proto-disciples from the classroom group, teaching to the "top of the class," or lecturing in take-it-or-leave-it fashion, but undergraduates are not their only clients and teaching them not their only tasks. Even the anonymous instructor, teaching in the most parochial college, can turn to his books and away from his students, under the guise of "scholarship." Only in graduate school, and then only when the thesis is being written, does a student attain many of the same rights as those enjoyed by the client *vis-a-vis* the free professional.

b) School goals and client aims. To this point, I have argued that the involuntary assignment of students to teachers combines with the affective quality of teaching and the opaque reputations of teachers, as teachers, to produce in most schools recurrent problems of student trust. Each new teacher that the student encounters is potentially un-trustworthy, while during the involuntary association the teacher tries over and over to "reach" even the least trusting. Moreover, after the early grades, the teacher confronts a student society with a shared per-spective on the trustworthy teacher that must be satisfied before trust is forthcoming.

I have discussed these factors as they bear on the relations between teaching in these grades, the "good-will" of young children, and the students' decisions about whom to trust among a school's faculty. Of course, these relations also vary in scope, as for example, between a narrowly task centered academic classroom and the more diffuse bonds that may link an athletic coach and the members of his team. These variations are largely a function of differences in the organizational structure of schools, and there are in addition, important differences in the scope of the student role itself that require broader or narrower grants of student trust, as between residential and day schools. In the primary grades, as I have already suggested, the questions of the intensity and scope of student trust are one, given the heavy affective loading of teaching in these grades, the "good-will" of young children, and the classroom-centered quality of pupils' lives. Beyond these grades, how-ever, decisions about whom to trust and what to take in trust are more

---

[14] Burton Clark, *The Open-Door College* (New York: McGraw-Hill, 1960).

distinct, and the latter becomes an issue especially of those factors that may lead students to commit themselves to their schools. Most important among these factors are the school's goals (i.e., the kind of education it seeks to provide) and students', or parents', aims for schooling.

Clearly the constraints on the willingness of students to commit themselves to their schools center on the involuntary status of most student bodies. If, at the outset, a school cannot select its students, it must accept them without clear evidence of their willingness to grant the legitimacy of the school's authority, that is, the authority of its administrators and teachers. The procedures used to cope with this problem appear to depend especially upon the school's power relative to parties whom it more or less directly serves—parents, the state, and the students themselves. Where its power is relatively great, it may establish a probationary period, during which students may be induced to commit themselves to the legitimacy of staff authority, after which they are either fully admitted as students or sent away.

The power of private schools *vis-a-vis* parents and students nearly always permits this, unless the flow of new students is insufficient. Moreover, they can screen student applicants, although the less eminent may be forced to take almost everyone who applies. But *vis-a-vis* the state, the public school has less power to expel, and none at all if the schooling is compulsory. In this situation, a school that does not by virtue of its locale draw already committed students may either tend toward a custodial function or mount long-range efforts at inducing student trust, granting full client-membership without clearcut probation and in the face of uneven results.

Above the school-leaving age, public schools vary markedly in their ability to screen or later reject student recruits, a variation that occurs primarily according to their eminence and the availability to students of alternatives for schooling or jobs. Thus, the great state universities freely reject students, both before and after matriculation, while many junior colleges "cool-out" the recalcitrant, as well as the over-ambitious, into other forms of post-high school training or into the labor force.

It is difficult for selective schools, in their admissions procedures, to make a detailed assessment of student commitment, since students often do not know precisely what they want, or are being sent to school at their parents' behest. The screening effort consequently is limited to evidence of general favorability to the school and of some minimal desire for the kinds of education the school provides. If the prospective students are fairly sophisticated, complex statements of purpose may be required, or plans concerning specific programs of study. These items of information provide at least indirect evidence that the student is taken sufficiently with the reputation of the school or, better, of its faculty and sufficiently eager for its particular brand of teaching to respond, if not whole-heartedly at least without complaint, to the guidance or direction of his teachers and to the necessities of the school's curricular or residential arrangements. That is, initial commitment is taken by the school as a reasonable sign of readiness to trust any of the school's staff and to take in trust whatever school policies may require.

Probation involves a search for early evidence of a student's trust at once firm and broad enough to span the student role as the school defines it—for example, compliance to school rules, "citizenship" (which may include the beginnings of an extra-curricular career), and the level of initial academic performance (on the assumption that admission to the school indicates the ability to perform adequately). Similarly, efforts at socializing students to the student role typically stress generalized loyalty to the school (i.e., grants of trust of generous amount and scope), through assemblies, athletics, and other collective rituals. With older and more sophisticated student bodies, these efforts may also stress the distinctive educational mission of the school or eminence of its faculty (undoubtedly, for example, one of the chief purposes of the college freshman "orientation week").

The position of the student's parents in the choice of school also must be considered. Where the student himself has chosen, parental wishes are of no more than secondary importance, as they support or contradict, and thus may strengthen or weaken, the student's own aims. At times, parental wishes may be unknown or no longer relevant, as in the various forms of adult education. If the parent has chosen, his conception of desired schooling is of paramount importance. It affects the kind of school to which the child will be sent, which may or may not coincide with the child's wishes. Also, according to the child's openness to parental influence, the parents support or confound the school's efforts to socialize the child to the student role and maintain his trust. Here one must consider not only direct parental influence, but also indirect influence resulting from wider kinship circles and the normative quality of the family's neighborhood and other circles of affiliation.

If neither the student nor his parents has acted on preference and the child appears at school simply by virtue of attendance laws, parental attitudes toward education may be as indeterminate as those of the student and may be forecast and subsequently used, ignored, or hopefully altered so that the school will have parental support. The school may try to establish a bond of trust with the parents, while it attempts to socialize the student. Parental sentiments more often are ignored and prime reliance placed on capturing the student's good wishes because negative parental attitudes place parents at some social distance from the school. The traditional apartness of schools—their lack of community involvement and cooperation with other government and voluntary agencies—compounds the problem.

In our earlier discussion, we suggested four characteristics of client-serving organizations as variables that affect the intensity and scope of client-member trust:

1) the prestige of the organization
2) its reputation
3) the level of client-member sophistication
4) the degree to which the client-members perceive their needs for help as critical

With respect to schools, as other client-serving organizations, the effects of organizational prestige and reputation are straightforward: the more prestigious the school and the more favorably regarded its educational services, the more ready student trust will be across the full range of school activities. Reputation and prestige are likely to have greater effects on student trust if the student body is knowledgeable concerning the aims and techniques of their education, but the child culture of almost every neighborhood creates a reputation for the local school. I have noted that the same propositions hold for individual teachers, so that the quality of a school and of its faculty, which are usually related positively, have mutually reinforcing effects on both the scope and intensity of student trust.

For individuals, the need for education never becomes as critical as may the need for medical or legal help. Instead, the student, or his parents, will think that he "needs" schooling to the extent that his own aims for education and those of some available school coincide. The effects of school goals and student and parent aims, like those of school prestige and reputation, differ with the level of student sophistication. Sophistication, I have suggested, is a function of the student's prior exposure to schools and teachers and thus varies directly with age. Students' cumulative school experience and acquired conventional student wisdom are major determinants of their identification with the school, their compliance to school or classroom rules, and their vulnerability to teacher, peer, and parental influence.

Student age is also related to variation in two of the important organizational conditions of school life: the agent to whom the school is most immediately responsible—the state, parents, the student himself—and the social structure of the school grades—from the relatively undifferentiated classroom society of the primary grades to the highly differentiated complex of relations to teachers and peers in multiple academic and residential settings during college and university. Because these differences define for the student the organizational world of the school, they profoundly condition the formation of trust in school and teacher.

In the first years of schooling, the classroom is, in effect, all that school means to the child. Students venture infrequently beyond the boundaries of the classroom and almost never for instructional purposes. Even on the playground, they are rigidly segregated by age and often by classroom group. Thus school authority is the teacher's authority, and the peer society is very largely a segment or extension of the play relationships of the neighborhood. In contrast to the more socially heterogeneous and structurally complex student societies in high schools and colleges, the classroom group in the primary grades is cohesive and undifferentiated, its members unselfconscious of their collective identity as students (in part because all their age-mates undergo the same experience of school). In these classrooms, teachers can foster a family-like classroom culture especially conducive to the growth of broad and intense student trust. As I have noted, the child's trust in school is formed among students upon his first encounter with school essentially as the establishment of trust in his own teacher. The teacher *is* the school.

The organizational character of higher schools is very different. Here the collective quality of schools becomes more real to students; they are engaged from the outset with the school as a corporate unit. If one must apply, he applies to the school, not to a person, and is accepted or rejected by the school. Upon matriculation, he enters not a classroom but the school itself and within its walls forms multiple affiliations. In the high school, for example, he is involved with several teachers and class groups, with extracurricular activities, with a distinctive friendship circle, and perhaps a specific track or course of study. His work is

59

judged by standards that to some extent override the judgments of individual teachers, while his progress toward graduation is governed by some form of corporate decision.

As he enters the school (assuming some consistency in sophistication among the student entrants to any given school), his initial commitment to the student role and willingness to submit to school authority are determined, as I have suggested, largely by the school's prestige and reputation (its facilities and evidence in the form of his impression of the character of its total faculty and student body) and by his conception of what he wants and what the school has to offer. As he continues his studies, he can compare teachers, courses, and curricula, establish his identity as student by reference to a student sub-culture more or less engaged with the work of the school, and compare his experiences with those of his fellows, both within and outside his own peer circle.

From these considerations, two conclusions can be drawn about student trust at post-primary levels of education. First, in the general case, both the formation and maintenance of trust, in intensity and scope, will respond more to the collective character of schools as organizations and student societies than to relation of students and individual teachers. This is not to gainsay the recurrently problematic question of trust in individual teachers, discussed earlier, or to deny that particularly skillful, attractive teachers may have powerful effects on certain students. But as a student participates in his school, his differential perceptions and evaluations of teachers and peers and of his own experiences compared with those of his fellows are of especial importance to trust. Second, trust is a collective attribute of student bodies, as well as an individual trait of students. As student bodies are more or less trustful of their schools, or as peer circles differ in levels of trust, individual students, according to their peer affiliations, are induced to trust or suspect the school and its teachers. Now we can return to the problem of variation in school goals and in student and parent aims, especially as these variations affect student readiness to make broad grants of trust to their schools.

## Variation in School Goals

Particularly relevant to the present argument is the relative stress given by a school to expressive or instrumental socialization. By instrumental socialization I mean the acquisition of motor or intellective skills or items of information that will be used as tools in enacting specified social roles. A curriculum with a strong instrumental emphasis consists primarily of subject areas differentiated both in content and instructional technique.

At higher levels of schooling, the instrumental curriculum usually prepares for social roles (Weber's "specialist" form of education [15]). This curriculum is most clear-cut in graduate and professional education. In high schools and colleges, it is reflected in the differentiation of faculties and courses according to subject matters. In elementary schools, these divisions are less clear, although still present in the form of "subjects" or "units" that divide the school day. But the relevance of these subjects to adult destinations is nonetheless pervasive; for example, preparing for multiple adult settings (e.g., arithmetic for work and family) or for more generalized adult destinations (e.g., citizenship). By high school or late in elementary school, differing instrumental curricula are linked to social class differences and are ranked as are the classes (e.g., in high school, vocational and collegiate tracks, among colleges the differential prestige ranks of four-year and junior colleges).

By expressive socialization, I refer to the development of beliefs and various forms of sensibility. A curriculum that stresses expressive socialization may be more or less differentiated with respect to styles of life, affected especially by the level of schooling and degree of social selection in the student body. Thus one finds, for example, an emphasis on "character building" in the early grades, on commitment to political responsibility in high school, and on preparation for responsible leadership or the pursuit of gentlemanly leisure in the "elite" colleges.

It is important to note that the instrumental and expressive forms of socialization are not strictly dichotomous. While instrumental content can be taught without much reference to belief or sensibility, expressive teaching almost always accompanies instrumental content and is concerned at least in part with the formation of certain evaluative or appreciative orientations to the content of the instrumental curriculum.

The two kinds of socialization involve distinctive incentives for student performance. Instrumental socialization can rely heavily on sanctions that are extrinsic to the content taught—grades, prizes, and the like. Among older students, already somewhat knowledgeable and sophisticated, trust centers especially on the teacher's competence, as it

---

[15] Max Weber, *From Max Weber*, Hans Gerth and C. W. Mills (eds.), (New York: Oxford University Press, 1946), p. 243.

legitimates his award of extrinsic sanctions. Because such teaching involves mainly didactic instruction or coaching, the relation of teacher and student is specific to the instructional act and need not involve diffuse acceptance by the student of the teacher as an attractive or admirable person (although such acceptance may foster an acceptance of teachers' judgments, whatever their intellectual or pedagogical skills). The requirements for student trust are correspondingly narrow, centered on the specific instructional task and the student's willingness (whether because of his own aims or the teacher's competence) to do the work that it requires.

In the lower grades, the incentive system is mainly expressive, reflecting the instrumental-expressive mix in the curriculum. In these schools the growth of trust centers on the establishment of a family-like climate that capitalizes on students' earlier affective experiences. The teacher is in a diffuse relation to her students. Trust requires acceptance of her as a person, in response not to her competence but her friendliness and nurturant qualities. In fact, for young children, what to take in trust from the teacher and how much to trust her are not really questions—as a mothering adult the teacher is extremely powerful.

Expressive socialization at whatever level of schooling, because the teacher functions as an agent of persuasion or as a moral exemplar, rests on a generalized acceptance of the teacher's moral authority— whether as a maternal surrogate in elementary schools, or as an eminent scholar or charismatic lecturer in universities.[16]

Expressive socialization requires not only strong affective bonds between teacher and students but an intensity and scope of involvement of students with one another greater than that required for instrumental purposes. Expressive outcomes are generated not so much by the teacher's indoctrination of students as by their participation in the school as a prototype of the moral order for which they are being prepared.[17] Here the teacher is only one among a number of role models, although a preeminent one, and sentiments and perspectives are learned largely as they are experienced in daily life of the school.

---

[16] Durkheim noted that a teacher's effectiveness as an agent of expressive socialization rests mainly on his own evident and exemplary commitment to the moral order. At the higher levels of education, where expressive teaching centers more than in the lower grades on specific belief systems or life styles, the teacher's commitment must be equally firm, though more narrowly focused. Cf. Emile Durkheim, *op. cit.*

[17] Durkheim, *ibid.*

The school, to be a powerful model of an adult moral order, requires not only students' identification with teachers, but also a more general acceptance of the legitimacy of its immediate normative structure. As I have noted, after the early grades the presence of numbers of students uncommitted or antagonistic to the school's expressive aims fosters a moral order that will socialize students to sentiments quite different from those sought by the school, both within alien student sub-cultures and through the medium of latent hostility or open warfare between students and teachers.

Clearly then the demands on student trust are more absolute and more pervasive in scope in expressive-oriented classrooms or schools than in those centered on instrumental training. The whole round of life in school is potentially the means of instruction, where the effectiveness of moral teaching is a function of the scope as much as of the strength of student-trust. I have already noted how favorable primary classrooms are for moral teaching because of their child client-membership. At higher school levels, the scope and intensity of student trust that moral teaching requires suggests that its effectiveness will depend on the selection of the student body with respect to initial levels of commitment (e.g., self-selection by students or their parents into denominational schools, or indirect self-selection according to the life style of the school community) and on the degree to which the school staff and, collectively, the student body live up to the moral sentiments they seek to teach.

The two forms of education, instrumental and expressive, are tied to different aspects of the stratification system: expressive to styles of life, instrumental to occupations. Hence, the mobility goals of students or their parents have quite different effects on student trust—as education is conceived by student or parent as fostering mainly occupational or "cultural" modes of mobility or status maintenance. One would expect, as a result, students of lower social origins to have greater trust in instrumentally-centered schools, those from families of higher rank to have greater trust in schools with expressive goals. Stress on sensibility, the humanistic ideal, and student involvement in, say art or music beyond the classroom, may seem irrelevant or alien to the student-vocationalist. These effects, however, will be more marked in the post-primary years of schooling.

These two forms of education also appear to be linked to sex-typing; to the sex roles that parents expect their children to assume and to the students' own emergent sexual identities. These linkages are intertwined

63

with the effects of social class and students' and parents' educational aims. But in general it would appear that boys, after learning early to be indifferent to schooling, become vocationalist and centered on instrumental forms of education. Girls, at first compliant and academically competitive, tend to lose their competitive drive and to withdraw into the more explicitly expressive fields of study. I shall consider these points in greater detail in the next section.

## Educational Aims of Students and Parents

Children, I have said, enter elementary school with a diffuse expressive orientation. Young children are prone therefore to trust schools and teachers from the outset, providing adequate ground for expressive socialization and for developing responsiveness to such extrinsic incentives as grades. But parental aims are more varied and are linked to social class. Moreover, they are salient because young children are not supposed to know what is good for them and in any case have no legal right to choose. Although parents can select elementary schools by residential mobility or by paying tuition, these options are closed to families of scant means and restricted information. At the same time there is increasing evidence that working class parents tend to stress instrumental aims for schooling (e.g., the 3 R's, acquisition of specific information) and are likely to be antagonistic to efforts at "character-building or individualized instruction." [18] These parents are least likely to participate in PTA's, while the public schools' traditional aloofness from other community agencies restricts their channels for influencing or persuading such parents.[19] Students in these circumstances may learn at home not to trust their schools or teachers.

Middle-class parents, on the other hand, are less concerned with instrumental and more with expressive factors, such as attention to aesthetic sensibilities and social skills. And as Litwak has noted, the problem these parents pose for schools is to keep their interest in their children's education within manageable proportions.[20] On these grounds

---

[18] Sam Sieber and David Wilder, "Teaching Styles: Parental Preferences and Professional Role Definitions," *Sociology of Education,* 40 (1967), 302–315.

[19] Eugene Litwak and Henry Meyer, "Administration Styles and Community Linkages to Public Schools," A. J. Reiss, Jr. (ed.), *Schools in a Changing Society* (New York: The Free Press, 1965), pp. 49–98.

[20] Sieber and Wilder, *op. cit.*

alone, one would expect parental tolerance, or enthusiasm, for more encompassing forms of schooling (whether at the extremes boarding *vs.* day schools, or between varieties of moral socialization or more narrow "academic" or subject-centered instruction) to be a direct function of social class—whatever the additional effects, for example, of family income.

In upper elementary grades and particularly in high schools, I suspect that there is a decline in expressive orientations on the part of both pupils and parents and a rise in instrumental aims centered on preparation for either work or college. This parallels the increased achievement emphasis and subject-specialization at these levels, and in this sense facilitates student trust based on teacher competence, while at the same time narrowing the limits within which trust is given.[21]

But in less selective junior or senior high schools, the narrower scope of the student role does not insure adequate levels of student trust. For students in these schools, whether any trust will be forthcoming is problematic, let alone how broad a grant will be made. One problem of trust in these schools involves the content of students' instrumental aims. Students with relatively unfavorable life chances may reject the more humane subjects and college-centered curricula that still dominate most high schools and find the extra-curricula irrelevant, while at the same time they resent the low prestige and meager resources of vocational or "basic" tracks or schools. These attitudes are likely to be mirrored in parental sentiments. Another problem results from the failure of a certain proportion of students to become responsive to extrinsic school sanctions. The more instrumental curriculum of the high school is likely to produce in these students low levels of interest and effort, while the seeming irrelevance of the curriculum to probable adult destinations makes it difficult for the high school to re-socialize them to the student role.[22] And of course, the now-ascendent peer society will reinforce these tendencies, where there are sufficient numbers of uncommitted or hostile students for contra-cultures to emerge.

---

[21] Teacher competence, however, has a somewhat imprecise link to the growth or maintenance of trust. First, above the early grades teachers inherit students already socialized, albeit imperfectly, to the student role and responsive to such extrinsic sanctions as grades, however poor or indifferent the teacher may be. Second, the intellectual or motor performance involved in learning instrumental content may be rewarding in itself, so that the student works independently of the teacher's incentives.

[22] Arthur Stinchcombe, *Rebellion in a High School* (Chicago: Quadrangle Books, 1965).

High schools faced with such failures of trust, in fact, must reconstitute the moral order of the school in directions that support student discipline and effort and recast its instruction to be more immediately related to students' life chances.[23] But public high schools typically are constrained from doing so, given the persistent heritage of the academy, the subject centered training of the large majority of high school teachers and administrators, and their responsibility to a public that is itself often traditional in outlook and suspicious of apparent efforts to "water down" high school programs.

Among American colleges, one finds at least as great a diversity of student aims as of organizational goals, reflecting the multiple occupational and status destinations to which colleges lead, students' more and differentiated interests, and their greater freedom of choice. Although there is a very imperfect fit between what students want and what their own colleges provide, there is nonetheless a noticeable strain to consistency when student aims and college goals are ordered on the instrumental-expressive continuum. This fit is a complex function of such variables as college selectivity; the constraints of information, money, and sophistication of college choice; and parental preferences and influence.

In any event, among colleges that can exert some control over admissions, relative to high schools, aggregate levels of initial student commitment by students to colleges should be high, especially when instrumental purposes have governed college choice. Such choices are based largely on students' anticipatory commitments to their specialist role destinations and their more or less informed judgments about the quality of facilities and faculty competence in one or another academic subject matter. When colleges are selected on expressive grounds, students evince a more generalized form of trust, centered less on the specific competence of teachers or school quality, more on the college's presumed linkages to status groups or on diffuse "styles," "climates" or "tones" presumed to inhere in the school. Such forms of trust are problematic, for conceptions of expressive education are less clear-cut than ideas about technical preparation, and are likely to be at variance with those of the faculty. These disagreements may have to do with both the tentativeness and scope of trust. The faculty expects "commitment"; the students wait to see whether the school will live up to its promise

---

23 Cf. Morris Janowitz, "Institution Building in Urban Education," *Working Paper*, Center for Social Organization Studies, University of Chicago, 1968.

and whether the expressive content of the curriculum in fact will be personally satisfying. They also may try to reserve a domain of privacy against the moral imperialism of a faculty seeking a "total" educative environment.[24]

When expressive socialization is at issue, then, whether in first grade or college, student trust is more emergent than explicit. At the college level, however, its explicitness varies with the clarity of the adult life style or status destination in view. In societies, for example, where college education prepares for or validates claims to a well-defined gentlemanly status, students are likely to have quite firm commitments to expressive forms of education. The decline of the gentleman, however, may be accompanied by declining student commitment to liberal aims, a greater tendency to be seduced by instrumental-vocational goals, and a struggle, even in select colleges, to preserve a humane tradition and re-socialize students to the gentlemanly ideal.

These matters are complicated by the sex composition of student bodies, but differently at the several school levels. These differences arise as students learn what peers and parents expect of them as boys and girls or men and women. Little clear-cut evidence exists on the effects of sex-typing for schools. There is some reason to believe, however, that in the elementary grades (beyond the earliest years when sex roles are quite diffuse), boys tend generally to reject teacher demands for competitive academic performance and to resist involvement in the more explicitly expressive aspects of the school curriculum—art, music, and the like.[25] Both parents and peers reinforce this boyish masculinity, which weakens and narrows boys' trust in schools and teachers. Girls, on the other hand, as they learn to be docile and compliant, tend to be broadly trusting in school and to excel academically.

By high school, these tendencies are accentuated, partly because the male student society becomes more tightly integrated (around athletics, for example), while girls, involved in the "rating and dating complex"

---

[24] Probably more destructive of student trust has been the assumed necessity for college administrators to safeguard the morals of students, a task abandoned by the faculties, in deference to presumptive parental, or community, standards. Not clearly related to the college's academic programs (signified especially by faculty unconcern), these efforts have been challenged increasingly by students no longer deferent to *any* parental demand and unwilling to trust colleges in areas not clearly related to instruction.

[25] Eleanor Maccoby, *Development of Sex Differences* (Stanford, California: Stanford University Press, 1966).

can afford, or may be forced, to be academic competitors.[26] This competitiveness, however, may be less among girls from working class families, whose parents are likely to find home more than school the appropriate arena for learning womanly responsibilities.[27] At the same time, a cleavage may appear among male students between those for whom the instrumental aspects of schooling are a sensible preparation for jobs or college and those for whom school is a senseless barrier to full-fledged adulthood.[28] In general, then, the effect of sex typing among middle-class high school students is to reinforce among boys the tendency toward instrumentally-centered narrow grants of trust, while encouraging trust of greater scope among girls. Among working class students of either sex, it may cause generalized failures of trust in school.

By college and university, the effects of sex typing have changed. Women appear to withdraw from the rigors of academic competition, especially in the more "masculine" instrumental subjects, and in co-educational schools. On the average, they do less well in these settings than men of equal ability.[29] They are found in disproportionate numbers in the more expressive fields—not only education, but, for example, the humanities and more humane social sciences.[30] These fields are defined as less "masculine" and also seem to give freer rein to the "creative," "artistic," and nurturant impulses suitable to the female role.[31] Men now begin to excel in the "tougher," and more instrumental areas of the curriculum, as the competitive rigors of the higher occupations make themselves felt both in the curriculum and in sex-typed performance.[32]

About the effects of these phenomena on college student trust, one can only speculate. But, recalling that college student bodies are more or less self-selected (on grounds of social class, motivation, ability, and the like), the effect of sex identities appears to be less on the level than the scope of trust, as women are drawn into the more diffuse, expressive fields and there find greater stimulus to academic performance than in

---

[26] Gordon, *op. cit.,* J. S. Coleman, *The Adolescent Society* (New York: The Free Press, 1961).

[27] Cf. Herbert Gans, *The Urban Villagers* (New York: The Free Press, 1962).

[28] Stinchcombe, *op. cit.*

[29] Maccoby, *op. cit.*

[30] *Ibid.,* also James A. Davis, *Undergraduate Career Decisions* (Chicago: Aldine Press, 1965).

[31] Jesse Bernard, *Academic Women* (University Park, Pennsylvania: State University Press, 1964).

[32] Maccoby, *op. cit.*

68

the more specific, instrumental areas in which men come to excel. If this is so, it should be more difficult to maintain a viable "total" educational environment in a college the greater the proportion of men it enrolls. For this assertion I have no real evidence. It is interesting, though, that men's colleges in America have not had notable success as peaceful or human student communities, while the women's colleges purportedly have been more successful at capturing and manipulating the loyalties of their students. Current student demands from the women's colleges for coeducation may be only a new statement of the expressive orientation, with the resistance of the alumni and faculty of these colleges as the sign of a persistent sense of community.*

---

* I am grateful especially to Eliot Freidson for his helpful comments on an earlier draft of this chapter.

# IV DOMINANT PROFESSIONS, BUREAUCRACY, AND CLIENT SERVICES

*Eliot Freidson*

FOR AT LEAST A CENTURY WE HAVE BEEN TREATED TO THE USE OF THE word "bureaucracy" as an epithet. Indeed, we have tended to take as self-evidently true the assertion that the rationalization and systematization of work, governed by formal administrative authority and written rules, leads to a fragmentation of experience, a loss of meaning, and a sense of alienation. Bureaucratic principles have come to dominate the process of industrial production and increasingly dominate the commercial organization of sales and many personal services. Even more recently, in the case of health, education, and social welfare services, bureaucratization has been growing. In such settings, too, where the organization justifies its existence by the benefits it provides clientele, clients are said to suffer a sense of helplessness, anxiety, and resentment over the way the organization of services has led to their depersonalization and loss of dignified identity. The culprit is thought to be the organizing principle of bureaucracy—orderly, systematic administrative procedures designed to ensure that work is done efficiently, honestly and fairly.

In contrast to the negative word "bureaucracy" we have the word "profession." This word is almost always positive in its connotation, and is frequently used to represent a superior alternative to bureaucracy. Unlike "bureaucracy," which is disclaimed by every organization concerned with its public relations, "profession" is claimed by virtually every occupation seeking to improve its public image. When the two terms are brought together, the discussion is almost always at the ex-

71

pense of "bureaucracy," and to the advantage of "profession." The principles underlying the two are said to be antithetical, the consequences of one being malignant and the other benign.

Over the years the literature has emphasized the differences between the two. Parsons pointed out that Max Weber, in his classic discussion of rational-legal bureaucracy, failed to distinguish between the authority of administrative office (generic to rational-legal bureaucracy) and the authority of expertise (generic to profession).[1] Making use of that distinction in the context of a study of a gypsum plant, Gouldner suggested that conventional, monocratic, and "punishment-centered" bureaucratic rules may not be so effective in ordering human effort in organizations as may rules based on expertise and consented to by all parties involved.[2] Elaborating on Gouldner's discussion, Goss[3] and Smigel[4] have developed conceptions of "advisory" and "professional" bureaucracy in which expertise is critical in creating and enforcing the rules. Many other writers, Thompson[5] and Blau[6] among them, have suggested that the principles of expertise and professionalization may constitute more efficient and more personally satisfying modes of organizing work than the classical principles of rational-legal administrative coordination. By virutally all writers, expertise and professions are equated with a flexible, creative and equalitarian way of organizing work, while bureaucracy is associated with rigidity, and with mechanical and authoritarian ways. There are, however, two important problems overlooked by that literature.

First, it seems to assume that technical expertise, unlike "arbitrary" administrative authority, is in some way neutrally functional and therefore so self-evidently true as to automatically produce cooperation or obedience in others and the efficient attainment of ends. In Gouldner's analysis, for example, we are told that so long as the *end* of technical expertise is accepted by workers, the expert's recommendation of means to that end will also be accepted automatically or at least without serious

---

[1] Talcott Parsons, "Introduction," in Max Weber, *The Theory of Social and Economic Organization* (New York: The Free Press of Glencoe, 1964), pp. 58–60.

[2] Alvin W. Gouldner, *Patterns of Industrial Bureaucracy* (New York: The Free Press of Glencoe, 1964).

[3] Mary E. W. Goss, "Patterns of Bureaucracy Among Hospital Staff Physicians," in Eliot Freidson, ed., *The Hospital in Modern Society* (New York: The Free Press of Glencoe, 1963), pp. 170–194.

[4] Erwin O. Smigel, *The Wall Street Lawyer* (New York: The Free Press of Glencoe, 1964).

[5] Victor Thompson, *Modern Organization* (New York: Alfred A. Knopf, 1961).

[6] Peter Blau, *The Dynamics of Bureaucracy* (Chicago: University of Chicago Press, 1959).

72

question in a "representative" or "expert" bureaucracy.[7] The implication is that when all workers can participate in setting ends in a complex organization, technical expertise can guide the way production is carried out without the necessity of exercising "punishment-centered" authority. Similarly, the implication in Parsons' comparison [8] of the authority of office with the authority of expertise is that while the former arbitrarily compels obedience, the latter is in some way naturally compelling by virtue of the fact that it is expertise and not office which is giving "orders."

But as I have shown elsewhere,[9] the authority of expertise is in fact problematic, requiring in its pure functional form the time-consuming and not always successful effort of persuading others that its "orders" are at once true and appropriate. As a special kind of occupation, professions have attempted to solve the problem of persuasion by obtaining institutional powers and prerogatives which at the very least set limits on the freedom of their prospective clients, and which on occasion even coerce their clients into compliance. The expertise of the professional is institutionalized into something similar to bureaucratic office. The implications of this fact have not been considered in the literature comparing "bureaucratic" and "professional" modes of organizing the performance of work.

Second, virtually all past work has compared an organization as a whole, from top to bottom and across all specialized tasks organized by bureaucratic administration, with a single specialized work group or profession within that larger organization and the way its members are ordered by their occupational norms. Such comparison illogically contrasts a whole with a part. What is required logically is comparison between 1) the ordering and mobilization of *all* types of workers in the organization's division of labor by office-holders who have administrative but not necessarily technical or productive expertise with 2) the ordering of the *complete* division of labor in an organization by the principle of technical expertise independent of bureaucratic office.

As I shall point out in this chapter, holding in mind characterizations of rational-legal, monocratic bureaucracies as wholes, when one looks at the *total* collection of workers among which professionals are found in some organizations, and when one examines how their interrelations

---

[7] Gouldner, *op. cit.*, pp. 221–22.

[8] Parsons, *op. cit.*

[9] See Eliot Freidson, "The Impurity of Professional Authority," in Howard S. Becker, *et al., Institutions and the Person: Essays Presented to Everett C. Hughes* (Chicago: Aldine Publishing Co., 1968).

are ordered by the authority of professional expertise, one finds distinctive properties which qualify considerably the significance of traditional contrasts between the consequences of bureaucracy and of profession on the experience of both workers and clients, and on the distribution of services to clients. I wish to suggest that the division of labor has a social organization distinct from any "external" or "artificial" authority imposed on it by "administrators." That social organization is constituted by the relations which occupations within a division of labor have to each other. Such relations are not merely determined by the functional interdependence of those occupations, but also by the social characteristics of the occupations themselves. The social organization of the division of labor is especially distinctive, I believe, when occupations with a special professional status are involved. Indeed, a division of labor ordered by professional rather than by administrative authority contains within it mechanisms and consequences similar to those described as the pathologies of bureaucracy.

Concentrating on the field of health, which is the most highly professionalized area of work to be found in our society, I shall suggest that many of the rigid, mechanical, and authoritarian attributes, and much of the inadequate coordination said to characterize the health services, may stem more from its professional organization than from its bureaucratic characteristics. In my discussion I shall deal with the influence of such organization on client experience as well as on the division of labor as such. Starting with a concrete organizational setting, I will point out how one kind of professional organization produces a non-bureaucratic but nonetheless real rigidity and authoritarianism which may be as much if not more responsible for the tribulations of the patient than the specifically bureaucratic elements of the health organization. Furthermore, I will point out how the place of the dominant profession in the health-related division of labor influences other workers, the emphasis of health services, and the facility with which the client receives services. But I must first clarify what I mean by the word, "profession."

## PROFESSION AS ORGANIZED AUTONOMY

A great many words have been consumed by discussions of what a profession is—or rather, what the best definition of "profession" is.[10]

---

[10] E.g., Morris I. Cogen, "Toward a Definition of Profession," *Harvard Educational Review,* XXIII (1953), 33–50.

Unfortunately, discussion has been so fixed on the question of definition that not much analysis has been made of the significance and consequences of some of the elements common to most definitions. The most critical of such underexamined elements are organizational in character, dealing with the organization of practice and of the division of labor. Such elements are critical because they deal with facets of professional occupations which are independent of individual motivation or intention, and that may, as Carlin has suggested for law,[11] minimize the importance to behavior of the personal qualities of intelligence, ethicality and trained skill imputed to professionals by most definitions. The key to such institutional elements of professions, I believe, lies in the commonly invoked word, "autonomy." Autonomy is said to mean, "the quality or state of being independent, free and self-directing." [12] In the case of professions, autonomy apparently refers most of all to control over the content if not the terms of the work. That is, the professional is self-directing in his work.

From the single condition of self-direction, or autonomy, I believe we can deduce or derive virtually all the other institutional elements that are included in most definitions of professions. For example, an occupational group is more likely to be able to be self-directing in its work when it has obtained a legal or political position of privilege that protects it from encroachment by other occupations. This is one of the functions of licensure,[13] which provides an occupation with a legal monopoly over the performance of some strategic aspect of its work so as to effectively prevent free competition from other occupations. In the United States, for example, the physician is virtually the only one who can legally prescribe drugs and cut into the body. Competitors are left with being able to talk to the patients and to lay hands *on* the body, but they may not penetrate the body chemically or physically.

Second, an occupational group is not likely to be able to be self-directing if it cannot control the production and particularly the application of knowledge and skill to the work it performs. This is to say, if the substance of its knowledge and skill is known to and performed by others, the occupation cannot be self-directing because those others can legitimately criticize and otherwise evaluate the way it carries out its work, thereby limiting autonomy by having the last word. The extended period of education controlled by the profession is an exclusively

---

[11] Jerome Carlin, *Lawyers' Ethics* (New York: Russell Sage Foundation, 1966).
[12] *Webster's Third New International Dictionary* (Springfield, Mass.: G. & C. Merriam Co., 1967), p. 148.
[13] Cf. W. K. Selden, *Accreditation* (New York: Harper, Row, 1960).

segregated professional rather than liberal arts school, and in a curriculum which includes some *special* theoretical content (whether scientifically proven or not), may be seen to represent a declaration that there is a body of special knowledge and skill necessary for doing the occupation's work which is not presented in colleges of arts and sciences or their specialized departments. The existence of such self-sufficient schools in itself rules out as *legitimate* arbiters of the occupation's work those with specialized training in the same area, but training received from some other kind of school. The professional school and its curriculum also, of course, constitute convenient institutional criteria for licensure, registration, or other exclusionary legal devices.

Third, a code of ethics or some other publicly waved banner of good intentions may be seen as a formal method of declaring to all that the occupation can be trusted, and thus persuades society to grant the special status of autonomy. The very existence of such a code implies that individual members of the occupation have the personal qualities of professionalism, the imputation of which is also useful for obtaining autonomy. Thus, most of the commonly cited attributes of professions may be seen either as consequences of their autonomy, or as conditions useful for persuading the public and the body politic to grant such autonomy.

## AUTONOMY AND DOMINANCE IN THE DIVISION OF LABOR

Clearly, however, autonomy is not a simple criterion. One can think of many occupations which are autonomous merely by virtue of the esoteric character of their craft or the circumstances in which they work. Nightclub magicians and circus acrobats, for example, form autonomous occupations by virtue of their intensive specialization in an area of work that is itself narrowly specialized without at the same time constituting part of an interdependent division of labor. Other occupations are fairly autonomous because their work takes place in a mobile or physically segregated context such as to prevent others from observing, and therefore evaluating and controlling performance. In these cases we have *autonomy by default.* An occupation is left wholly to its own devices because there is no strong public concern with its work, because it works independently of any functional division of labor, and because its work is such (in complexity, specialization or observability) as to preclude easy evaluation and control by others.

Where we find autonomy by default, we find no formal institutions in existence which serve to protect the occupation from competition, intervention, evaluation and direction by others. Should interest in such an autonomous occupation be aroused among other workers or in society, its autonomy would prove to be fragile indeed without the introduction of such institutions. In short, most stable and relevant to professions is *organized autonomy.*

When we turn to look at occupations engaged in such a complex division of labor as is found in the field of health, however, we find that the only occupation which is truly autonomous is medicine itself.[14] It has the authority to direct and evaluate the work of others without in turn being subject to formal direction and evaluation by them. Paradoxically, its autonomy is sustained by the *dominance* of its expertise in the division of labor. It is true that some of the occupations it dominates —nursing for example—claim to be professions. So do other groups which lack either organized autonomy or dominance claim the name— schoolteachers and social workers, for example. Surely there is a critically significant difference between dominant professions and those others who claim the name but do not possess the status, for while the members of all may be committed to their work, may be dedicated to service, and may be specially educated, the dominant profession stands in an entirely different structural relationship to the division of labor than does the subordinate. To ignore that difference is to ignore something major. One might call many occupations "professions" if one so chooses, but there is a difference between the dominant profession and the others. In essence, the difference reflects the existence of a *hierarchy of institutionalized expertise.* That hierarchy of office to be found in rational-legal, monocratic bureaucracies, can have the same effect on the experience of the client as bureaucracy is said to have. Let me briefly indicate how.

## THE CLIENT IN THE HEALTH ORGANIZATION

Unlike education, where most services are given within complex organizations, in the field of health most personal services have been given in settings that are, organizationally, analogous to small shops. For a

---

[14] See Eliot Freidson, "Paramedical Personnel," in *International Encyclopedia of the Social Sciences* (New York: Macmillan and Free Press, 1968), Vol. X, pp. 114–120, for a more complete discussion of the division of labor as a social organization.

number of reasons, however, the proportion of personal health services given in complex organizations like hospitals seems to be increasing. And it is the service in such organizations that has been most criticized for dehumanizing care. But is it bureaucratic office or institutionalized expertise which produces the client experience underlying that criticism?

Some of the complaints, such as the cost of hospitalization, reflect the method of financing medical care in the United States rather than the organization as such. Other complaints—such as those about poor food, noise, and general amenities—seem to reflect the economic foundation and capital plant of the institution rather than its organization. For our present question, two sets of complaints seem most important—those related to the physical treatment for sickness, and those related to the discomforts of being in a patient role in medical organizations.

Clearly many complaints about the depersonalization of the client in the medical organization are complaints about what some technical ostensibly therapeutic procedures do to people.[15] Simply to be strapped on a rolling table and wheeled down corridors, into and out of elevators, and, finally, out into an operating room for the scrutiny of all is to be treated like an object, not a person. To be anesthetized is to become literally an object without the consciousness of a person. And to be palpitated, poked, dosed, purged, cut into, probed, and sewed is to find oneself an object. In such cases, it is the technical work of the profession, not "bureaucracy," which is responsible for some of the unpleasantness the client experiences in health organizations. That unpleasantness is partly analogous to what is supposedly suffered by the industrial worker when the machine he works on requires him to make limited, repetitive motions at some mechanically paced speed. It is directly analogous to what is suffered by the raw materials shaped by worker and machine in productive industry.

Such discomfort may easily be excused by the outcome—that is, improvement or cure is generally thought to be a product well worth the discomfort of being treated like an object. The problem, though, is to determine exactly how much of that treatment has any necessary bearing at all on the technical outcome. There is no doubt that some of the management of the patient has little or no bearing on the purely technical requirements for treatment. Some practices bear on the bureaucratic problem of administering services to a number of individ-

---

[15] Important in this context is Erving Goffman, "The Medical Model and Mental Hospitalization," in Erving Goffman, *Asylums* (Garden City: Doubleday and Co., 1961), pp. 321–386.

uals in a manner that is fair, precise, predictable and economical. Other practices bear on the convenience of the staff, medical or otherwise, and while they may be justified by reference to staff needs as workers, such justification has no bearing on staff expertise as such. Without denying the role of formal bureaucratic organization in creating some of the problem, it is the role of the professional worker himself I wish to examine more closely if only because, in medical and other organizations, the professional worker is specifically antibureaucratic, insisting on controlling the management of treatment himself. The question is, how do professional practices contribute to the unhappy experience of the patient?

The best way of beginning to answer that question seems to lie in recalling the difference I made between an object and a person. An object does not possess the capacity for understanding, and its behavior cannot be influenced by communication or understanding. When a person is treated *as if* he were an object, he will nonetheless behave on the basis of his understanding of that treatment. Naturally, his understanding is formed in part by what he brings with him into the treatment setting. It is also formed by the sense he himself can make of what is happening to him in the treatment setting. Since the treatment setting is presumably dominated by specialized, expert procedures, however, the most critical source of his information and understanding lies in the staff and its ability and inclination to communicate with the patient. If the staff does not communicate to the patient the meaning of and justification for what is done to him, it in essence refuses him the status of a responsible adult, or of a person in the full sense of the word.

The extent to which the staff withholds information from the patient, and avoids communicative interaction with him, has been a common criticism of the operation of such medical organizations as hospitals.[16] The complaint is that no one tells the client what is going to be done to him, why, and when. And after he has been treated, no one tells him why he feels the way he does, what can be expected subsequently, and whether or not he will live or die. The charge is that so little information is provided him that the patient cannot evaluate the meaning of the manner in which he is being treated. Experience is mysteriously

---

[16] For example, see the following: Julius A. Roth, "The Treatment of Tuberculosis as a Bargaining Process," in A. M. Rose, ed., *Human Behavior and Social Processes* (Boston: Houghton Mifflin Co., 1962), pp. 575–588; Jeanne C. Quint, "Institutionalized Practices of Information Control," *Psychiatry*, XXVIII (1965), 119–132.

meaningless, including long waits for something unknown to happen, or for something that does not happen; being awakened for an apparently trivial reason; being examined by taciturn strangers who enter the room unintroduced; perceiving lapses in such routines as medication and feeding without knowing whether error or intent is at issue. Surely this experience is little different from that of Kafka's antibureaucratic hero of *The Castle.*

In commercial organizations, "personalized forms," and other superficial means are employed to acknowledge their clients' status as responsible adults capable of intelligent choice and self-control. In the hospital situation, explanations by the staff would supply such acknowledgements, yet they do not occur. Part of the reason may stem from the necessity to treat clients in batches standardized by their technical status and by the services they require. Some reason may also be found in understaffing and overwork, which excuses the minimization of interaction with some in order to maximize it with those who have more "serious" problems. But these reasons do not explain why *bureaucratic* solutions to the problem of communication are not adopted—for example, distributing brochures explaining and justifying hospital routines, describing the experiences of "typical" cholycystectomies, mastectomies, or heart patients from the first day through convalescence, and including answers to "commonly asked questions." The prime reason for the failure to communicate with the patient does not, I believe, lie in underfinancing, understaffing, or bureaucratization. Rather, they lie in the professional organization of the hospital, and in the professional's conception of his relation to his clients.

In the medical organization, the medical profession is dominant. This means that all the work by other occupations which is related to the service of the patient is subject to the order of the physician.[17] The dominant profession alone is held competent to diagnose illness, treat or direct the treatment of illness, and evaluate the service. Without medical authorization, little can be done for the patient by paraprofessional workers. The client's medication, diet, excretion, and recreation are all subject to medical "orders." So is the information given to the patient. By and large, without medical authorization paramedical workers are not supposed to communicate anything of significance to

---

[17] E.g., Albert F. Wessen, "Hospital Ideology and Communication Between Ward Personnel," in E. G. Jaco, ed., *Patients, Physicians and Illnesses* (New York: The Free Press of Glencoe, 1958), pp. 448–468.

the patient about what his illness is, how it will be treated, and what the chances are for improvement. The physician himself is inclined to be rather jealous of the prerogative, and is not inclined to authorize other workers to communicate information to the patient. Consequently, the paraprofessional worker who is asked for information by a patient is inclined to pass the buck like any bureaucrat—"You'll have to ask your doctor," the patient is told.

The dominant professional, then, is jealous of his prerogative to diagnose and forecast illness, holding it tightly to himself. But while he does not want anyone else to give information to the patient, neither is he himself inclined to do so. A number of reasons are advanced for this disinclination—the difficulty of being sure about diagnosis and precise about prognosis being perhaps the most neutral and technical of them all. Another reason is the physician's own busy schedule—that he does not have the time to spend in conversation with the patient, that more serious cases need his attention. But the reasons of uncertainty and of time-pressure are rather too superficial to dwell on. In the former case, the fact of uncertainty can constitute a communication, though as Davis has shown [18] it can be asserted to avoid communication; in the latter case, the task can merely be delegated if the doctor is lacking time. For our present purposes, the most revealing argument against communication is based on characteristically professional assumptions about the nature of clients as such. The argument, which goes back at least as far as Hippias' defensive remarks in the Hippocratic Corpus, asserts that, lacking professional training, the client is too ignorant to be able to comprehend what information he gets, and that he is in any case too upset at being ill to be able to use the information he does get in a manner that is rational and responsible.[19] From this it follows that giving information to the patient does not help him, but rather upsets him and creates additional "management problems" for the physician. Thus, the patient should not be treated like an adult, but rather like a child, given reassurance but not information. To do otherwise would only lead to the patient being upset and making unnecessary trouble for the staff. Characteristically, the professional does not view the client as an adult, responsible person.

In addition, it is worth pointing out the implications of the profes-

---

[18] Fred Davis, "Uncertainty in Medical Prognosis, Clinical and Functional," *American Journal of Sociology,* LXVI (1960), 41–47.

[19] See, for example, the material in Barney G. Glaser and Anselm L. Strauss, *Awareness of Dying* (Chicago: Aldine Publishing Co., 1965).

sional insistence on faith or trust rather than persuasion. The client, lacking professional training, is thought to be unequipped for intelligent evaluation of or informed cooperation with his consultant. Essentially, he is expected either to have faith in his consultant and do what he is told without searching questions, or else to choose another consultant in whom he does have faith. To question one's doctor is to show lack of faith and is justifiable grounds for the doctor to threaten to withdraw his services. Such insistence on faith, I believe, rests on more than the purely functional demands of an effective therapeutic or service relationship. It also neutralizes threat to status. The very special social position of institutionalized privilege that is the profession's is threatened as well as demeaned by the demand that advice and action be explained and justified to a layman. If the professional must justify himself to a layman, he must use grounds of evidence and logic common to both professional and layman, and cannot use esoteric grounds known and subscribed to by the profession alone. Insistence on faith constitutes insistence that the client must give up his role as an independent adult and, by so neutralizing him, protects the esoteric foundation of the profession's institutionalized authority.[20]

# OTHER WORKERS IN THE PROFESSIONAL ORGANIZATION

Thus far, I have pointed out that in medical organizations if the client is alienated the source is professional rather than bureaucratic authority.[21] Some alienating characteristics of professional authority may lead to practices with a curiously bureaucratic look to them, including such notorious practices as passing the buck, and such a notorious problem as (in the form of requiring doctor's orders) red tape. In this organization the client's position is similar to that which he is said to suffer in civil service bureaucracies—handled like an object, given little information or opportunity for choice, and unable to feel like a responsible adult. And what of the subordinate worker in this setting dominated by a profession?

---

[20] For a more extensive discussion of the professional ideology see Eliot Freidson, *Profession of Medicine* (New York: Dodd, Mead and Co., 1970).

[21] For a rare study of patients using a measure of alienation, see John W. Evans, "Stratification, Alienation and the Hospital Setting," *Engineering Experiment Station Bulletin,* No. 184, Ohio State University, 1960.

As I noted at the beginning of this paper, it has been felt by many writers that the worker as well as the client suffers from the bureaucratization of production by a monocratic administration. Lacking identification with the prime goals of the organization, lacking an important voice in setting the formal level and direction of work, and performing work which has been so rationalized as to become mechanical and meaningless, functioning as a minute segment of an intricate mosaic of specialized activities which he is in no position to perceive or understand, the worker is said to be alienated. In contrast to the bureaucratized worker, however, the professional is said to be committed to and identified with his work so that it retains meaning for him, becoming in fact a central life interest. This may be true for dominant professions, but what of the other occupations working in the organization which the professional dominates? Are they not prone to alienation?

By and large, this question has not been asked in past studies, for the emphasis has been more on the positive response of "professionalism" than on the negative responses of alienation. What evidence there is, however, indicates that there are serious problems of worker morale in professional settings. Available studies are fairly clear about the existence of hierarchy in the professional health organization, and about a decrease of participation in decision-making the farther down the hierarchy one goes. Neither the ends nor the means of their work seem to be a matter for legitimate determination by lower level workers, though of course they do have their sometimes very strong informal influence on such determination. Furthermore, even in situations where the stated official expectation is free participation by all workers in conferences about the running of such units as wards, participation has been observed to be quite unequal.[22]

The paraprofessional worker is, then, like the industrial worker, subordinated to the authority of others. He is not, however, subordinated solely to the authority of bureaucratic office, but also to the positively superior knowledge and judgment of professional experts. In some studies this authority is characterized as a kind of stratification,[23] in

---

[22] For example, see the findings in William Caudill, *The Psychiatric Hospital as a Small Society* (Cambridge: Harvard University Press, 1958).

[23] See M. Seeman and J. W. Evans, "Stratification and Hospital Care," *American Sociological Review*, XXVI (1961), 67–80, 193–204, and Ivan Oxaal, "Social Stratification and Personnel Turnover in the Hospital," *Engineering Experiment Station Monograph*, No. 3, Ohio State University, 1960.

others as a function of status.[24] In very few if any of such studies is that status or stratification said to be of administrative or bureaucratic origin. It is instead largely of professional origin. In a few studies the notion of alienation has been specifically cited.[25] Clearly, while there is no comparative evidence to allow us to determine whether more or fewer workers are alienated from professional than from bureaucratic organizations, neither hierarchical nor authoritarian tendencies are missing in the professional organization of the division of labor, nor are alienation, absenteeism, low morale and high turnover insignificant problems. Just as is true for the patient, so is it true for the worker that the professionally organized division of labor has pathologies similar to those said to stem from bureaucracy.

## SUBSTANTIVE BIAS IN CLIENT SERVICES

Thus far I have compared the influence of professional authority with the influence of bureaucratic authority on the experience of both client and worker in the physically limited corporate body we usually call an organization. Since, however, inter-organizational relations may themselves be seen as organization, and since the production of particular goods and services is rarely limited to the confines of a single corporate body, requiring a variety of functions from outside "the" organization, it seems useful to continue my comparison in the rather broader context of planning and coordinating service as such. I have already noted that the common assumption is that the expert authority has a neutral, functional foundation rather than, like bureaucratic authority, the foundation of arbitrary office. If this is so, then we should expect that the influence of expert authority on the support and planning of services would be highly functional, lacking arbitrary bias from the special vantage of bureaucratic office. Our expectation is not so met in health services. There, the dominant profession exercises great influence on the disposition of

---

[24] See E. G. Mishler and A. Tropp, "Status and Interaction in a Psychiatric Hospital," *Human Relations,* IX (1956) 187–205, and William R. Rosengren, "Status Stress and Role Contradictions: Emergent Professionalization in Psychiatric Hospitals," *Mental Hygiene,* XLV (1961) 28–39.

[25] See Rose L. Coser, "Alienation and the Social Structure: Case Study of a Hospital," in Freidson, *Hospital in Modern Society, op. cit.,* pp. 231–265, and L. I. Pearlin, "Alienation from Work: A Study of Nursing Personnel," *American Sociological Review,* XXVII (1962), 314–326.

resources which make services available for clients. The character of that influence does stem from professional views of the purely functional considerations of what service is needed to accomplish some desired end, but those views have been distorted by the lenses of a special occupational perspective.

To understand how resources get distributed to the varied health services sought or required by the client, we must keep in mind the fact that the medical division of labor is not functionally complete. It is composed solely of those occupations and services controlled by the dominant profession. Outside of it are some which perform work that is functionally and substantively related to the profession, but not subject to the profession's authority. In matters of health in the United States, such occupations as dentistry, optometry, chiropracty and clinical psychology exemplify by their independent existence the functional incompleteness of the medically ordered division of labor. Furthermore, these are occupational groups whose work is often at least partly related to health problems, but which are not recognized medical occupations—schoolteachers, specialized training and guidance personnel, social workers, and even ministers may be cited here. These are not part of the medically ordered division of labor either. Thus, while the profession stands as the supreme authority in the medical division of labor, the medical division of labor does not encompass all health-related activities of the large health-related division of labor. Nonetheless, the distribution of support and resources tends to move disproportionately through the medical division of labor.

I have argued for the distinction of a type of profession that has ultimate authority over its work in such a way that it is self-directing or autonomous, and dominant in a division of labor. In the case of medicine, a strategic facet of its authority is its delineation of pathology, of the definitions of health and illness which guide the application of knowledge to human ills. The physician is the ultimate expert on what is health and what illness, and on how to attain the former and cure the latter. Indeed, his perspective leads him to see the world in terms of health and illness, and the world is presently inclined to turn to him for advice on all matters related to health and illness irrespective of his competence. Given the highly visible miracles medicine has worked over the past century, the public has even been inclined to ask the profession to deal with problems that are not of the bio-physical character for which success was gained from past efforts. What were once recognized as economic, religious and personal problems have

85

found redefinitions as illness, and have therefore become medical problems.[26] This widening of medical jurisdiction has had important consequences for the allocation of resources to client services.

No philanthropies today seem to be able to attract more financial support than those devoting themselves to an illness, particularly one that affects children. If the label of illness can be attached to a problem, it receives extensive support. And it also becomes dominated by medical institutions even when there is no evidence that medical institutions have any especially efficacious way of dealing with the problem. By virtue of being the proprietor of notions of illness and health, medicine has in fact become a giant umbrella under which a disparate variety of workers (including sociologists) can be both financed and protected from overclose outside scrutiny by virtue of their semantically created connection with health. But those that do not or cannot choose to huddle under the umbrella, even though their work is health related, tend to find it difficult to obtain support.

One rather obvious consequence is the uneven distribution of resources to health-related activities. For example, it was pointed out recently that heavy financing has been given to medical research into mental deficiency, only a small amount of which is biologically or genetically caused, while *educational* facilities for the training and teaching of mental deficients have been solely underfinanced.[27] Less obvious and more important to public welfare is the extent to which this uneven distribution of resources emphasizes some hypotheses and investigatory and therapeutic models at the expense of others equally plausible. For example, it was recently pointed out that work in rehabilitation has come to be pulled in under medical supervision, the result of which has been the inappropriate emphasis on the traditional authoritarian therapeutic relationship of medicine which I have already discussed.[28] By and large, within the well-financed division of labor dominated by the profession and under its protective umbrella, most work is limited to that which conforms to the special perspective and substantive style of the profession—a perspective that emphasizes the

---

[26] For an extended discussion of the relative place of notions of health and illness in modern society, see Eliot Freidson, *Profesion of Medicine, op. cit.*

[27] George W. Albee, "Needed—A Revolution in Caring for the Retarded," *Transaction*, V (1968) 37–42.

[28] Albert F. Wessen, "The Apparatus of Rehabilitation: An Organizational Analysis," in Marvin B. Sussman, ed., *Society and Rehabilitation* (Washington: American Sociological Association, 1966), pp. 148–178.

individual over the social environment, the treatment of rare and interesting disorders over those that are common and uninteresting, the cure rather than the prevention of illness, and preventive medicine rather than what might be called "preventive welfare"—social services and resources which improve the diet, housing, way of life and motivation of the people without the necessity for each to undertake consultation with a practitioner. In short, I suggest that by virtue of its position in the public esteem, and in its own division of labor, the dominant profession of the field of health exerts a special and biased influence on the planning and financing of the services of the general field within which it is located. The prime criterion for determining that emphasis is not necessarily functional in character, but social and structural—whether or not the services can be dominated by or be put under the umbrella of the dominant profession. The consequence for the client is an array of differentially supported services which may not be adequate for his needs and interests.

Finally, I might point out that given this array of health-related services, differentially developed and supported by functional and other considerations, still further qualifications of the kind of service a client is likely to get is exercised by the dominant profession. In general, I wish to suggest that when some of the relevant services lie outside of the medical division of labor and some inside, serious problems of access to relevant care and of the rational coordination of care are created by the barriers which the profession creates between that segment of the division of labor it does dominate, and that segment it does not.

Perhaps the simplest way of discussing those barriers is to examine the process by which clients move through the division of labor. They move in part by their own choice and selection of consultants, and in part by their consultants' choice of and referral to other consultants or technicians. To the extent that the client moves through the division of labor by his own volition, he is responsible for his own care and his consultants are dependent on him for relevant information about his problem. But to the extent to which the client is being guided by consultants, the character of his experience and care is dependent on the substantive direction of his consultants' referrals, and on the exchange of information among them bearing on treatment. Here is where the professionally created barrier is found. Within the general health division of labor, the referral of clients tends to go on in only one direction— into the smaller medical division of labor, without also going from the medical into the larger system. This is also generally true of the transmission of information about the client. To put it more bluntly, teachers, social workers, ministers and others outside of the medical division of labor refer to physicians, and communicate information about the client to them, but physicians are not likely either to refer clients to them or to provide them with the results of medical investigation.[29]

By the same token, physicians do not routinely refer to clinical psychologists, optometrists, chiropractors and others outside of the medical division of labor but clearly within the health division of labor. They are likely to refer only when they are sure that solely the limited services they may order and no more will be performed—psychological testing rather than psychotherapy, spectacle fitting and sales rather than refractions, and minor manipulations for medically untreatable muscular-skeletal complaints rather than for other complaints. They are also, wittingly or not, likely to discourage such workers' referrals to them by reciprocating neither referrals nor information about their findings. And from at least one study there is evidence that they are prone to reject the patient if he comes to them from an outside source.[30]

By and large, physicians refer to and communicate extensively only with those who, within the medical division of labor, are subject to their prescription, order or direction. Indeed, physicians are likely to be very poorly informed about any of the institutional and occupational resources that lie outside of their own jurisdiction. And, as is quite natural for people who have developed commitment to their work, they are likely to be suspicious of the value of all that lies outside their domain, including the competence and ethicality of those working outside. Their commitment leads them to deprecate the importance of extramedical services and their position as a profession encourages them to restrict their activities to the medical system they control. So long as this is all their clients need or want, no harm is done save for the possibility that the professional's response to outside services may encourage those outside to avoid or delay in referring clients to the physician. If services from outside are necessary for the client's well-being, however, referral to them may be delayed or never undertaken, and the client's interests unprotected.

---

[29] For work bearing on these statements see Elaine Cumming *et al., Systems of Social Regulation* (New York: Atherton Press, 1968). And see Eugene B. Piedmont, "Referrals and Reciprocity: Psychiatrists, General Practitioners, and Clergymen," *Journal of Health and Social Behavior,* IX (1968), 29–41.

[30] See David Schroder and Danuta Ehrlich, "Rejection by Mental Health Professionals: A Possible Consequence for Not Seeking Appropriate Help for Emotional Disorders," *Journal of Health and Social Behavior,* IX (1968), 222–232.

# PROFESSION, BUREAUCRACY AND THE CLIENT

I began this chapter with the comment that "bureaucracy" has become an epithet. From what I have said about "profession" in my exposition, you might think that I am attempting to make it, too, an epithet. This is not true. It is true, however, that I have attempted to remove the word from the realm of the normative, where most usage has been prone to keep it, and to move it into a realm of reality which is subject to logical and empirical investigation. In this effort, I have chosen first to use the word to refer to a way of *organizing work* rather than, as is common, to refer to an *orientation* toward work or a *body of knowledge*. By that criterion I suggested that we might distinguish between what are commonly (and, I believe, meaninglessly) called professions, and those which are dominant, directing others in a division of labor and being themselves autonomous, subect to direction by no other. Medicine is one of those dominant professions.

After discussing the implications of this usage for the other variables commonly attached to the notion of profession, I then went on to suggest some of the ways the medical profession influences health services. First, I suggested that the experience of the client in the medical organization—particularly the hospital—is created less by the bureaucratic elements in those organizations than by the work as such and by the perspective of the dominant profession which orders the activity of most of the occupations in the organization. Second, I suggested that the experience of the worker in the medical organization suggests alienation similar to that said to exist in bureaucratically organized settings. Third, I suggested that the planning and distribution of health resources tends to be weighted by the dominant profession's structural position in the division of labor as well as by the functional problems of health and illness as such. Finally, I suggested that in the cooperative exchange and referral of clients which is a prerequisite for the expeditious delivery of all necessary health-related services, the physician neither reciprocates referrals nor communicates with those who work outside of his own division of labor. In all four cases, and perhaps in more, I suggest, the relations between clients and organizations, and the relations between clients and the services they need are influenced strongly by the dominance of a single, autonomous profession. Insofar as there is pathology, much stems from the profession, not bureaucracy.

Thus, I suggest that the dominance of client services by the principle of expertise which is embodied in a professionally ordered division of labor is, analytically and practically, fully as problematic as is domi-

89

nance by the principles of rational-legal bureaucracy. Expertise institutionalized into a profession is not, as much writing seems to assume, an automatically self-correcting, purely task-oriented substitute for "arbitrary" bureaucracy. The definition of the work—that is, how the client should behave and what other workers should do—is a partial expression of the hierarchy created by the office, and of the ideology stemming from the perspective of the office as well as of the purely technical character of the work itself. And when that work involves personal services of some importance to the welfare of the client, both the ideology and the technology combine to produce bureaucracy-like consequences for his fate.

It may be said that my analysis, fixed as it has been on one profession, does not reflect all professions. This is true. Of all the established professions, only medicine has developed such an elaborate and complex division of labor. The division of labor in college teaching, for example, is positively primitive, though more so in the teaching of some subjects than others. So is the division of labor in the ministry. And in the case of law, while there is a fairly complex division of labor, most of it in the United States has as yet escaped dominance by the profession. But I believe it can be argued that medicine provides the most important even if not the most representative case of the professions because its dominance is the model toward which (and against which) ambitious occupations are now struggling. We may expect to see many more cases like medicine in the future.

## LIMITATIONS ON THE PROFESSIONAL PERSPECTIVE

Finally, I must say that my intent here has not been to find villains on whom to blame the problems confronting the organization and presentation of client services. Both professional and bureaucrat have, by and large, the best of intentions. Both, like everyone else, are creatures of their perspectives, and those perspectives are limited by training, by commitment, and by personal work experience which comes to be regarded as wisdom. This is not some easily remedied defect, but something inherent in the nature of social life requiring countervailing pressure from other perspectives more than better intentions from within. One serious difference between professional and bureaucrat, however, lies in the very existence of legitimate countervailing pressures.

90

As Parsons pointed out in distinguishing between the authority of office and the authority of expertise, a critical difference between bureaucrat and professional lies in the foundations for their authority. One is largely a creature of the organization itself and the laws which establish it, answerable to the organizational rules and to a legal order that stands outside of him, his colleagues and the organization in which he works. His client has recourse to both sets of rules and, in our society at least, has specific civil rights in that order. While it is a serious problem of our time how we can make such a formal, rational-legal order actually work efficiently, fairly, and humanely, the principles of the order are designed to protect both worker and client, giving them the basic right to be recognized as responsible adults.

Such protection does not exist unequivocally in professional organizations. Unlike the bureaucrat, who may on occasion attain autonomy by *default,* the professional has gained *organized autonomy* and is not bound by rules which stand outside of his profession. His performance, however, can produce the same barriers to communication and cooperation within a functional division of labor, the same structures of evasion and the same reduction of the client to an object which have been attributed to bureaucratic organization. In the name of health the client may be stripped of his civil status, a status which is as much if not more an element of his welfare as is his health. But unlike bureaucratic practices, which in rational-legal orders are considered arbitrary and subject to appeal and modification, professional practices are imputed the unquestioned objectivity of expertise and scientific truth, and so are not routinely subject to higher review or change by virtue of outside appeal. There is no generally accepted notion of due process for the layman— client or worker—in professional organization. And in theory, the lack of review or due process is as it should be, since the professional's arbitrary authority is not supposed to be that of bureaucratic office. In practice in the everyday world, though, there is no such thing as pure knowledge or expertise—there is only knowledge in the service of a practice.

Here is the crux of the matter. Expertise is not mere knowledge. It is the *practice* of knowledge, organized socially and serving as the focus for the practitioner's commitment. In this sense, it is not merely mechanical skill which like the cog of a machine, automatically fits itself into Durkheim's organic order. The worker does not see his work as merely different than another's. He develops around it an ideology and, with the best of intentions, an imperialism which stresses the technical superiority of his work and of his capacity to perform it. This imperialistic ideology is built into the perspective that his training and practice create. It cannot be overcome by ethical dedication to the public interest because it is sincerely believed in as the only proper way to serve the public interest. And it hardens when an occupation develops the autonomy of a profession and a place of dominance in a division of labor, and when expertise becomes an institutional status rather than a capacity. The pathology arises when outsiders may no longer evaluate the work by the rules of logic and the knowledge available to all educated men, and when the only legitimate spokesman on an issue relevant to all men must be someone who is officially certified.

# V MEMBERS AS RESOURCES IN VOLUNTARY ORGANIZATIONS

*Charles Perrow*

THERE ARE THREE THEMES IN THIS PAPER: FIRST IS AN ATTEMPT TO find some way to distinguish voluntary from nonvoluntary organizations. One is easily dissatisfied with the basis upon which most distinctions are made and I have tried to formulate a more effective criterion. Second, assuming some modest success with such a distinction, I might illuminate the problem of the role of voluntary associations in society, a matter which has been discussed at considerable length by pluralists. Third, I hope to shed some light upon perhaps the most distinctive organizational concern in this area, democracy and oligarchy in voluntary associations.[1]

In general I approach these organizations as organizations rather

---

[1] The reader will note that there are very few footnotes in the paper, and perhaps I should apologize for violating a long standing and generally sound, if tedious, convention of giving due credit to those who have been the first to put into print ideas (no matter how obvious) or discussions of topics (no matter how brief). I so apologize; unobvious and thorough discussions of all my topics have appeared before. I direct the interested (and uninformed) reader to a good survey of this literature and a quite full bibliography contained in David Sill's essay, "Voluntary Associations: Sociological Aspects," *International Encyclopedia of the Social Sciences* (New York: The Macmillan Company and Free Press, rev. ed., 1968), Volume 16, pp. 362–379.

In addition, I wish to acknowledge the emergency help rendered by a contentious group of graduate students at Wisconsin: Kenneth Bryson, Roy Gesley, Karl Magnusen, and Anthony Tillett. Finally, such conference participants as Eliot Freidson, Norton Long, Talcott Parsons, and William Rosengren pointed out several important problems I haven't solved.

than as elements in a theory of political process, integrating devices, or value maintaining or generating institutions. To do so I start with a conception of organizations as mechanisms for transforming raw materials into goods or services that are consumed by persons or groups. This model has a no-nonsense, rationalistic flavor which smacks of economic analysis. This is intentional; we should "retreat" to values, norms, ideologies, and so forth only when our steps falter. I shall so retreat frequently, but do not intend to commence with a normative view of voluntary associations.

# DEFINING THE VOLUNTARY ORGANIZATION

The category of voluntary associations is one of the grossest and most poorly conceptualized in the field of organizational analysis. The variety and diversity of organizations that can be considered by any one of several definitions to be voluntary associations is enormous. Almost any defining characteristic, such as goals, runs immediately into the problem that there are many exceptions and there are organizations which are obviously not voluntary which have the same defining characteristics. This suggests that most of our criteria for classifying organizations involve intersecting continua. It is not just that voluntary organizations are non-profit, they are also not governmental organizations. It is not just that they are private, they also have certain tax status not available to other private organizations. But it is not enough to say they are private, nonprofit organizations, for so are voluntary hospitals, which are usually not included. Therefore, one adds another criterion—most of their members do not receive salary or wages for their work. But for that matter, neither do investors in economic organizations, though they are legally considered members since they are owners. Investors have no guarantee of dividends or stock appreciation, whereas salary and wages are guaranteed by the law of contract. This suggests adding a criterion that eliminates organizations with economic goals, but that would rule out trade associations and investment clubs and farmers' organizations. Perhaps the answer is simply that voluntary associations do not have involuntary members. But there are many involuntary members of the American Medical Association and National Association of Social Workers, even though most would agree that these are voluntary associations.

The definitional problem might be solved through a conceptual "factor analysis" of multiple intersecting continua with fairly arbitrary cutting points on each one, but I would doubt that it would be worth the effort. We are interested in voluntary associations from some point of view, not just as a taxonomic exercise. The possible continua are usually anchored in fairly standard points of view or criteria that we apply to organizations such as the relationship to the larger social system, the official goals or actual output, legal status, public or private status, the motives of participants, and so on.

Now that scholars have the license to "do their own thing," I will enjoy that privilege myself and define voluntary organizations in terms of the nature of the raw material that it transforms in order to survive and meet various output expectations. This is a much neglected, but hopefully useful, characteristic of all organizations. Viewed in this light, the voluntary association is a distinctive beast in that most of its resources, or most of its raw materials, are also direct consumers of a good part of the product.

Let me elaborate. In one sense, all or most members of most organizations are also consumers of its products. The man who works for U.S. Steel also owns an automobile or refrigerator or garbage can that can have steel from "his" company in it; the clerk in the social security administration is contributing to social security, and so on. In a wealthy and interdependent society such as ours there are bound to be many of these dual roles. (The Chilean peasant also contributes to our cars and refrigerators, but does not consume them, nor is he counted in the figures on wage costs or value added in the U.S. Copper industry.) But, the steelworker does not join U.S. Steel in order to have access to motor cars built with its steel; he gains that access through the impersonal medium of money, through a wage. The clerk could participate in social security by working in one of Barry Goldwater's enterprises as well as by working for social security administration. Obvious enough; but what this leads to is the provision that consumption of some part of the output must be available only to members of the organization. Map routings provided by the American Automobile Association are for members only. But, on the other hand, when the AAA lobbies for more and more superhighways many people benefit (or suffer, depending upon your viewpoint). Red Cross volunteers need not expect themselves to benefit from war or disaster relief, but neither do they become members of the organization just to work during war or disasters. Their membership provides a number of rewards that are not attained by non-members—satisfactions of noblesse oblige, fulfilling social class and community expectations, using up leisure time in a meaningful way, meeting people, holding office, etc. Despite its aims, the organization survives and remains busy in periods of peace and quiet, and even survives competitive threats from large scale governmental alternatives ranging from the PX to the Corps of Engineers. Thus, some of the output must be exclusively available to members, but not all. In addition, the output is generally in a non-monetary medium of exchange—you do not receive money which then can be used to purchase a different output. I say generally because an investment club can be classified as a voluntary association, yet the output occurs in the form of dividends and stock appreciations. Except for making your own collective decisions regarding the investments, this is no different from a mutual fund, which is an economic organization.

The important distinction between these two is not the collective decision—for in that case, many voluntary organizations have no viable mechanism for collective decisions—but rather the legal status of the member. The member of a voluntary association has few if any legal claims that flow from his contribution; members of non-voluntary associations have rights which are protected by law. One may sue, in civil court, the managers of a mutual fund for mismanagement, but it would be hard to do so in the case of an investment club, and the charge would have to be a criminal one.

The legal status of voluntary associations appears to reflect the resource-consumption criterion I have been proposing. In non-voluntary organizations contributions must be matched by returns to the contributor or he has grounds for civil action. This is not so in voluntary associations, though I am sure that there are some grey-area exceptions. Any return to the member can be deferred indefinitely or never realized and is not controlled by law, because the category of contributor and consumer is identical. (This, incidentally, greatly enhances the opportunities for oligarchy and goal displacement in the organization.) The recourse of members is to leave the organization and form another one or join another one. This criterion also differentiates investors in firms from voluntary members of organizations. Investors give voluntarily of their money to the firm, receiving stock in return, which has the form of an unspecified return—it may or may not pay dividends, appreciate, or be worth anything if the company goes bankrupt and uses its assets to pay off other creditors who have first claim. However, investors can sue in courts for malpractice by the officers of the firm because they are, under law, owners rather than voluntary members.

To sum up then, voluntary associations can be distinguished from other organizations by virtue of the fact that members are both a primary source of raw materials for the organization and also consume a substantial part of the output; and that a substantial part of the input, and all of the output consumed by members, is in a non-monetary medium. These differences are reflected in their legal status.

What, then, about non-voluntary associations? I will consider that there are three types of organizations in the U.S.: governmental, economic, and voluntary. The differences between them lie not in their goals or structure or technologies, but in their relationship to resources and to consumers of their goods and services. Governmental organizations secure resources through *coercion,* or the threat of force. They tax, condemn land, draft soldiers, and so on. The output of governmental organizations is in the form of public goods, available to all. The consumer, then, is an *involuntary* consumer. All citizens who meet certain criteria must consume specific outputs. The citizen cannot remove the policeman or the street lights, nor refuse to spend the night in the jail built with his funds if he is to be jailed.

Economic organizations *purchase* their resources from profits from their sales or from invested capital. They sell to consumers who voluntarily purchase their goods and services, but do not have to belong to the organization to do so. Economic organizations cannot, in general, limit consumption to classes of consumers defined on arbitrary grounds.

Voluntary associations, as we have seen, get their resources from their members, and a good part of their output is consumed by members only. Furthermore, they can restrict membership, and thus consumers, on arbitrary grounds.

Some organizations, of course, are hard to categorize. The 4-H clubs are surely voluntary organizations, but they are sponsored by, and to some extent are controlled by, the Extension Service of the Agriculture Department. There are many examples of organizations which combine characteristics of business and governmental organizations, e.g., the T.V.A. Universities are a striking example of combining elements of all three types at once, and universities vary considerably in the relative domination of one or the other of the three types of resource supply and relationship to the consumer. Some can be seen primarily as voluntary organizations of scholars and students, whereby the students pay their dues, invest their time and effort in the productive function of the organization, and consume a good part of the product. One gathers from the esoteric nature of conferences, journals, and books that scholars are the primary consumers of their scholarly output in these institutions. Some universities or colleges are in reality tax supported governmental institutions, socializing citizens and generating public goods. It's not quite true that participation is involuntary, but it often looks that way in some state colleges and junior colleges. Some colleges are economic organizations, producing a service for a fee paid by the client and also receiving funds from organizations that hire their output. The difference between the technical institute set up by General Motors and the vocationally oriented commuter college is faint; indeed, one of GM's technical schools recently became a public institution receiving support from tax payers, clients, and industry. These very exceptions clarify the importance of the criteria used to distinguish the three types of organizations, for it is in terms of resources and consumers that we can best analyze the hybrid and changing types.

# FUNCTIONS OF VOLUNTARY ASSOCIATIONS

It has long been noted that voluntary associations mediate between the individual and society, or between groups within society, and that they represent group interests that are best met by cooperative action. The discussion of their role in this sense (not, it should be noted, the individual motives for joining) has not been very systematic. I propose that it is best seen in relationship to the other two types of organizations. The major categories of functions are as pressure groups to alter the behavior of governmental or economic organizations and as alternatives to governmental or economic organizations, either because members are reluctant to have services provided by these other types, or because the other types have failed to provide services. Any one voluntary association may serve in more than one of these roles; there are few pure types in this sense among the large voluntary associations.

## Alternatives to Government Action

Governmental action is repugnant to trade associations, for example, because they fear it will lead to greater restrictions on business behavior. Therefore, they seek to regulate business behavior in their own terms, keeping it just barely consistent with what they think the government will tolerate. Professional associations, recreation groups, and private social welfare organizations also have as a part of their reason for existence the control over activity that they are reluctant to see the government engage in.

Trade associations also engage in internal policing in the industry that they feel will not be carried out by the government—informal price setting, for example. Foundations and charity groups frequently pick up services that they feel the government might well perform, but is not likely to perform. (Recent activity by the government, however, has threatened the existence of many private health and welfare groups.) Defense groups such as the NAACP or the Anti-Defamation League attempt to persuade or threaten individuals or groups to behave differently (for example, by boycott or publicity) because they recognize that the government is not likely to take such action.

## Alternatives to Economic Organizations

Just as many voluntary associations perform functions the government is not likely to provide, so do they occasionally provide functions that commercial or economic organizations are not likely to provide. As I recall, the investment clubs sprang up well before their economic counterpart, the mutual funds, and probably stimulated the latter. No oil company was providing map routings, ratings of motels or emergency road service until recently, and the American Automobile Association fulfilled that service. One frequently finds the co-existence of the two types of organizations in the same area, since commercial entrepreneurs are not often slow to see a potential market. Thus, we have non-profit neighborhood swim clubs and commercial ones in housing developments.

But the main advantage of voluntary associations in potentially commercial areas has been the repugnance for members to "buy" services—mainly when the service is recreation, culture, self-fulfillment, or physical culture. There are cultural norms which make commercial alternatives distasteful or suspect. However, these norms often change rapidly and economic organizations move in, just as governmental organizations have moved into the charitable, welfare, and health field.

Voluntary associations such as the venerable Y's used to provide dancing lessons, gymnasiums and self-beautification services; now these are more frequently purchased from profit-making organizations. Not only has repugnance at commercial alternatives declined, one also suspects that the alternatives are more efficient, as witness the growth of charm schools and dancing schools. "Key" clubs have probably taken over the functions that some veteran and fraternal organizations played for some members. There have always been taxi dance halls, hired companions, and prostitution as last resorts for those who could not find personal gratifications in voluntary associations. Yet there are countless voluntary associations that serve interests that one does not wish to pay for outright through a commercial transaction and which one does not want anyone with the money to be able to muscle in on and buy.

## Pressure Groups

Many voluntary associations include within their functions that of attempting to change the behavior of economic and particularly governmental organizations. Sometimes these are defensive moves, such as the lobbying activities of the American Iron and Steel Institute or the National Rifle Association. Sometimes they are offensive moves, designed to get the government to do something that no voluntary or economic group could do, as with the Anti-Saloon League or the racial or ethnic defensive groups. The alternative to the NAACP or the Anti-Defamation League is governmental action in areas of discrimination and injustice. Only to a limited degree can they perform services that the government will not perform, as when they boycott stores. More important, they wish the government to forbid and punish discriminatory behavior.

Though the examples are rather scanty, there is also pressure upon economic organizations. One gentleman, when bumped once too many times from an Eastern Airlines flight attracted attention by standing in front of the plane and delaying its departure. Given the publicity, he formed the We Hate Eastern Airlines Club—the WHEALS they were called. They had a good deal to do with changes in policy and top management in the airline. However, even here it was the Federal Aviation Authority that was as much a target as Eastern Airlines.

I would not like to give the impression that voluntary associations exist simply because economic and governmental organizations do not perform the functions that the voluntary associations are interested in, or that it would he repugnant for them to do so for moral reasons. In the course of producing services, voluntary associations provide gratification to members which they would not otherwise receive. Indeed, these gratifications are often more important than official outputs, and constitute the operative goals of the organizations.[2] Therefore, it seems unlikely that all voluntary associations would disappear from U.S. society even if the role of private enterprise and government were greatly expanded to undertake the functions voluntary associations now serve.

In addition, it should be noted that voluntary associations have been able to generate laws which encourage and protect voluntary associations. They pay no taxes on their surplus in addition to many other tax breaks, thus maintaining a competitive advantage over economic organizations. Furthermore, a member's financial contribution is tax deductible in the case of many, though not all, voluntary associations. Thus, the government in effect subsidizes all voluntary associations that receive tax breaks. The government must forego that revenue and collect it from the general public instead. (Since most members of voluntary associations are middle and upper class, and since a taxation system is somewhat regressive, this means that the lower classes provide a substantial part of the subsidy. This makes it unlikely that the laws will be changed to make voluntary associations less attractive.) In this way, for example, corporations can require general support by the public of lobbying groups such as trade associations and chambers of commerce, and even quasi-political right wing pressure groups by recovering about one-half of their contribution to the group through the tax system. This income for the government is foregone and must be secured elsewhere.

## MEMBERS AS RESOURCES

Having defined voluntary associations, distinguished them from non-voluntary associations, and examined their functions in terms of non-voluntary associations, we now must look more carefully at the resource problem. In what ways are members resources of these organizations? What are the differences among voluntary associations in terms of the resources they obtain?

I propose four basic forms of contributions from members: name,

---

[2] This has been argued most vigorously in the case of Negro voluntary associations, but the reward of pomp and official standing extend right up the social and racial ladder. See Nicholas Babchuk and Ralph V. Thomson, "Voluntary Associations of Negroes," *American Sociological Review,* 27:5 (1962), pp. 647–55.

money, manpower, and personality (or self). These are vague enough to suggest an exhaustive classification of resource contributions, but specific enough to distinguish among voluntary associations to some degree.

But first some of the inevitable caveats. Some groups mobilize a group of volunteers once a year and seek house-to-house contributions. We will not consider these once-a-year volunteers, nor the contributors, as members of the organization. One might do so, but it is stretching things rather far to talk of the output consumption of March of Dimes women or the people who "voluntarily" give a dime.

Furthermore, all groups utilize all of the four resources to some extent; we are speaking only of more or less good examples of one or the other. Finally, we will defer for a time a discussion of layers of organizations where one form of resource predominates in the mass of members, and another in the core of members who do most of the work.

## Names

Giving one's name is not necessarily the most minimal contribution one can make to a voluntary association, as the existence of an Attorney General's list of supposedly subversive organizations indicates, but it takes the least time and in some cases, once done it does not have to be repeated. The most familiar examples are Referendum Petition committees, committees of 100 or whatever for this or that cause, and honorary societies. The important implication of committees of 100 is not only that you subscribe to the goals of the organization, but that if things got sticky you would be expected to back up your name with action—manpower. Since I know little about these groups, as pure types, I will assume that they are not terribly important in the scheme of things and henceforth lump them together with the next category— money groups. However, the subject of names is too interesting to let go that quickly, so some general remarks.

Names are important for all voluntary associations, and much of the potential power of a pressure group or a union or a church rests not only with gifts of money and manpower, but the sheer size of the membership list, and, of course, the presumed "quality" of the names. When a leader "speaks for" a thousand church members in a community, or three million veterans in the nation, he speaks with authority. He has access to these names and can presumably mobilize them. Since he is elected, or, in the case of the church, his leadership is acknowledged as legitimate and potent, he presumably reflects the members' views.

There are non-voluntary alternatives to acquiring this resource. Names, of course, can be purchased, as in paid testimonials. A survey some years ago indicated that a surprisingly large percentage of the population felt that testimonials in advertisements were volunteered. Paid or not, the association of the name or face of a public figure of some renown with a cause or product is a valuable resource, whether it is Dr. Spock's name at the head of a list of sponsors or as honorary chairman, or a group of football players who use a certain kind of toilet water. (Names are also sold; firms pay a good price for the mailing lists of magazines or credit card organizations, or indeed, the names of members of voluntary associations. To be inundated with junk mail after joining a voluntary association is to perform a peculiar kind of service to the organization.) The value of names as a resource for commercial or governmental or voluntary organizations is further suggested by their variable worth. The discount rate of an inveterate honorary chairman of right wing cause groups is high; while the name of a Bishop Sheen on an Anti-Vietnam War Committee would have a solid ring. Eisenhower added more valuable names of private citizens to his administration than did Truman.

The return to the member—his consumption of part of the organization's output—includes not only gratification of having supported, with his name, the cause of the organization, but the valuable right to list his membership in advertisements for himself, as in a vita, a casual conversation, a lapel pin on his business suit, credential lists in political campaigns, and so on. If he is willing to contribute sufficient manpower and receive a title in the organization the benefits are increased. One of the pleasant things about voluntary organizations is that both the individual member and the organization can benefit from each other even with a minimal transformation or effort. One of the unpleasant things is that if the nature of the organization changes, or your perception of it changes, or people of whom you do not approve give their names, you may be stuck. Generally, once given, a name is best hidden in these cases. Withdrawal may only call attention to your name. Many liberals became aware of this in the Joseph McCarthy (Republican, Wisconsin) era. Rarely had a name seemed to be so important a contribution.

# Money

Giving money generally means giving your name too (though there are some who support unpopular causes through money but who refuse to give their names). Here identification with the aims of the organization is not necessarily an associated quality, for voluntary organizations have their involuntary aspects. This is particularly true of professional associations. It is increasingly hard to be employed by a large social agency without a membership in the National Association of Social Workers, for only then can you be accredited. Through this device the income and size of the agency was presumably greatly increased. The same has long been true of the American Medical Association, where access to most non-governmental hospitals and to the very important resource, malpractice insurance, has depended upon membership. Thus, money, a prime resource of any organization, buys protection and services for the member in some cases. But one suspects that for most social workers or doctors, membership would be voluntary even in the absence of the sanction.

For most organizations money is the most desired form of resource. In the terms suggested by Selwyn Becker and Gerald Gordon in their discussion of business firms,[3] money is a general resource which can be easily stored. That is, it can be used to purchase other resources at will—such as manpower—and does not require that personnel be stored in the organization, with the associated costs of providing continual rewards in the form of consuming the output. A general resource gives greater power to the leaders or officials of an organization, whereas a specific resource such as manpower or personality can lead to control problems. Thus, most mass organizations rely primarily upon monetary contributions, and dues or contributions of at least a nominal amount are found in almost all voluntary associations. That I have little to say about the actual use of my contributions to the ACLU, NAACP, or even the American Sociological Association is perhaps irrelevant. My contribution is small, of course, so my consumption of the output may be correspondingly small (though not necessarily). Yet, by contributing to these organizations I receive moral satisfaction that I would forego if I did not contribute; I also receive a kind of character reference which I can use with appropriate groups.

---

[3] Selwyn W. Becker and Gerald Gordon, "An Entrepreneurial Theory of Formal Organizations Part I: Patterns of Formal Organizations," *Administrative Science Quarterly* (December, 1966), pp. 315–44.

## Manpower

Compared to most nations, we may be a nation of joiners, but we are more likely to give our names and money rather than our time and effort to organizations. Surveys show that the proportion of members of voluntary associations who do any more than attend an occasional meeting is quite small. Yet our dominant image of a voluntary association is one of giving one's energy, or participating actively with a smallish group of others to effect change or provide a service.

Manpower provides more effective legitimation than donations and names; the fact that people are willing to work for something strongly suggests it deserves a place in the sun. Yet there is no clear association between manpower associations and other characteristics, such as goals, which are generally thought to distinguish organizations. The Junior League and a small revolutionary group such as the Students for a Democratic Society both rely upon manpower; so do service clubs such as the Kiwanis, the Planned Parenthood Federation, the Woodlawn Organization in Chicago, or Fite in Rochester, spawned by Saul Alinski. Little Leagues would not exist without this contribution nor would countless brief-lived demonstration and confrontation groups.

Those groups which rely predominantly upon manpower for their resources tend to be either small or fairly autonomous parts of federated organizations. This resource cannot be easily stored and is specific rather than general—specific skills in a specific time and place are required. Furthermore, these resources are self-activating, sentient, and potentially recalcitrant as well as voluntary so they have greater say regarding the output of the organization, part of which they consume. Consumption varies as widely as the organizations themselves, from fulfilling the imagined obligations of a social position and using up leisure time, to satisfying burning resentments and desires for social change. For some groups there is little opportunity to hire the manpower because of the controversial or illegal nature of the task, or the high degree of commitment required to avoid goal displacement. Revolutionary change groups would find it difficult to hire people to picket business organizations which discriminates or to storm the Pentagon. (Unions, however, have used hired thugs rather than members at times, but the paid spy or informer is generally the product of governmental and economic organizations.) For others, only certain social roles or statuses are appropriate for membership, as in the Junior League. For still others, there are comparable services for hire, but having the Woman's Auxiliary run the hospital snack bar and gift shop enhances the voluntary status of the private, non-profit hospital despite the admitted inefficiencies.

## Personality

A significant element of most voluntary donations of manpower is also access to other's personalities through giving access to one's own. Furthermore, even those organizations we would class as primarily personality or self-oriented must have an important element of manpower involved, as in bridge clubs. Yet the distinction is useful, since these are consummatory or internally directed groups, as they have been called in the literature, with almost all the production being consumed internally. Some examples are recreational or psychotherapeutic groups, fundamentalist religious organizations, Alcoholics Anonymous, and Synanon. (Ideally, according to dogma, all religious organizations would be personality groups. However, it would seem that names and money play a big role in most, manpower in some, and personality in only a few. Like any other large, heterogeneous clump of groups distinguished in terms of official goals, they actually run the gamut. Unions are another example.)

Strong elements of personality are found in parts of other types of voluntary organizations, as in the patriotic, fraternal and veterans' organizations who have a steady group of members who are oriented primarily towards sociability *per se,* while other members join primarily to receive access to the only bar in town, help with the Veteran's Administration, business contacts, or validation of their political loyalty (e.g., for political career purposes). There is no reason the benefits cannot be multiple, of course, or one lead to another. Some members of manpower groups expect to receive personality-oriented services through association with specialists and others with similar problems, as in community mental health associations, or the polio foundation.

As with manpower organizations, resources in personality-oriented groups are specific and cannot be stored—relationships deteriorate with lack of use. Even more than in manpower organizations, however, the resource is free to determine the output of the organization. While manipulation is possible and frequently practiced, it costs more and is less effective than in manpower organizations, not to mention money and name organizations.

# SOME CONSEQUENCES
# DERIVED FROM THE MODEL

This completes our taxanomic exercise. I have tried to distinguish voluntary associations from non-voluntary associations, relate them to non-voluntary organizations in terms of their general functions, and categorize them on the basis of resources. Like all such exercises in sociology, it may be somewhat interesting, but the question always is, so what? Can important problems be addressed in a different way or seen in a new light as a consequence? Can issues be resolved? Without promising any success in this respect I will make at least a try at illuminating one of the most generic problems in this area—the tension between hierarchical distribution of power and democratic participation in voluntary associations.

Voluntary associations should be, if any organizations are, democratic, since the members volunteer their membership, provide resources, and are free to drop out without presumed penalty. This is not true of governmental or economic organizations. What then of goal displacement, or of the iron law of oligarchy? To address this issue we must step back a little and look at the nature of organizations in general for a moment.

Among other things, organizations are mechanisms for generating power. Some of this power is used to pursue official goals; goods or services are produced by organizations and consumers of the goods or services make some sort of contribution to the organization in return. But organizations generate considerably more power than is used to produce official goods or services. They have a number of other contingencies that must be met and they devote resources to these; that is, part of their production is utilized to meet these. One is legitimacy. As Parsons reminds us, the output must be legitimated for some groups of consumers, and this is not an automatic process. Therefore, some resources are utilized to create, establish, or convince people of the legitimacy of the output. Organizations, in this sense, have what I have called elsewhere [4] societal goals and output goals. In order to

---

[4] Charles Perrow, "Organizational Goals," *International Encyclopedia of the Social Sciences* (New York: The Macmillan Company and the Free Press, 1968), Volume 11, pp. 305–11.

attract resources, voluntary organizations sometimes expend a good deal of power establishing legitimacy.

Organizations also have to meet the need of investors. In the case of voluntary associations these are, in most cases, the members themselves, but in the case of the United Fund, or Red Cross or the many other organizations that rely upon donations from non-members, some modicum of return is expected. The organization may merely publish lists of causes supported or organizations helped. Still another use of organizational power is to insure survival and perhaps growth under certain conditions and restrictions. For the Townsend Clubs, survival meant dropping social change goals and substituting recreational or personality goals; for the Women's Christian Temperance Union it meant shifting from opposition to drinking *per se,* to opposition to the immorality of the middle class in general.

Finally, there are, of course, the actual product goals of the organization—characteristics of the goods or services produced.

But after all these needs are met, organizations still have areas of decisions, or the power to make decisions, which go beyond any of these other goals. Organizations employ people, so they can be selective in their employment and, for example, not employ minority groups, or women, or people beyond certain ages. They have a physical location, and there is power derived from the ability to decide upon that location or change it. They purchase supplies and equipment, and can decide who shall be rewarded with the contract. They can seek to develop or enfeeble their employees, propagandize them or make certain kinds of behavior—e.g., a decent contribution to a voluntary association—an implicit condition of employment or promotion. The list is large, but we rarely concern ourselves with it explicitly, except perhaps when we talk vaguely about the social responsibilities of business. But much of the literature on goal displacement focuses not on the official or product goals of organizations, but goals that are derived, wittingly or unwittingly, from merely being in existence. We shall label this area derived goals, distinguishing it from societal, output, investor, system and product goals.

Derived goals, or the use of this almost latent or residual form of power, has always played a large role in the literature on voluntary associations. What strikes observers of AMA, the farm organizations, patriotic and veterans' associations, and recently even the character-building organization such as the Scouts or the Y, is the extent to which they have power to pursue goals which are beyond the area legitimated by their character or public image, and sometimes do not even reflect the views of their members. Some years ago a student of mine, Merwyn Greenlich, simply went through the convention resolutions of a few large professional and occupational and veterans' associations looking for resolutions which had no apparent connection with the official aims of the organizations.

He examined the policy statements of the American Bar Association, American Dental Association, Farm Bureau Federation, American Hospital Association, American Legion, American Medical Association, National Education Association and the Chamber of Commerce of the United States. Only two of these groups, the American Hospital Association and the American Dental Association made no policy statements outside of their announced sphere of competence. (The American Legion has announced its sphere of confidence as being so broad as to include almost anything, but we shall consider its legitimate concern to be veterans' affairs.)

The ABA has taken stands on federal aid to highways, federal development of atomic power, the National Science Foundation, control of venereal disease, suppression of prostitution, restricting immigration, government medical care, limitation of taxation power, tideland oil rights for states, compulsory social security coverage, the Bricker amendment to limit the treaty making powers of the President, and the international trade organization.

The House of Delegates of the AMA passed a resolution stating that it shall not take a position on legislation not bearing directly upon medicine, yet they opposed daylight saving time, federal housing for indigents, favored limitations on federal taxation powers, and the Bricker amendment, opposed collectivism in schools, minimum wage standards, and compulsory social security coverage. The Chamber of Commerce concerned itself with the establishment of Indian reservations in Alaska, Alaska-Hawaii statehood, the UN, medical care for indigents, federal aid to education, immigration laws, animal experimentation, the Bricker amendment, and so on. The Legion, of course, ranges far and wide: mental health programs, reforestation of lands, international labor organizations, alcoholic beverage advertisement limitations, federal aid to education, compulsory health insurance, immigration, tideline oil, the Bricker amendment and the Ku Klux Klan. The Farm Bureau considers itself an authority on the mutual security program, medical care under social security, federal aid to education, right to work laws, minimum wages, selective service system, the United Nations, civil service system and tideland oils. Even the National Education Association, which states that only resolutions "national in scope and education in nature" will be considered in its national conventions, found this to include the U.N., the voting age, the Korean War, national defense issues, limitations on the federal power to tax, and the issue of equal rights for men and women.

Where more than one of these organizations takes a stand on one of these issues, the stand is generally consistent, except for easily understood exceptions. Thus, five of the six took stands on the government's role in medical care and all were opposed, four of the six felt it within their province to speak out on the Bricker amendment and all were for it. But the issue is not the content of their position, but the use of organizational resources to support a position, whatever the position was. We know from journalistic accounts that these organizations provide more than a resolution and the implied support of one and one-half million members of the Farm Bureau Federation or three million members of the Legion; they also lobby actively, spend money on propaganda, trade support with other voluntary associations, and demand and receive political goods of a varied sort for their support of a position.

Recently there was a lively debate within the American Sociological Association as to whether it was legitimate or not for the Association, as an organization, to take a stand on the Vietnam War. Despite disapproval by a large majority of those members returning ballots of the war itself, the majority thought the Association should not itself take a stand. This would be an illegitimate derived goal—using the prestige of the organization to try to influence a political decision that was not relevant to the avowed purposes of the association, the majority seemed to think. Other members felt, of course, that by not taking a stand, the power of the association was implicitly being used to support the war. The issue is a recurrent one in voluntary associations, raising questions of derived power and of elevating derived goals to product goals.

Less dramatic are the hiring practices, headquarter location decisions, convention location decisions (this has become a more common issue, as witness to threat by the American Sociological Association to persuade the American Psychological Association to withdraw its convention from a St. Louis hotel that was found, contrary to stated policy, to discriminate), supply purchases (a hot issue in corporation-land, as witness the Chrysler case in 1966) and so on. But if less dramatic they still concern the basic characteristic of organizations, their ability to generate power.

One can readily see that it is in the voluntary associations that rely heavily upon names and money that leaders have the greatest freedom with respect to the uses of these kinds of powers. General, storeable resources lend themselves to flexible usage. In the organizations emphasizing manpower, and in particular those emphasizing personality, the resources, being specific and consumed more or less on the spot, do not permit much freedom to the leaders. The power is still there; it is the basis of decisions on how it is exercised that is different. The distinction between the two is compounded by the differences in size that are likely to obtain. Only rather small units can coordinate and control voluntary contributions of manpower and self; therefore, as noted, these are likely to be smaller organizations or federated units. Money and names can be easily aggregated, their use coordinated and controlled. The presence of factions, schisms, internal squabbles that amount to sabotaging the effectiveness of organizations is not limited to, but probably concentrated in, those that use manpower and personality as major resources. They will also probably have more frequent product goal changes, and in stances of derived goals being elevated to product goals, since what the members do constitutes, more than in the other types, what the organization does.

Note that the issue is not whether name and money organizations necessarily pursue derived goals to which their members might be opposed, only that a wider latitude of choice is given to the leaders without the necessity of checking with, or having the blessings of, members. Probably most doctors were themselves in favor of limiting the powers of the president in international affairs, and most Legionnaires feel the communist threat is overwhelming. Where these organizations have taken public stands that most members oppose, they have found that they must modify their stands. According to opinion surveys, most doctors were for social security for doctors and the AMA gave up its effort to convert them and modified its stand. The Legion leadership was forced to back down on veterans' bonuses during the 1930's, and cease their attack upon popular General Bradley who was appointed to head the Veteran's Administration during World War II. He was, incidentally, somewhat opposed to having the Veteran's Administration completely dominated by Legionnaire personnel, but this was not the issue for the Legion members. He was simply a popular general to them. Perhaps they did not realize how important it was for the Legion to control the Veteran's Administration in order to get Legion members preferential treatment.

# THE OPTIMUM STRATEGY

Name and money groups have the advantages of general and storeable resources which can be used flexibly, but the disadvantage that, in their pure state, they must purchase staff and leadership manpower. They lose the advantage of the committed member. Manpower and personality groups have the advantage of the committed member, but lack the general and storeable resources. Furthermore, name and money groups are able to resist divisiveness and unstable goals that may plague the manpower and personality groups, but the latter have the legitimacy and prestige accorded to "truly voluntary" efforts, while the former does not. The sensible thing is to try to combine the advantages of both sets and minimize the disadvantages. The great and powerful voluntary associations in our country have succeeded in doing this. The strategy is sufficiently similar in the powerful professional associations such as the AMA, the three major farm groups, and the two major veteran's associations, to present a fairly clear picture.

At the bottom of the organization is the mass of members who receive services, or in some cases income protection, through dues, payments and contributions. Receiving the services or eliminating the threat to income is automatic upon joining; no further commitment is required (though the payments may go up, as when the AMA levied special assessments to fight Medicare). Thus, a valuable general and storeable resource is acquired by the organization. However, there are further rewards available for increased participation—that is, for contributing manpower. Contributing one's personality may be an entire factor, as descriptions of local meetings suggest, but this is not significant beyond that level. Business contracts such as medical referrals, insurance customers, political contacts, and so forth are initially important and remain so. For the modestly successful businessman, doctor, lawyer, or politician an office in the voluntary association may be the only means of upward mobility.

Another set of rewards depends more upon the names and money contributed by the mass of members, for the organization itself has a good deal of power lying around for those with the wit to use it. Thus, those who contribute manpower—go to the meetings, hold offices, carry out tasks—can influence decisions that shape the derived goals of the organization. With the association standing behind them they may receive commissions or important appointments to public offices; they may be rewarded by interested economic or governmental organizations in countless ways for shaping decisions of the association accordingly. As the member mounts the levels of the association—typically county, district, state, regional and national officers—his rewards, of course, increase. At some point he may find it more lucrative to become a paid officer, but it is not the income that matters, I suspect, but the ability to use the resources of the organization. Of course, he is carefully screened by those who have preceded him, and there is a good deal of self-selection operating at each level such that if he were not in sympathy with his superiors, there is no point in going higher. Thus, once you reach the middle levels of those organizations there is probably little difference in commitment and ideological conformity than one finds among the members of manpower organizations. However, since it rests upon a much more secure and flexible resource base—membership lists and money—you have the best of both worlds.

There will be threats to the leadership at each level, of course. Organizations generate power, and power is always contested. But beyond the personal and group contests where each seeks the same prize, there have not been many contests over the character of the prize, or the character of the organization. The few rump groups that have appeared in the AMA, American Bar Association, American Legion, Farm Bureau Federation, etc. have been interesting but not significant phenomena. Generally, these groups have split off and formed ineffective rival organizations. It should not be assumed that these are always left-leaning alternatives, such as the Lawyer's Guild. Recall that the American Dental Association took no stands that were not consistent with its concern with dental matters. However, in 1963, the Association of American Dentists filed for incorporation in Amarillo, Texas. Its official goals were to "promote, encourage and perpetuate the highest standards of dental care within the United States of America," yet it immediately found that this was consistent with support of the Bricker amendment, opposition to social security, and the international labor organization, federal aid to education, support of right to work laws, and so on and on. If the American Dental Association refused to behave like the AMA, they would start their own group. They knew the power of names and money.

Splinter groups generally complain that they have been defeated in their attempts to change policies of voluntary associations by undemocratic methods. In one sense this is often true; strong-arm methods are not unknown when the ability to speak for three million veterans and the ability to use their dues is at stake. But in a more important sense the issue of democratic control seems irrelevant.

## DEMOCRACY AND VOLUNTEERS

And this brings me finally to my main point—oligarchy and democracy in voluntary associations. One gathers the impression that internal struggles that are suppressed by undemocratic methods, or complaints by participants, critics or social scientists about undemocratic structures and tactics in voluntary associations, rarely concern the character of the output consumed by members. While it is only a suspicion, it is not unreasonable to suspect that even where the issues appear to be the efficiency, quality, or quantity of services to members, as in internal struggles in unions, the real issue is the spoils that will go to the victors. The polio foundation, as studied by David Sills and the Bureau of Applied Social Research, was not democratic, even though local members thought it was. But there was no quarrel with its services to members or its product goals. There may have been some quarrel over its derived goals had the members, or the Bureau, taken a close look at the national headquarters, but they were indifferent to such concerns. Worthwhile services are produced by professional associations, farm groups and veteran's organizations, and members retain their membership, even though most of these organizations are far from democratic. Why? Because the issue of democracy or oligarchy is mainly confined to areas where there is dispute about the uses to which power shall be put beyond those outputs which are consumed by members.

Framed in terms of resources and the characteristics of voluntary associations, the issue of democracy is no longer the Schumpeter-Lipset formulation of ability to throw the bastards out,[5] or even the older issue of "no taxation without representation" since it is primarily the "unrepresented" outputs that are involved. In fact, I am forced to conclude, there should be no issue of democracy at all. Ironically, democracy is only really an issue in involuntary associations, where resources are obtained through coercion and all persons are involuntary consumers,

---

[5] Joseph Schumpeter, *Capitalism, Socialism and Democracy* (New York: Oxford Press, 1942), p. 269, or Seymour M. Lipset, *Political Man* (New York: Doubleday, 1959), p. 45.

and this is the state itself. In economic organizations and voluntary associations the only issue is who shall have what Selznick calls that fundamental prize of organizational life, control over the character of the organization.[6] The prize is up for grabs and those who fail to take it cry foul.

It is true that in manpower and personality-oriented voluntary associations there is more room for members to influence the character of the organization, for derived goals are always on the verge of becoming, or are candidates for, product goals, which have more or less official status. This is because when you make your contribution you do so "in person," so to speak, and it is utilized at that time. Thus, you are able to see to what ends it is put and to withhold it if you disagree too strongly. But this is not the essence of democracy in the Schumpeter-Lipset formulation (though it is closer to the "no taxation without representation" formulation). More important, there is no need for all of these groups to be democratic. Synanon and Alcoholics Anonymous are probably anarchistic; some revolutionary (manpower) groups are admittedly dictatorial; other groups are laissez faire.

But even these slogan-concepts—anarchistic, dictatorial, laissez faire—seem strangely irrelevant in our context. This is not surprising, since I have defined these organizations in terms of an input-output model, wherein most of the resources are contributed by members and most of the output is consumed by them. In these terms we could only state the issue of democracy as the conditions under which those who contribute resources have control over the uses of those resources *which are relevant to them*. Relevance varies among levels and within levels of participation. Only in small, personality-oriented groups are all outputs possibly relevant to all contributors. Only here is the power generated by the organization at all consonant with the resources contributed. For example, the power to exclude persons who might be potentially undesirable members is quite important here, and is controlled by the contributors; but this is far less true of all other types. There the issue of democracy and oligarchy in voluntary associations concerns primarily the content of derived goals and the struggle to legitimize them, or to put it differently, control over a power that goes beyond product and system goals.

Viewed in this light the usual variables which are supposed to in-

---

[6] Philip Selznick, *TVA and the Grass Roots* (Berkeley and Los Angeles: University of California Press, 1949), p. 181.

fluence the degree of democracy in groups—the authority structure (e.g., election procedures, distribution of rewards and sanctions, control of the agenda, etc.), the social status of members and alternative employment for disposed leaders, presence of organizational skills, rate of attendance at meetings, member interest and identification, etc. take on a new aspect. They are largely dependent variables, or merely irrelevant. That is, they are not subject to significant manipulation without a change in the resource base. They may affect the efficiency of the organization or the extent to which one group rather than another may pursue derived goals or give the appearance of democratic procedures, but they will probably reflect, more than shape, the character of the organization. Yet those are our traditional divining rods of democracy and oligarchy.

# VI THE CAREERS OF CLIENTS AND ORGANIZATIONS

*William R. Rosengren*

IT IS POPULAR TO SAY THAT FORMAL ORGANIZATIONS ARE UBIQUITOUS and salient in the lives of people. The so-called "organizational" society may well distinguish contemporary modernized societies from the "gemeinschaft"-"gesellschaft" typology which preoccupied social scientists for so long. To borrow Earl S. Johnson's words: [1]

> With gemeinschaft I associate *natural, sentimental, kinship,* and personal; with Gesellschaft I associate fabricated, rational, contrived, and impersonal. We must, and likely do, understand that the Community Chest, the Red Cross, the Peace Corps and other institutional agencies we now use at home and overseas lack, in significant ways, the warmth and intimacy of the simple face-to-face and private charitable devices of the parish.

That, perhaps, is the profound issue in service organizations: how to strike a working balance between the rational structures of bureaucracy, and the ethic of conviction which tends to make all organizations something less than bureaucratic.

But rationally fabricated organizations are more than the meeting place of Gemeinschaft and Gesellschaft. They are the ground upon

---

[1] Earl S. Johnson, "Gemeinschaft-Gesellschaft Perspectives on the Human Experience," Kermit Eby Memorial Lecture, Manchester College, January 15, 1968, p. 1 (dittoed).

which the individual as a person confronts his social institutions and his social structure.

Some might even argue that large scale organized efforts are *the* distinctive earmark of modern societies—signaling their historic drift, shaping the lives of people in all of their facets whether workers or clients, and bearing the prevalent values which inform relations between persons and their social institutions.

To say this, however, fails to give much of a clue to four main problems with which organizations—service organizations in particular— are now confronted.

The first has to do with Weber's wise observation that the bureaucratic organization represents efficiency and effectiveness par excellence. But at the same time it arises out of conditions of democratization and egalitarianism and hence is pressed to serve humanely and effectively. Michel Crozier's fine analysis of the French bureaucratic system could be turned to this theme to the extent that the members of that system attempt to eke out a sphere of personal autonomy in opposition to the system; the American system leans more toward favoritism and the growth of informal cliques which may subvert the system; British bureaucracy retains an element of elitism which harks back to an earlier era of traditional authority.[2] Each cultural setting, in its own way, seems to manage some degree of accommodation between the ethics Gemeinschaft and Gesellschaft.

The second problem I want to explore has to do with the ways and extent to which organizations change over time. Although the empirical evidence is scanty, I entertain the idea that organizations—like people— live out a career which has discernible stages from beginning to end even though the larger social order may remain very much the same throughout. Hence we must ask what the career followed by service organizations is; to what social forces turning points in the organizational career may be traced; and what the posture of an organization is likely to be as it passes through its career-cycle towards those with whom it is involved, especially in regard to technical imperatives on the one hand, and humanistic expectations on the other.

---

[2] See for example, Michel Crozier, *The Bureaucratic Phenomenon* (Chicago: University of Chicago Press, 1964); Talcott Parsons, "Definitions of Health and Illness in the Light of American Values and Social Structure," in E. Gartly Jaco, Ed., *Patients, Physicians, and Illness* (Glencoe: The Free Press, 1958), pp. 165–187; Morroe Berger, *Bureaucracy and Society in Modern Egypt* (Princeton: Princeton University Press, 1967).

Thirdly, there is a related set of issues which springs from the second general theme of this symposium—inter-organizational collaboration, and especially organizations as "members" of other organizations. Organizations of all kinds are presently forced to respond not only to the demands of client groups, but are also called upon to alter their historic patterns of isolation from one another and established loyalties to special segments of the communities in which they exist. The question that I wish to pursue here is the following: if organizations change in discernible ways as they age, what consequences may this have for the *kind* of inter-membership activity of which they are capable?

Finally, I want to mention just briefly one last aspect of organizations. That has to do with the degree to which clients are "taken-in" to organizations more or less as full participants. In recent years service organizations of all kinds have "invited" clients to take a more active part in organizational life. The fact that this democratization of bureaucracy has in some cases opened Pandora's Box is hardly surprising: mental hospitals, for example, through devices such as patient government, family visitation, community advisory groups, and others have drawn the patient (and other quasi-members) into the organizational system in quite real and sometimes authoritative ways. Schools—universities especially—seem well along the way to transforming student power into student authority in ways which can wrought significant changes in the functioning of educational institutions. Welfare agencies—largely through OEO—have taken welfare recipients *directly* into their membership, thus breaking through the hallowed crust traditionally separating staff from clients. Prisons also have been toying for a long time with ways of engaging inmates in the work of the organization.

In short, client-serving organizations may well be quite far along the road to becoming—at least in an approximate sense—*voluntary associations*—in the sense that the needs and expectations of the "clients" become the goals of the organization staff and the determinants of the patterns of work which develop. As a result they are likely to contain many of the processes that Charles Perrow has described.

So by way of introduction, these four issues are certain to constitute a rich mix: (1) the dual demands for efficiency and humanism; (2) the possible presence of quite inexorable organizational careers; (3) the increasing demand for—under various names—inter-organizational contact and collaboration; and (4) the increasingly flirtatious relationship between organizations and their clients.

# ORGANIZATIONAL CAREERS AND ORIENTATIONS TOWARD CLIENTS

A first task is the labeling process itself—how shall organizations be referred to at each stage of their growth and development? These labels are not totally arbitrary, for they obviously must be ones that I can work with, and which can be of some utility in addressing the four issues just posed. I draw upon what has, by Mark Lefton and myself, been called the "client-biography" model.[3] This derives from the proposition that the internal structure and dynamics of organizations are closely related to the manner by which organizations intervene in the life course of their clients—both present and future. To re-cap this perspective simply: organizations may choose to interrupt the contemporary life-space of their clients in either a highly focused, specific way, or more diffusely and broadly in an attempt to alter—if you will—the whole person. Mark Lefton and I (in stubborn opposition to the pleas of friends and colleagues) persist in referring to this social space dimension of the client biography as "laterality." A general hospital might typify the "non-lateral" specific focus, while a family counseling agency is called to mind as a more 'laterally' or broadly oriented institution.

Organizations may also choose to intervene in the lives of their clients in either the short or long run. Those which attempt to attach themselves, perhaps even permanently, to their clients' future lives are termed "longitudinal." Those which detach themselves from clients after but a truncated period of time are called 'non-longitudinal.' Hence, such a perspective yields four analytic types of organizations, each expressing a distinctive orientation towards its clientele. Using these types as the bench-marks, I wish to pursue—in turn—the following questions: (1) What type are organizations likely to be when they are new, and toward what type are they likely to drift as they age? (2) What are some of the internal features of new and old organizations? (3) With what kinds of collaborative activity are old and new organizations most compatible, and what implications may this have for present-day preoccupa-

---

[3] Mark Lefton and William R. Rosengren, "Organizations and Clients: Lateral and Longitudinal Dimensions," *American Sociological Review,* 31 (December, 1966), pp. 802–810; William R. Rosengren, "Organizational Age, Structure, and Orientations Toward Clients, *Social Forces,* 47 (September, 1968), pp. 1–11; William R. Rosengren and Mark Lefton, *Hospitals and Patients* (New York: Atherton Press, 1969); Carl Gersuny, "Servitude and Expropriation as Dimensions of Clienthood," paper presented at the Annual Meetings of the Eastern Sociological Society, April, 1969 (mimeo).

tions with service programs predicated upon inter-organizational membership?

# ON NEWNESS

I want to pursue the argument that organizations of the "service" variety are likely to begin with a broadly focused and short-term style of intervention. In doing this, I thoroughly expect to be making a number of inferences, some of which may not be totally justified.

## Contending with Liabilities of Newness

In his discussion of the "liabilities of newness" Stinchcombe makes the point that new organizations must rely heavily on establishing social relationships with strangers, and that their initial relationships with strangers tend to be highly unstable and subject to change.[4] The aim is to standardize and routinize these relationships and—in the interests of economy and efficiency—to reduce these relationships to the smallest possible number. (This is not unlike the point made by James Thompson that organizations, when operating under norms of rationality, attempt to seal off their "core-technologies" from environmental influences).[5]

One manner by which organizations may overcome this initial liability and establish tentative and temporary ties with strangers is to offer services of a broad-based kind, addressing as it were multiple sectors of the community by focusing upon multiple aspects of the client's life space. This will serve not only to attract a heterogeneous clientele, hopefully one large enough to sustain the new organization as an economy, but will also serve to link the new institution to a large organizational set. As some of these strangers come to be colleagues, associations with others are terminated. With this comes a more specific focus in the organizations' orientations towards its clients: the stabilization process has begun.

At the same time, during the early unstable period, the organization is unlikely to adopt a long-term orientation precisely because of the

---

[4] Arthur L. Stinchcombe, "Social Structure and Organizations," in James G. March, Ed., *Handbook of Organizations* (Chicago: Rand-McNally, 1965), pp. 142–193.
[5] James D. Thompson, *Organizations in Action* (New York: McGraw-Hill, 1967).

tentative nature of its external linkages. Over time, however, and in accompaniment to its drift toward a specific orientation, the institution is likely to attempt to retain a continuity of clientele through intervening for a long period of time in the client's biographical career. This is consistent with what Thompson has called "smoothing" out-puts in an effort to reduce uncertainties. For as the organization's focus becomes more specific, it reduces its alternatives, becomes less capable of shifting its goals, and can reduce some of the organizational uncertainties produced by these facts by retaining clients as organizational property for longer periods of time. As Stinchcombe says, "One of the main resources of old organizations is a set of stable ties (*lateral/longitudinal,* italics mine) to those who use organizational services." [6] And, "the stronger the ties between old organizations and the people they serve . . . the tougher the job of establishing a new organization." [7] One way by which new organizations may break into the existing organizational set is by altering the customary pattern and codifying their relationships in accord with the prevailing specific and long-term pattern.

A further contingency of newness has to do with the fact that clients can sometimes be attracted away from existing old organizations by holding out the appeal of full organizational membership and participation to them. Hence, new organizations may initially begin by becoming, in Charles Bidwell's terms, "Moral-Associational" in nature, with clientele acquired by being "inducted" into the institution on a quasi full-membership basis.[8] However, at least some students, David Mechanic, for example,[9] argue that lower level participants may be quite effectively insulated from organizational effectiveness and authority, and these organizations take the form of what Bidwell terms "Technical-Communal." In short, the new organization may achieve this ultimate effect by beginning in a broad lateral fashion, and then later effectively limiting the participation of lower-member-clients by focusing more specifically upon them and for a longer period of time. Hence, the initial contract between the client and the organization may be normative, turning later into a technical imperative.

Stinchcombe also points out that new organizations arise out of an

---

[6] Arthur L. Stinchcombe, "Social Structure and Organizations," *op. cit.* p. 149.

[7] *Ibid.,* p. 150.

[8] Charles E. Bidwell and Rebecca S. Vreeland, "College Education and Moral Orientations," *Administrative Science Quarterly,* 8 (September, 1963), pp. 166–191.

[9] David Mechanic, "Organizational Power of Lower Participants," *Administrative Science Quarterly,* 7 (December, 1962), pp. 349–364.

effort to meet needs which are presently unmet and to introduce a technology, or series of technologies, not currently being made available.[10] Perhaps as a result of this, new organizations are likely to begin life with a relatively untried and untested technology, the efficacy of which is yet to be demonstrated. In the absence of a viable and specific technological repetoire (already achieved by more stable and mature organizations) an intensive technology is likely to form the basis of organizational operation—the utilization of multiple and uncoordinated efforts to achieve through *scope,* what cannot yet be achieved through *depth.* Hence, services are likely to be offered initially on a broad lateral basis. One can only speculate that the original short-term orientation may also arise because of an awareness of the temporary character of the first "technology" and the likelihood of its radical reduction in scope of kind as the organization ages.

There is yet another factor which might account for an early broad orientation toward clients. This has to do with the need for new service organizations to acquire both a clientele and a patronage. The relation of both of these imperatives to the kind of service credo that develops has been suggested by both Eisenstadt and Perrow.[11]

One way by which new service organizations can attract clients and patrons is to offer services on a broad lateral basis. This serves not only to attract the attention—and potential support—of multiple groups in the community with rich and varied interests at stake, but it also serves to present a unique cluster-appeal to clients who may already be the property of organizations with more routine service patterns.[12]

In short, new organizations must somehow break through the crust of the existing organizational set. They can do this best by offering "novel" combinations of services to clients. But the economies of newness invite a tentativeness about this, and hence result in a short-term orientation toward clients.

With a beginning such as this, I want to turn now to the question of the factors—both internal and external to the organization—which might

---

[10] Arthur L. Stinchcombe, "Social Structure and Organizations," *op. cit.*

[11] See for example, Ray Elling, "Organizational Support and Community Power Structure," *Journal of Health and Human Behavior,* 3 (Winter, 1962), pp. 257–269; Charles Perrow, "Goals and Power Structures," in *The Hospital in Modern Society.* E. Freidson, Ed. (New York: The Free Press, 1963); S. N. Eisenstadt, "Bureaucracy, Bureaucratization, and Debureaucratization," in *Complex Organizations.* A. Etzioni, Ed. (New York: Holt, Rinehart and Winston, 1961), pp. 268–277.

[12] Elaine Cumming, *Systems of Social Regulation* (New York: Atherton Press, 1968).

account for a subsequent drift toward a specifically focused and long-term orientation toward clients.

## Some Processes of Organizational Change

Let us assume once again that organizations—especially as they mature —increasingly come to pay homage to the "norms of rationality," not only for economic reasons but for organizational control purposes as well. In this sense (and as Thompson has pointed out) organizations attempt to seal-off their core technologies from environmental contingencies. The laterally oriented organization is acutely vulnerable to environmental contingencies. This is due largely to three structures which tend to accompany a broad focus toward clients. First, a multiple technology system demands the presence of multiple professionals with varied technical and varied ideological persuasions. Secondly, the lateral organization inducts more of the client's social personality into the organization. This institutionalization of client latent roles is potentially disruptive to the organization. Thirdly, a broad lateral orientation normally means that the organization draws support from many different groups in the community. This is potentially a divisive pattern because it leads to competitive processes among supporters, with the organization itself as the target for manipulation and control. So, factors such as these will tend to reduce the organization's broad scope orientation and give rise to a more specific and delimited service ideology.

In addition, and drawing once again upon Stinchcombe's discussion, one characteristic of formal organization is an effort to "achieve" predictability of future benefits or outcomes. This, according to Stinchcombe, is consistent with Weber's repeated emphasis upon calculable law, calculable taxation, etc., in the growth of rational enterprise. So a presumed penchant for predictability will not only reduce the organization's scope of interest in the client, but will tend to stretch it out in time as well. A single technological focus is more easily calculable than are several, and a long-term attachment to the client is more easily calculable than are several, and a long-term attachment to the client more easily assures that calculability will be realized. At the same time, as an organization becomes more stable, i.e., ages successfully, it may calculate its own "survival" in terms of long-time spans, while the young and unstable organization is more likely to seek for measures of adequacy more immediately in the here-and-now. Furthermore, a drift toward a more specific and long-term orientation allows an accommodation of standardized routines, while a broader and short-term perspective mitigates against a "norm of rationality" such as this.

I mention only parenthetically the fact that an increase in organizational age cannot help but be accompanied by increased urbanization of the environment in which the organization undergoes the aging-process. And it is now axiomatic that urbanization is equivalent to population density, and that population density is equivalent to functional specialization.[13] One can only add that functional specialization is consistent with a differentiation among organizations along the non-lateral dimension.

A not unrelated argument stems from the proposition that organizations of all kinds attempt to effect some kind of *change* upon the people whom they serve. Organizations are instruments of alteration, and *service* organizations attempt to alter materials which are highly reactive— people. On the whole, "technical" changes are more easily wrought than are changes in ways of life; the first involves the manipulation of some specific aspect of the human material, while the latter must engage the material's conscious desire and cooperation in altering himself.[14] The broadly oriented *lateral* organization, as a matter of fact, attempts to bring about these ways of life-changes, while the specifically focused *non-lateral* organization addresses itself to the problem of technical change. And to bring to fruition changes in the total configuration of people is more difficult organizationally, more costly in terms of resources, and less conducive to organizational stability and permanence, than are those interventions which elect to change some specific part of the human resource. As a result, surviving new organizations will tend to renounce their original broad focus and zero-in on a specific mechanism, a technologically accessible aspect of their materials. Changing human persons also demands that the alteration be made more or less permanent: hence as the organization becomes more stable in terms of its own survival capacity, it will elongate its specific orientation toward the client in an attempt to make its technical change as irreversible as possible.

As the new organization enters the set, resource scarcity, (or the perception of its presence) becomes increasingly an issue. As a result, or-

---

[13] The Durkheimian axiom is too frequently neglected.

[14] Oliver P. Williams, *et al., Suburban Differences and Metropolitan Policies: A Philadelphia Story* (Philadelphia: University of Pennsylvania Press, 1965).

ganizations which become set members—that is as they age and survive —must compete at two levels.

Inter-organizational competition first occurs for what Levine and White have called goals-priorities—laying down some special claim or service or competence which shall insure a source of clients and a support fund: hence a drift toward a specific non-lateral focus once the initial survival problem is overcome.[15] Secondly, competition develops over set domination—how directly to effect the relations among the set members so that the distribution of set resources is not left either to the whims of the present dominant nor to the mysteries of *deus ex machina*. One good way to achieve set domination is for the organization to extend itself in the "social time" of its clientele, thus achieving some leverage in the organizations which may later be held responsible for departed clients. This arena of set domination competition may also account for the fact that the long-term oriented institution tends to be one which contains a large number of discretionary job-holders at the administrative level called upon to alter their conduct depending upon the existing pattern of power relationships amongst set members. Younger short-term oriented organizations are often ignored in this pattern, thus allowing them to become full participating members in the organizational set.

These are but some of the external processes and forces which move new organizations from a plus-lateral/minus-longitudinal to a minus-lateral/plus-longitudinal service orientation. Some internal forces may also be at work leading to a similar result: the first has to do with the ambiguities for staff roles which accompany a broad orientation toward clients as reflected in the unspecialized division of labor which such an organization usually contains. Role expectations are ambiguous and poorly defined. Tasks are highly discretionary, demanding creativity, imagination, and commitment, especially on the part of lower level personnel. In Caplow's terms,[16] new organizations of this type tend to have too little stratification, too high interaction, ambiguity, loss of autonomy for the individual, and too much flexibility and goal deflection as far as the organizational system is concerned.

In addition, new multiple-technology organizations face serious coordination problems. Priorities are competitive at best and unclear at worst. Criteria as to final results are similarly confused and perhaps in

---

[15] William R. Rosengren, "Organizational Age, Structure, and Orientations Toward Clients," *op. cit.*

[16] Theodore Caplow, *Principles of Organization* (New York: Harcourt, Brace & World, 1964).

conflict. Due partially to this, the organization is likely to drift to a more specific orientation toward clients, hence solving problems deriving from an initial broad orientation toward clients.

Problems of control are yet a further issue faced by the new plus-lateral organization. Specifically, the new broadly oriented institution is unable to achieve worker compliancy through its structural division of labor. Rather, it turns to supervisory management tactics to achieve through styles of leadership what its unspecialized division of labor has failed to achieve.[17] This, in turn, means that much administrative time and effort must be devoted to overseeing and supervising the work of operative personnel. Parenthetically, it may be in this early stage of organizational life that the oft noted conflict between operatives and administrators is most acute and disruptive to the organization. On the other hand, a more specifically focused orientation obviates the need for direct supervisory controls, hence mitigating, to some extent, potential conflict between operatives and administrators. At the same time, the development of a longer-run interest in the client requires that administrators devote more of their time and energies to "future" contingencies rather than to work-a-day routines. Hence, a drift towards a minus-lateral/longitudinal orientation helps to resolve both internal conflict and external contingencies.

## Some Characteristics of End-State Organizations

At a general level, I think that old organizations of the type discussed—specifically and long-term oriented—contain quite contrasting ideologies in the operational as compared with the administrative sphere. Indeed, this kind of terminal organization is likely to contain classic rational bureaucratic (Gesellschaft) elements at the operational level, but more Gemeinschaft characteristics at the administrative level. Operative activities are likely to be informed by rationalization while the latter by humanism. Operations are likely to be integrated through specialization, while administration by means of esprit de corps;[18] control of operative personnel is likely to be accomplished by means of structural authority while compliancy of administrators is likely to be achieved through

---

[17] William R. Rosengren, "Structure, Policy, and Style: Strategies of Organizational Control," *Administrative Science Quarterly*, 12 (June, 1967), pp. 140–164.

[18] Peter M. Blau, *Bureaucracy in Modern Society* (New York: Random House, 1956).

strategies of managerial supervision; [19] the day-to-day routines of the operative wing are likely to be conducted on the basis of rules and regulations, while the administration is likely to be oriented more towards incalculable contingencies uncovered by pre-existing rules. Finally, the face-to-face relationships between operative workers are likely to have the impersonality signaled by Weber, but the administrative wing will be permeated by the pressures of latent cultures and the demands of many latent roles. In sum, the old organization has a specific focus on the client, and from this can devise a single technology around which it can organize a rational and bureaucratic division of labor. But, on the other hand, it has also a long-term, perhaps incalculable time-interest in future contingencies and must therefore conduct its administrative work more in terms of the ethic of commitment, rather than of rational calculation. In short, the specific focus of the mature organization permits the structures of bureaucracy to develop within the operational line, while the diffuse and long-term commitment to future unknown contingencies results in a more de-bureaucratized administrative system.

Furthermore, under the assumption that age leads to a specific and long-term orientation towards clients, it might also follow that the old organization is characterized by *member involvement* of an "exchange" variety at the operational level, but to "commitment" at the administrative level.[20] If the exchange bargain which is struck is adequately negotiated and satisfactory, then the organization can probably anticipate "efficient but personally detached" work. It is more likely to be the case however, that old and specifically focused organizations will increasingly contain "early-ceiling" occupations in which the economic structure of the larger social order will rather effectively mitigate *against* continually altering the bargain to raise levels of worker satisfaction. In short, the old organization is—in Caplow's terms—likely to result in high stratification and low valience, hence boredom and low productivity, alienation and sabotage, anomie and apathy, coercion and rebellion.[21]

This pattern is generally consistent with Udy's comparison of *bureaucratic* and *associational* production systems.[22] In this sense, the older

---

[19] Herbert C. Kelman, "Compliance, Identification, and Internalization," *Journal of Conflict Resolution,* 11 (March, 1958), pp. 51–60.

[20] This is not inconsistent with Etzioni's "compliancy theory": Amitai Etzioni, *A Comparative Analysis of Complex Organizations* (New York: The Free Press, 1961).

[21] Theodore Caplow, *Principles of Organization, op. cit.*

[22] Stanley Udy, Jr., *Organization of Work* (New Haven: Human Relations Area Files Press, 1959).

organization is likely to contain what Udy refers to as technical salience at the operational level, but to organization membership in the administration. Hence, the specifically focused and long-term organization will be technically integrated—and its operatives technically motivated, but it will be normatively integrated at the administrative levels, and its administrators more subject to ideological values. Let me emphasize that later I hope to argue the importance of these patterns for inter-organizational relationships.

Assuming, furthermore, that the old organization does become specifically and long-term focused, it is also likely to develop what Thompson refers to as a "long-linked" technology with *certain inputs* (a controlled predictable source of clients) but with uncertain out-puts.[23] In some sense, this kind of organization receives its human materials usable in their presenting form, but the long-term intervention which is intended may well mean that the organization is seldom fully satisfied that it knows when the job is finished. Hence, tremendous concern for and ambivalence about moving clients *out* of the organization while still retaining some degree of interest in or even control over them. What is involved here is probably better said by suggesting that the new organization is not quite sure what its doing, but it knows when its job is finished; the old organization is more certain about what its doing, but not quite sure when the job is over.

In addition, the old organization, with its specific and long-term orientation, has little difficulty in inducting its clients into the organization, but must devote much staff effort and organizational resources to "outducting" them. Not only must they contend with the problem of delineating the precise time at which clients ought to be discharged—they must also determine the suitable places to which clients ought to be sent. All of these problems are essentially administrative in nature and result in judgments which may be more system maintenance in nature than service oriented. For example, in an organizational "set," in which the members mature to the end state, the out-put needs of one can very easily come to be resolved by input needs of another institution.

There are, undoubtedly, many other characteristics of old organizations which are worth pursuing: (1) a focused and single technology exists at the operational level, but multiple and uncoordinated technologies exist at the administrative level; (2) authority informs staff relations at the operational level, but power and attractiveness is the

---

[23] James D. Thompson, *Organizations in Action, op. cit.*

bench-mark at the administrative level; (3) clienteles are regarded as exclusively the organization's own at the operational level, while there is great awareness of overlapping clienteles at the administrative levels. In short, the new organization is likely to be preoccupied with *perfecting* its core technology more than with accommodating large inter-organizational problems. On the other hand, the aged organization is more likely to preoccupy itself with accommodating its administrative melange to the power setting, having already settled on its technological tour de force.

If these patterns are true, it could be argued that they hold important implications for present programs in the fields of human welfare which currently press upon us. I turn lastly to this issue.

## Current Demands Upon Service Organizations

I want to indicate what I understand to be five aspects of recent federally inspired programs in health and welfare: *first,* such programs call for innovations, departures from the present practices in both operational and administrative spheres. *Second,* most federal programs ask for rather dramatic alteration in the work load of existing organizations. Inducements are offered, of course, but these must be balanced against out-puts. *Third,* the success of these programs demands a minimum of conflict between organizations. *Fourth,* and perhaps the base issue, these opportunities usually call for broad based and long-term engagement of multiple organizations in the community—a collectivized plus-lateral/ plus-longitudinal orientation. *Fifth,* and finally, many of the new programs seem to be moving in the direction of renouncing the traditional organizational complexes in favor of those which can enhance inter-agency collaboration.

On the whole, I think it is fair to say that new collaborative programs tend to be initiated through the established, i.e. old, organizations in a community. It is the dominant, viable, large, and visible institutions to which funding agencies normally turn. As a result, local community mobilization for new programs tends to fall in the hands of those organizations which have certain structural limitations as far as adequate implementation is concerned.

One cannot ignore Caplow's contention that decisive innovations tend to be introduced into the organizational set by organizations of intermediate prestige and power—those which are younger, less firmly established, less visible, and otherwise less established in the total organizational complex. We are talking, of course, about technical as well as ideological innovation, and in this sense a prime dilemma is posed: the old organization with its specifically focused interest *is* capable of accommodating technical changes, but its extensive external administrative linkages to an established organizational set tend to prohibit dramatic ideological changes. On the other hand, new "zealot" organizations are often founded on the problem of perfecting their core technologies, but are fertile ground for ideological transformation. Hence, the old and the new: the first capable of and in a set position to innovate at one level, the second capable of another kind of innovation but not in a set position to do it.

I think it is also fair to say that as organizations age and mature, they tend toward a stabilization of work roles and work loads. This occurs not only through rationalization and formalization processes, but also as a result of collective negotiation between workers and management which, over time, come to acquire the character of precedents. In old organizations, the answers to questions such as who shall do what work, at what pace, for what rewards, and even for what purpose tend to be quite inflexible. The reverse is the case in the new laterally oriented organization. The problem, of course, is that most of the new programs in health and welfare—if *properly* implemented—demand drastic alterations in work role and work loads. Paradoxically, perhaps, it seems that new organizations, broadly oriented toward the client's biographical career, *are* capable of conducting the work called for by the new programs, but incapable of effectively engaging themselves.

On the other hand, the old and established organizations are capable of mobilizing the necessary inter-agency contact and dialogue, but least capable of responding meaningfully to the appeal for a more diffuse orientation toward clients.

Thirdly, an obvious component of most federally inspired programs—explicit in some cases—is a renunciation of inter-agency conflict and divisiveness in the interests of mobilizing the collective energies of multiple agencies toward common problems. Organizations, however, especially mature ones with a specific and long-term interest in their clienteles are probably less capable than others may be of responding to this call. I would entertain the hypothesis that as organizations become specifically focused they increase their inter-agency competition for scarce operational resources. And as organizations attempt to maintain an interest in their clients for a longer period of time, they compete for dominance in the set concerning what the final or long-term goals ought to be.[24] Moreover, established organizational sets in a community tend to constitute prestige sets as well—some organizations are thought to be more desirable to work in and to be serviced in than are others. As Caplow has pointed out, this self-aggrandizing tendency of set members effectively mitigates against precisely the kind of inter-agency "rank-equality" which full collaboration calls for: [25] it also minimizes the likelihood of sharing of scarce personnel, a process often regarded as critical to the success of forward-looking programs. In fact, one might suppose that the very enunciation of the principle of non-conflict has itself brought to the fore aspects of intra-set conflict which were before only occasionally visible when the barriers to inter-agency isolation were not challenged.

Fourth, most of the new programs call for what we have termed a lateral and longitudinal orientation toward clients. Yet the dominant and mature members and those to which granting agencies usually turn for leadership, for some of the reasons set forth here have a structural incapacity to deal with client problems in this global way.

An alternative, of course, and one that has been followed in many communities, is to allow the aged organizations to go their own way and construct new organizations to deal with the clients in the broad fashion desired. The difficulty here, of course, is that new organizations are hardly able to break through the hard-crust of the organizational set and fulfill the constituent demands for interagency collaboration and integration. The effect can be only that of introducing *another* service sector into communities which are already encumbered by the presence of multiple-organizational sets, the members of which engage in prestige ranking with their co-members, and are effectively insulated from other sets which deal with the similar clients and similar client problems.

One outcome of this embroglio has been to give the burden of responsibility to the least mature zealot new organizations without anchorage or leverage in the total organizational complex, and even more poignant, to turn to the clients themselves as a resource. And in this sense, new organizations, and even the clarion call of the new community programs themselves, tend toward voluntary associations in which the

---

[24] For a discussion of the "set" concept see, William M. Evan, "The Organization Set: Toward a Theory of Interorganizational Relations," in *Approaches to Organizational Design*, James D. Thompson, Ed. (Pittsburgh: University of Pittsburgh Press, 1966), pp. 173–191.

[25] Theodore Caplow, *Principles of Organization, op. cit.*

desires of those served become the goals of those who serve, and determine final organizational structure. The present trap in all of this, of course, is that the new organizational systems will themselves age. If they do so in the directions which I have suggested they will move toward a specific and long-term interest in their clients, a codification of their position within existing organizational sets, and all of the other patterns which I believe inhibit effective inter-agency contact and collaboration.

# SOME SPECIFIC PROBLEMS OF OLD ORGANIZATIONS AS EFFECTING INTER-AGENCY COLLABORATION

Let me mention just briefly and in propositional form a few specific characteristics of specifically focused and long-term oriented organizations as they bear upon collaborative demand, not *all* of which are as gloomy in outlook as what has previously been said.

First, age leads to non-discretionary jobs at the operational level and to highly discretionary jobs at the administrative level. Persons in discretionary jobs—in this case administrators charged with the responsibility for giving direction to inter-agency collaboration—attempt to maintain power over others in the task environment. This will lead to the development of coalition arrangements to maintain the status quo as persons in discretionary jobs in multiple-organizations seek to coalesce their powers in the face of threatening forces from outside.[26]

In addition age leads to the development of precarious values at the administrative level and to stablized values at the operational level. Persons in organizational sets subject to precarious values tend to become partners in organizational coalitions in an effort to codify their values and make them acceptable to the environment. On the other hand, inter-organizational coalitions can easily develop into "hold-actions" until the environmental heat is off.

Also, age results in an organizational occupational structure which involves up-grading through negotiation and collective action at the operational level, but through work visibility and prestige at the administrative level. Most new community programs, however, are of such a type as to be enhanced through prestige and work visibility at the oper-

---

[26] James D. Thompson, *Organizations in Action, op. cit.*

ational level and through rational negotiation at the administrative level. The conflict presented is obvious.

A final reference to Starbuck probably sums up in a global fashion much of what has been said: [27] the older an organization becomes the more resistant is its social structure to change. Demands for collaboration call for great changes in the structural arrangements of service organizations.

Let me sum up briefly my argument before a final remark on the Gemeinschaft-Gesellschaft distinction with which I began:

1. Many service organizations begin life with a broadly focused but short-term interest in their clients. This occurs because of the need to collect clients, garner community support, and to survive initially without access to the prevalent organizational set.

2. As they age, they tend toward a specific and long-term orientation toward clients. This happens because of the press of norms of rationality, perfection of technology, membership in the organizational set, and the need to retain a hold on clienteles in order to sustain relationships with other organizations in the environment.

3. Current federal programs call for a broadly focused and long-term commitment to clients. New organizations are operationally able to provide the first, but their weak set membership prevents them from accomplishing the second. Old organizations are incapable of shifting from a specific to a broad orientation toward clients, but *are* able to sustain their set dominance.

4. An alternative, represented in some of the CAP programs and which can easily be read as an admission of organizational defeat, is to turn to the clients themselves and ask them what to do and how to do it—to become voluntary in nature. Charles Perrow writes more authoritatively about the limits and possibilities of this strategy of making clients full participants in service organizations.

## OLD ORGANIZATIONS AND THE CONFRONTATION OF GEMEINSCHAFT AND GESELLSCHAFT

In Earl Johnson's words, for an organization to be natural, sentimental, kin-like, and personal it must be lateral in its orientation toward clients.

---

[27] William H. Starbuck, "Organizational Growth and Development," in *Handbook of Organizations, op. cit.,* pp. 451–533.

The taking-in of the total person in milieu psychiatric hospitals, in collegiate educational institutions, and in other such broadly oriented institutions represents an effort to inject these *kinds* of relationships between clients and the formal organizations which periodically touch the lives of people.

On the other hand, the technically elaborate and specifically focused minus-lateral organization more closely represents a Gesellschaft context —fabricated, rational, contrived, and impersonal.

But both gemeinschaft and gesellschaft must deal in their own unique terms with the person not only as he *now* is, but as what he shall be. Hence, the short-term minus-longitudinal organization opts for gesellschaft in the long-haul: the client—treated either personally or impersonally in the here and now—is soon cast off as a person as if he were never a member of the organization. In the long-term plus-longitudinal organization, however, the ethics of sentiment, natural, personal, and kinship follow him about from organization to organization for a very long time.

Perhaps with the enthusiasm of the Great Society, the new programs in human welfare call for the organization to deliver gemeinschaft in both the present and future tenses—organizations are asked to be sentimental and natural with regard both to the clients contemporary life space and future life course. This may be too much to ask. Old organizations may be able to deliver gemeinschaft in the long-haul because of their established linkages with other organizations which can deal with the client later on. New organizations may be able to give a context of gemeinschaft in the short run because of their zealot character. Unfortunately, I see no real evidence that gemeinschaft in the present as well as in the future can easily be accomplished for clients without more drastic organizational transformation than has as yet taken place. It will be very hard indeed to reconstruct the parish in the presence of bureaucracy.

But in spite of the obstacles to achieving the kinds of interorganizational memberships presently thought to be desirable by many, it is clear that there are systematic relationships between organizations. The analysis of these relationships as they are found to occur at the local community level is taken up in the following chapter.

# VII

## TOWARDS THE THEORY AND PRACTICE OF COORDINATION BETWEEN FORMAL ORGANIZATIONS

*Eugene Litwak*
*with collaboration of*
*Jack Rothman*

## INTRODUCTION

BY INTERORGANIZATIONAL ANALYSIS WE MEAN THE THEORIES WHICH indicate how two or more formal organizations relate to each other.[1] Put otherwise, we consider here those situations where one organization is the client of another. In sociology most work in organizational theory has been on the structure of a single organization. Usually the inquiry has been addressed to the question of which type of organizational structure is optimal to achieve a given goal.[2] More recently, attention has turned to the relationship between organizations and their environments, with the emphasis on how the structure of the organization might handle dif-

---

[1] In the present chapter we elaborate some ideas developed in an earlier work on interorganizational analysis: see E. Litwak, and L. Hylton "Interorganizational Analysis: A Hypothesis on Coordination," *Administrative Science Quarterly*, Vol. VI, No. 4 (March 1962), pp. 395–420.

[2] Max Weber, "The Essentials of Bureaucratic Organization: An Ideal-Type Construction," *The Theory of Social and Economic Organization*, trans. A. M. Henderson and Talcott Parsons, ed. Talcott Parsons (New York: Oxford University Press, 1947), pp. 329–340. Peter Blau, *Dynamics of Bureaucracy* (Chicago: University of Chicago Press, 1955), pp. 18–32. Charles Perrow, "A Framework for the Comparative Analysis of Organizations," *American Sociological Review*, 32 (April 1967), pp. 194–208. Amitai Etzioni, "Organizational Control Structure," *Handbook of Organizations*, ed. J. G. March (Chicago: Rand McNally, 1965), pp. 650–677.

ferent types of environments.[3] The other instructive thing about the studies just described is that they are generally not interested in the point of this paper—the forms of linkages which effectively join organizations to each other.[4] Here we are concerned with the circumstances under which organizations contact each other through formal and informal links, through adjudicatory versus communication strategies, through autonomous or dependent links, through authoritarian or collegial links.

# DIFFERENCES BETWEEN INTRAORGANIZATIONAL AND INTERORGANIZATIONAL ANALYSIS

## Intra and Interorganizational Continuum

Organizations can be classified on a continuum from a pole which is clearly intraorganizational to the opposite which is interorganizational (a confederation of semi-autonomous organizations). A small shoe factory by itself might fit on the intraorganizational pole of this continuum while General Electric with its multiple semi-independent divisions (radio, locomotive, generators, electric light bulbs, etc.) might be near the

---

[3] William R. Dill, "Environment as an Influence on Managerial Autonomy," *Comparative Studies in Administration,* ed. James D. Thompson et al. (Pittsburgh: University of Pittsburgh Press, 1959), pp. 131–161. Also in *Administrative Science Quarterly,* 2 (March 1958). P. R. Lawrence, and J. W. Lorsch, *Organization and Environment* (Boston: Harvard Business School, 1967), pp. 1–22, 133–158. J. D. Thompson, *Organizations in Action* (New York: McGraw-Hill, 1967), pp. 3–13, 39–82. B. R. Clark, "Organizational Adaptation and Precarious Values," *Complex Organizations,* ed. Amitai Etzioni (New York: Holt, Rinehart & Winston, 1965), pp. 159–167. Also in *American Sociological Review,* 21 (1956) 327–336.

[4] For some important exceptions: M. Aiken and J. Hage, "Organizational Structure and Interorganizational Dynamics," Paper read at A.S.A. Meetings, August 1967. W. M. Evans, "The Organizational Set: Towards a Theory of Interorganizational Relations, *Approaches to Organizational Design,* ed. J. D. Thompson (Pittsburgh, 1966), pp. 173–191. S. Levine and P. E. White, "Exchange as a Conceptual Framework for the Study of Interorganizational Relationships," *Administrative Science Quarterly,* V. 4 (March 1961), pp. 583–601. Richard R. Rubin and A. L. Stinchcombe, "Interorganizational Networks as Systems of Functional Interdependence," mimeographed paper read at the A.S.A. Meeting, August 1967. V. M. Sieder, *The Rehabilitation Agency* (Brandeis University, 1966), 77–118. Ray E. Johns and D. F. DeMarche, *Community Organization and Agency Responsibility* (New York, 1951), Chaps. 12–16.

middle. Also near the middle would be steel companies which are nominally separate organizations but in many areas act like one organization, e.g., setting prices and negotiations with labor unions. Typical of the interorganizational pole of the continuum would be a businessmen's association of shoe manufacturers. It is clearly a group of semi-autonomous organizations (i.e., cooperating in limited areas). The problem of describing what is unique about inter and intraorganizational structures is a bit like trying to differentiate between day and night. It is clear at the extremes that there *is* a day and a night, and they *are* different. However, it is difficult to say at what point day becomes night. For this reason, our analysis speaks to the differences at the extreme poles. When we speak about organizations with mixed characteristics we speak only about that part which deals with the issues we are discussing. Put more precisely, the more an organization approaches a confederation of organizations, the more interorganization analysis will hold while traditional intraorganizational analysis will hold for the opposite extreme.

The question might now be asked: what are the differences between intra and interorganizational analysis?

# DIFFERENCES IN VARIABLES STRESSED

The most obvious difference between a confederation of organizations and a single organization is that confederations lack strong central authority. As has been noted by various authors,[5] this has important implications for the factors central to confederations as compared to single organizations. The type of variables operating in the two situations might not differ radically; but their importance might. Thus, as Clark points out,[6] how one deals with poor performance, decisions to introduce an innovation, setting criteria for work, or determining who will be accountable for a given decision involves different processes within an organization as compared to a confederated situation. In a set lacking centralized decision-making, the apparatus is much slower and the processes are

---

[5] B. R. Clark, "Interorganizational Patterns in Education," *Administrative Science Quarterly*, X, 2 (September 1965), 224–237. Basil J. F. Mott, *Anatomy of a Coordinating Council* (University of Pittsburgh Press, 1968), pp. 75–104. Litwak and Hylton, "Interorganizational Analysis: A Hypothesis on Coordination," *op. cit.* J. D. Thompson, *Organizations in Action, op. cit.*

[6] B. R. Clark, "Interorganizational Patterns in Education," *op. cit.*

more likely to involve bargaining, negotiations, and conflict rather than administrative fiats. Basically, a decision process involves separately persuading each unit of the confederation.[7]

There is another feature of confederated interorganizational analysis which is less true of organizational analysis. The confederated situation involves mechanisms that maintain distance between units as well as mechanisms which integrate units with each other. If our reasoning is correct, we should be able to suggest an entire class of devices for maintaining distance which are little emphasized or pointed to as devices which are disruptive in the typical organizational analysis. We have in mind, for example, avoiding membership coordinating bodies, the maintenance of highly competitive relationships, and others.

## DIFFERENCES IN IDEAL FUNCTIONS

There is one very important difference between organizational and interorganizational analysis which from some points of view is central and which reflects the above differences. In general terms, confederated organizations deal with multiple goals or means not consistent with each other. By contrast, a single organization is designed to deal with one goal or one mean, or multiple goals and means, but only *if they are consistent or can be ordered in some rational way.* Thus, organizational analysts point out that when organizations have to in fact deal with multiple goals, they must find some process—optimizing, satisfying, maximizing, majority rule, historical trend, etc.—for reconciling or ordering them. Or if for some reason there are multiple means to choose from and there is no way to choose, then a series of strategies are suggested as to how to select one from the many, e.g., incrementalism, calculated risk, visibility, etc.[8]

By contrast, it is suggested that a confederation of organizations is ideally suited for maintaining differences. So wedded has the organizational analyst become to the problems of one organization that he sometimes overlooks the fact that society takes great precautions to insure that different values and means which are not completely consistent with

---

[7] Litwak and Hylton, "Interorganizational Analysis: A Hypothesis on Coordination," *op. cit.*

[8] R. A. Dahl and C. E. Lindblom, *Politics, Economics and Welfare* (New York: Harper, 1953), pp. 57–92. J. D. Thompson, *Organizations in Action, op. cit.,* pp. 83–98.

each other are preserved. Thus, the entire political theory of "checks and balances" is based on the idea that there are governmental processes which are different, not completely consistent with each other, and which must be preserved. One solution which seeks to preserve these separate functions gives each an independent organizational base. Similarly, it can be pointed out that ours is a society which believes in religious freedom, public education, freedom of the press, and the need to protect citizens from criminals. It is abundantly clear that these goals are not completely consistent with each other. In order to preserve these independent goals each was given an independent organizational base and forbidden to join in a common organizational structure. Nelson's suggestion that youth probation agencies and police should be kept separate,[9] or current suggestions that income maintenance and social services should be separated are representative of the same philosophy.

It can be pointed out that the goals and means need not be logically inconsistent to be in conflict. As economists have long noted, scarce resources can produce conflict between goals or means which are logically consistent. Thus it may be true that group work, casework, leisure time programs for children, and music programs might all in their way contribute to "good citizenship" and reduction of delinquent behavior. Yet, limited funds might force a community budget committee to treat them as competitors. Under such circumstances, if all were thought worthy of survival, it could be argued that each should have an independent base.[10]

There is a third circumstance in which confederation might be important, and this has to do with the economies of small scale.

It has been suggested by organizational analysts that the more unstandardized the task dealt with, the more important it is to have decentralized departments in a loose confederation.[11] Carried to its extreme, it could be argued that the costs of maintaining the kind of communication and centralized authority required by an organization might eventually become too great, leading to the splitting off of organizations into

---

[9] E. K. Nelson, Jr., "Organizational Disparity in Definitions of Deviance and Uses of Authority: Police, Probation, and the Schools," *Schools in a Changing Society,* ed. A. J. Reiss, Jr. (New York: Free Press, 1965), pp. 21–47.

[10] See Banfield's reasoning behind social and central decisions. E. C. Banfield, *Political Influence* (New York: Free Press of Glencoe, 1961).

[11] Lawrence and Lorsch, *op. cit.* Eugene Litwak, "Models of Bureaucracy that Permit Conflict," *American Journal of Sociology,* 57 (September 1961), pp. 173–183. Charles Perrow, "A Framework for the Comparative Analysis of Organizations," *op. cit.* J. D. Thompson, *Organizations in Action, op. cit.*

small units which coordinate with each other. More generally, where tasks are highly idiosyncratic or nonstandardized, a series of small organizations cooperating as a confederation might have much greater speed and flexibility than one large organization.[12] Without attempting to exhaust the reasons, it is hoped that the reader will follow the point; namely, that society seeks to maintain multiple goals and means at the same level rather than seeking to order them, reconcile them, or eliminate inconsistencies. Furthermore, one major method for doing so is to give to the various means or goals their own organizational base.

One reason for insisting on organizational autonomy is that organizations provide power. Each member of an organization often views its survival in its simplest form in terms of his immediate occupational survival. As a consequence, he is easily enlisted into the preservation of the organizational goals or means.[13] But, equally important, organizations have both professional expertise, legitimation, sanctions and physical resources which they can apply to preserve their unique qualities.[14] One has only to ask what happens when a single organization has under its auspices two or more contradictory goals to appreciate the importance of this point. Thus, it has been pointed out that freedom of the press and protection against criminals is often combined within the same organization, the police.[15] Given the inevitable conflict which arises between freedom of the press and "public safety," freedom of the press tends to be

---

[12] W. R. Dill, "Environment as an Influence on Managerial Autonomy," *op. cit.* Lawrence and Lorsch, *op. cit.* E. Litwak and J. Figueira, "Technological Innovation and Theoretical Functions of Primary Groups and Bureaucratic Structures," *American Journal of Sociology,* 73, No. 4 (January 1968), pp. 468–481. J. D. Thompson, *Organizations in Action, op. cit.*

[13] Peter Blau and Richard Scott, *Formal Organizations* (San Francisco: Chandler Press, 1962), Chapter 3. They point out that professionals often do not identify their occupational success with the survival of the organization with which they currently work. Philip Selznick points out that there is often a mismatch between organizational goals and individual needs and as a consequence organizational goals suffer (*TVA and the Grass Roots: A Study in the Sociology of Formal Organization* (Berkeley and Los Angeles: University of California, 1949), *in passim.* All would say is that for a large proportion of the population a threat to the organizational goals by another organization is viewed in terms of a personal job loss.

[14] John R. P. French Jr. and Bertram Raven, "The Bases of Social Power," Article 32 in *Group Dynamics,* eds. D. Cartwright and A. Zander (New York: Row, Peterson and Co., 1962, 2nd Edition), pp. 607–623. E. Litwak and H. Meyer, *Relationship between School-Community Coordinating Procedures and Reading Achievement* (December 1966), Final Report for U.S. Office of Education, pp. 1–17 and Appendix A, "Organizational Bases for the Use of Coercion, Legitimation, and Reference Power," pp. A1–A8.

[15] Litwak and Hylton, *op. cit.*

assigned a secondary place. It is our argument that where the press had an independent organizational base, it could more easily maintain its freedom on a par with public safety. Although somewhat the same analysis can be made within organizations, it should be understood that in most organizations there is a centralized authority, and parity depends on good will. However, in the case of a confederation, more than the good will of an executive is needed to guarantee parity.

There have been additional justifications for the maintenance of coordination among separate organizations. One of the most frequent is that the ability to use other organizations provides an organization with more resources.[16] This is far from universal, however. In all situations which approach a constant sum game the gain of resources by one organization will be matched by the loss of resources by the other. There are many instances when organizations do much better if they do not cooperate with others. For instance, the American Cancer Society has long refused to cooperate with community chest programs because they do much better alone. We do not believe that central to defining interorganizational effectiveness is the idea that cooperation adds new resources. We believe this will happen in limited situations, which we will describe below.

Having suggested some of the tasks performed by a confederation of organizations versus a single organization, we would not want the reader to assume that this is the only reason for the rise of confederated organizations. As Goode has pointed out,[17] organizations and societies are not necessarily guided by efficiency. As a consequence, confederations exist for many reasons other than the fact that they are ideally suited for accomplishing a given task. Thus, the very virtue of the organization for maintaining pluralistic values may also lead to avoidance of merger when in fact merger is called for. Thus, fear of loss of jobs or organizational imperialism might keep organizations apart which might benefit from economies of large scale. Somewhat related is the idea that there are cultural mandates which stress certain types of separateness as a good in itself. Thus, various business concerns are prevented from joining together under the antitrust laws. Although originally there might have been some theory of effectiveness for the autonomous organizations, what it might well reflect in current society is not so much effectiveness but a

---

[16] Aiken and Hage, *op. cit.* Levine and White, *op. cit.*

[17] W. J. Goode, "The Protection of the Inept," *American Sociological Review,* Vol. XXXII, No. 1 (February 1967), 5–19.

cultural value *per se*. Finally, it should be noted that the process of change is not instantaneous. At any moment in times an investigator might find two separate organizations in the process of merger or one organization in the process of splitting up. The fact that organizations may be joined or confederated for reasons other than effectiveness, and can survive at less than optimal effectiveness, means that to test our hypothesis one should have measures of effectiveness as well as type of structure.

Before launching into the next section of our paper a brief summary of the main points made so far is important. First, interorganizational analysis is different from organizational analysis because the absence of a centralized authority produces different decision processes in everyday activities such as changing personnel, setting up criteria for work, etc. In a confederation, the chief processes are negotiations and discussion, while in organizational analysis they tend to involve administrative fiat. Further, it was pointed out that studies of interorganizational analysis emphasize mechanisms for keeping subunits at a distance while typical organizational analysis is concerned more with mechanisms which bring subunits closer together. Finally, it was pointed out that interorganizational structures are ideally suited for dealing with problems of multiple goals, multiple means, and economies of small scale, where the desire is to maintain goals and means which are in partial conflict. What is considered the legitimate goal of interorganizational structures is considered deviant for the intraorganizational ones.

In the next section we should like to concentrate on the *types* of effective linkages which connect organizations and the conditions under which they are most effective. There are of course an indefinite number of ways by which social phenomena can be described. As mentioned above, we are interested in the following: the degree of organizational formality of the linkage, whether it is continuous or ad hoc, whether the linkage stresses communication or judicial functions, the extent to which the linkage procedure has functions which are autonomous from those of the member organizations, the extent to which linkage procedure is organized with an authoritarian structure or a collegial one, and the extent to which a network of linkages might affect the role of a particular linkage.

In our attempts to explain the various types of linkages between organizations, we shall confine ourselves to an elaboration of an approach suggested by Litwak and Hylton [18] and will therefore deal with the fol-

---

[18] Litwak and Hylton, *op. cit.*

lowing set of variables: (1) degree and type of organizational interdependence, (2) level of organizational awareness of interdependence, (3) number of organizations involved or the number of interorganizational transactions, (4) type of bureaucratic organization, (5) the extent to which the linkages deal with uniform or nonuniform events, and (6) the resources an organization has to commit to interorganizational linkages. What the reader must ask himself in considering such variables is the extent to which they occur in traditional organizational analysis and, insofar as they do, the weight they are given. Insofar as they do not occur in traditional organizational analysis, or insofar as they are considered trivial items in such an analysis, then we have provided the reader with a more specific statement of how confederated interorganizational structures differ from the intraorganizational ones.

# CONDITIONS UNDER WHICH FORMAL AND INFORMAL LINKAGES ARE MOST EFFECTIVE

## Continuum of Organizational Formality

A continuum of organizational structures can be envisioned from the monocratic bureaucratic organizations described by Weber [19] to the primary group structure described by Cooley.[20] In between these extremes would be the human relations type of bureaucracies, professional associations, voluntary associations, and semiformal social clubs such as family clubs. Without trying to specify each point on such a continuum, the reader can get the sense that there is such a continuum. Many different types of organizations might be located on such a continuum by suggesting that the extreme rationalistic end (the Weberian monocratic bureaucracy) might ideally be represented in terms of a completely automated industry. The only individuals necessary are those involved in policy making. Or put differently, the extreme pole of formality would involve coordination which takes place through explicit rules and virtually no need for direct interaction between members of the various organizations.

There are three illustrations of such formal types of linkages. Linkages between libraries for the purpose of exchanging books are almost

---

[19] Max Weber, *op. cit.*

[20] Charles H. Cooley, "Primary Groups," in *Small Groups,* eds. Paule Hare, Edgar F. Borgatta and Robert Bales (New York: Alfred Knopf, 1955) 15.20.

totally carried out through member organizations filling out printed forms. The entire procedure is spelled out in a three-to-five page document of rules and regulations. Linkages between social work agencies in very large cities such as New York are partly accomplished through printed directories of agencies which indicate the type of services, the telephone number, the address, and some of the leading personnel in all agencies. A member of any particular agency will often use this directory to aid a given client by determining which additional organizations he must deal with, where they are, how he should get in touch with them, etc. In a similar manner, cost of living escalation clauses in union-management contracts are linkage devices characterized by a priori rules. One has only to compare the way in which such clauses produce changes in the wage rate with what goes on in a regular wage negotiation between union and management to see that such linkages utilize a priori rules and regulations to coordinate the two groups.

A less formal type of linkage than rules would be a coordinating organization. For instance, various private social agencies in a large community may have a community chest organization which coordinates their fund raising or a community council which coordinates their service. These coordinating agencies have their own personnel and sometimes carry on autonomous activities (fund raising and research) for the service of the member agencies. Similarly, business concerns might have business associations which have paid functionaries who carry on the activities of linkages. If one considers doctors as really small business concerns, then the American Medical Association would be another instance of a linkage organization with permanent specialized personnel. Other examples might be governmental regulatory agencies, Councils of Education geared to coordinate university or public school systems, etc.

The informal pole of our continuum is represented by linkages which resemble primary group contacts between members of the agencies involved. Thus, it has been pointed out that much linkage between organizations takes place informally between executives of the organizations involved either over lunch or in presumably social situations (e.g., country clubs). Hunter, in his analysis of power, and Banfield in his analysis of political decisions both point out that informal "friendship" linkages of this type seem to be quite common.[21]

---

[21] F. Hunter, *Community Power Structure* (Anchor Books edition, 1963) pp. 61–113 (also Chapel Hill: University of North Carolina Press, 1953). E. C. Banfield, *Political Influence,* esp. discussion of Fort Dearborn, pp. 126–158 in hardcover edition, 1961.

What we hope is clear from this discussion is that linkages between organizations can vary from the extreme of impersonal rules, to the use of special linkage organizations, to informal "friendship" type of contacts. In what follows, we should like to suggest the social conditions which indicate under what conditions each type of linkage might be most effective. We emphasize the diversity of linkages because when considering interorganizational contact people often fixate on one type of linkage (e.g., official coordinating agencies) and overlook the tremendous amount of linkage carried on by rules as well as the more informal ones. The latter are often viewed as chance friendships rather than as being systemic in character. With these definitions in mind let us turn our attention to the factors which permit us to say which degree of formality is ideal.

We beg the reader's indulgence because there may be exceptions to our hypotheses when presented singly. Once the major factors are delineated we will present a multifactor hypothesis and we would argue there should be few exceptions. It is upon these multi-factor hypotheses that the argument in this paper rests.

## Partial Interdependence

We introduce the concept of interdependence at this point because it suggests the minimum condition for any form of linkage. By interdependence we mean that two or more organizations must take each other into account in order to best achieve their individual goals. In some sense, every individual affects another and all organizations can be considered interdependent. We mean by interdependent that the acts of one organization affect those of another in an immediate way. Although it would be hard to specify the exact point at which "long run" becomes "immediate," we think that in practice such distinctions can be made.

The question now is what states of interdependence provide the bases for linkages between two or more organizations. Our hypothesis would be that *partial* interdependence is the ideal basis for maintaining a confederation of organizations. Where there are complete states of interdependence between two or more organizations, the ideal solution would be organizational merger or the destruction of all but one organization. There would be no need for interorganizational linkages. The problem would become intraorganizational. Alternatively, if two or more organizations had no interdependence at all, the ideal solution would

147

be no linkage. To illustrate let us assume that a family agency and a child agency operate in the same area. Let us further assume that developments in therapeutic practices dictated that all members of a family must be dealt with as a unit, that treatment of children must also involve the parents. As a consequence, the workers in the two agencies must maintain very close continuous contacts. And in fact it could be argued that one worker handling both parent and child is most effective. Furthermore, there would be economies offered by virtue of sharing the same building and the same administrative staff. Thus, there is a powerful interdependence on clients, on professional knowledge, and on the economies of administration and housekeeping functions. Merger is the solution.

To illustrate no interdependence, take the case of private social work agencies joined together for fund-raising purposes. In one city, there was included among these agencies funds for the city symphony. The symphony had no interdependence in terms of services with any of the other agencies. Its clientele was unique, and in general it could draw on different sources of funds. Eventually the symphony left the community chest program and developed its own fund-raising operation. The two fund-raising operations could be carried on independently with no real friction, only indifference. From these two illustrations it should be clear that the key to interorganizational linkage is the notion of partial interdependence. There must be certain areas in which each organization is independent of the others while other areas are interdependent. Thus, private family agencies, delinquency control programs, youth leisure-time agencies, programs for senior citizens, and programs for dealing with sick and disabled are frequently heavily interdependent on each other for services and fund raising. On the other hand, their specialties are sufficiently distinct so that areas remain autonomous where they are.[22]

When we say that the ideal state for interorganizational linkages is partial interdependence, we include the concept of reciprocity or symmetrical exchanges. Put more precisely, there cannot be extreme asymmetry in aid. In cases of extreme asymmetry in interdependence, we would hypothesize no linkage at all or complete merger depending on the inclination of the non-dependent members. Thus in some communities the American Cancer Society refuses to join the local community chest, while the local community chest very much wants them to join. Here is a

---

[22] V. M. Sieder, *The Rehabilitation Agency, op. cit.*, has a very good illustration of this point.

good case of asymmetry in dependence. The American Cancer Society feels no dependence on other private welfare organizations. Its work involves sponsoring research and requires no services from the local agencies. Locating its clientele (in this case research subjects) again requires little if any cooperation from the local agencies. The studies can be done in foreign countries. The medical scientists to whom it disperses funds are not tied to local organizations. Finally, it is not dependent on the local agencies for fund-raising. Thus in any open competition for funds it can do much better than the community chest programs. However, by virtue of this last fact the community chest program is dependent on the American Cancer Society. For the more successful the campaign of the American Cancer Society, the less money there is for the community chest programs because they solicit from the same population. We thus have a case of asymmetrical interdependence. In such a case, the community chest will try to create mutual interdependence by setting up its own cancer organization. However, insofar as that does not succeed there is little that they can do. If the American Cancer Society's needs were infinite or if the community chest had no holding power, the community chest program would be destroyed. However, if the situation stabilizes, then we would hypothesize a minimum number of linkages approaching the pole of a situation similar to that of multiple organizations which are indifferent to each other. The reader should keep in mind that in this discussion we are dealing with extreme forms of asymmetry. In fact, modest forms of asymmetry are perfectly consistent with interorganizational linkages and are important determinants of their shape. But these have less to do with degree of formality and more with the concentration of power within the linkage organizations or relationships themselves. We would also suggest that symmetry of dependence need not involve a direct exchange of similar services at a given moment of time. Rather, it may involve limited time lags as well as an exchange of different services and very indirect paths of exchange.[23]

To sum up, the crucial consideration when relating interdependence to linkages between organizations is whether it is at a *partial state*. Complete interdependence and complete dependence tend to lead away from interorganizational linkages. Therefore, partial states of interdependence

---

[23] Peter Blau, *Exchange and Power in Social Life* (New York: John Wiley, 1964). Eugene Litwak, "Extended Kin Relations in an Industrial Democratic Society," Chapter 13 in *Social Structure and the Family Generational Relations,* Eds. E. Shanas and G. F. Streib (Prentice-Hall, 1965).

are minimum conditions for the discussion of all linkage mechanisms. Similarly, "effectiveness" only applies to situations where organizations must maintain actual states of partial interdependence.[24]

## Organizational Awareness of Interdependence

Partial states of interdependence will not by themselves tell us what form the interorganizational linkages will take. In addition, the organization must be aware of its interdependence. By organizational awareness we mean that the organization must, as a matter of policy, recognize its interdependence with another organization. In its extreme form this means that the organization assigns people or defines jobs to deal with other organizations. Sometimes individuals are aware of interdependence on other organizations but their *organization* does not recognize it. This is defined as low organizational awareness.[25] It is important that in fact organizations can be in actual states of interdependence and not recognize it. Thus, Buell, in a study of "hard core" welfare families, found that they might be involved with twenty or more agencies.[26] Furthermore, these agencies could be giving advice which had contradictory implications for the family and yet there was no official agency policy regarding cooperation with each other. It was only after his research was reported that agencies undertook to coordinate explicitly.

Furthermore, it is often true in social work professions and others heavily endowed with a classic planning orientation that there is a stress on interdependence where in fact none exists. Morris and Binstock have pointed out that all too often agency personnel meet with each

---

[24] We will elaborate our definition of effectiveness in the section following formality.

[25] Josefina Figueira McDonough has pointed out in a project memorandum (Fall 1968) that there are three distinct forms of awareness of interdependence: (1) the organization officially designates someone to coordinate, (2) the members of the organization are aware of the need for coordination, and (3) the larger public are aware of the need for coordination. These three forms are not necessarily correlated. A full understanding of awareness requires an examination of the interaction of all three types. In addition, Jim Ajemian points out that one would want to differentiate those organizations which officially do not recognize coordination because they are ignorant of other organizations from those who do so because they are knowledgeable about the existence of other organizations.

[26] Bradley Buell, *Community Planning for Human Services* (New York: Columbia University Press, 1957).

other and attempt to coordinate their activities when in fact there is not sufficient interdependence to warrant it.[27] The move for decentralized decision making in industry as well as in planning in the East European countries are evidence that in the past there was an awareness of felt interdependence above and beyond the degree of interdependence which in fact existed. As a consequence, although awareness of interdependence and actual states of interdependence may be correlated, they are sufficiently independent to warrant separate consideration. Our hypothesis is that where organizations are aware of their interdependence, formal modes of linkage are the most effective. The reasoning behind this hypothesis is that organizational awareness leads to assignment of special personnel and stress on permanent forms of coordination. These in turn are most consistent with formal modes of linkages (i.e., least likely to lead to conflict between linkages and organizational structure).

Levine and White in their discussion bring up the notion of "domain consensus." This concept includes the idea of organizational awareness and points up the need to consider the organizational awareness of both members of the linkage system.[28] Where organizational awareness is asymmetrical—one organization aware and the other not—then we would hypothesize that the most effective form of linkages will be semiformal. This would be a compromise between the pressures of one organization for formality and the other for primary group linkages. Thus, two or more organizations may use a regularly scheduled luncheon meeting which has a mixture of formality and informality.

## Uniformity or Standardization

Another factor which relates to interorganizational linkages is the standardization or changeability of the element to be coordinated. Thus, in the organizational literature there has been a series of studies which have argued that the more non-standardized an event, the more decentralized and collegial the structure for handling it, while the more standardized the event, the more rationalistic the organizational means for handling it.

---

[27] R. Morris and R. H. Binstock, *Feasible Planning for Social Change* (Columbia University Press, 1966).

[28] Levine and White, *op. cit.*

Perhaps the clearest empirical documentation for this point of view is by Lawrence and Lorsch.[29] They point out that in the plastics industry where technological change is very rapid, the organizational structure which was most effective was one which had decentralized decision making and much in the way of lateral interaction, while in the container industry which had been more or less stable, a more hierarchical rationalistic organization was most effective. We think that the same considerations would hold for linkage mechanisms, but we would carry the analysis still further and argue that extremely non-standardized situations will be best managed by primary-group-type linkages, while extremely standardized situations will be handled most effectively by linkages which consist of written rules.[30]

To clarify the meaning of the term non-standardization, we shall discuss some of the typical situations to which it might apply. First, it might refer to a complex situation. For as Levine and White point out, where organizations have many varied goals, it is likely that their linkages with similar organizations will have to involve some face-to-face negotiation. But when it has a simple goal, then the two organizations might link by virtue of having common orientations. In this case non-standardization is defined in terms of complexity of goals. The hypothesis is that the more non-standardized the event the more *face-to-face* (as opposed to rules) kinds of interaction are necessary to coordinate.[31]

Rubin and Stinchcombe also seek to indicate the circumstances under which face-to-face contact or close geographical proximity is essential for coordinating two or more organizations.[32] They point out the following circumstances: (1) coalition formation (e.g., a group getting together to buy a company) where detailed knowledge of the thoughts of other men are essential and where there is no necessary standard to go by, (2) comparison shopping where knowledge is imperfect and therefore comparison shopping is necessary, e.g., purchase of expensive art, purchase of stocks and bonds, purchase of women's apparel, (3) new industries where production deals with innovation and knowledge or relationship of product to market is unknown or uncertain, and (4)

---

[29] Lawrence and Lorsch, *op. cit.* E. Litwak, "Models of Bureaucracy that Permit Conflict," *op. cit.* Charles Perrow, *op. cit.* J. D. Thompson, *Organizations in Action, op. cit.*

[30] Litwak and Figueira, *op. cit.*

[31] Levine and White, *op. cit.*

[32] Rubin and Stinchcombe, "Interorganizational Networks . . ." *op. cit.*

information-gathering agencies where speed of communication and need to deal with the unexpected is pertinent. From their analysis, it is clear that sometimes they are speaking about situations which are so complex that standardized communication techniques cannot help, situations which are changing so quickly that standardization techniques cannot be devised or brought to bear in time, or situations where knowledge is so sparse that standardized techniques cannot be devised.

What is crucial for our analysis is that Rubin and Stinchcombe, as well as Levine and White, point out the importance of close face-to-face contact when the event to be communicated is non-standardized. Face-to-face relations are of course one ingredient of a primary group relationship. However, a close look at Rubin and Stinchcombe's analysis indicates other dimensions as well. Thus in such situations of uncertainty, the development of trust is also necessary as well as diffused non-instrumental orientations.

Form and Nosow, in their analysis of a disaster, point out that in the most nonuniform moments of the disaster (the first hour or so of a tornado) coordination between agencies tends to take place on the spot and in a face-to-face contact between members of the respective organizations.[33] However, as the time periods become longer, the event can be sorted into more uniform categories. Organizations then tend to evolve more formalistic modes of coordination.

Banfield points out in his analysis of community decisions that efforts to coordinate organizations frequently floundered because there was no knowledge upon which to base decisions. Moreover, the members of the various organizations were not in sufficient personal contact nor did they trust each other sufficiently to coordinate through formal channels. He points out that in order to start an urban renewal project the city had to agree to move its offices into a proposed city-county building, insurance companies had to agree to put up the initial capital, the federal government had to locate its offices in the proposed new building, and the government had to certify the project eligible for urban renewal grants. If any one of these organizations had taken the first step, then it would have been likely that others would follow. However, none took the first step and the project never began. We would speculae that the various groups involved had only a formal mode of linkage and did not have the continuous personal face-to-face contact such a

---

[33] W. H. Form and S. Nosow, *Community in Disaster* (New York: Harper, 1958).

nonstandardized situation requires if each organization is to coordinate with another.[34]

Where situations can be standardized, it is easy to specify a priori rules. Where they are not standardized detailed rules cannot be written. This is the basis for our hypothesis that standardized acts are most effectively coordinated by formal procedures while nonstandardized events are best coordinated by informal ones, especially those which stress face-to-face relations.

It is possible, as Thompson and Perrow have done, to combine the various forms of non-standardization—heterogeneity, knowledge and change—and come up with finer distinctions among non-standardized events.[35] Such developments are worthy. But given the number of variables dealt with in this paper, we shall leave this refinement to others and classify all complex rapidly changing situations, and situations for which there is no knowledge as non-standardized.

## Number of Organizations or Number of Interactions

It is our hypothesis that the larger the number of organizations, the more effective will be formalistic modes of coordination. This hypothesis is based on the simple notion that the larger the number of organizations, the more difficult it is to establish communication between them unless one hires special people or has special communication machinery. Furthermore, to insure that members of a large number of organizations can meet together, it is necessary to schedule meetings well in advance. The employment of specialists in communication and the development of special equipment for communication are almost by definition the building blocks of formal linkages. By contrast, where few organizations are involved, arrangements for meetings can be made on an ad hoc basis and by personnel already in the organization. Furthermore, optimum flexibility is obtained, e.g., meetings can be called exactly when needed rather than arbitrarily scheduled. The variable "numbers of organizations" stresses one special aspect of formality; organizational links must be externally visible to be effective as well as traditional ties involving special personnel, written agenda, etc.

Similar reasoning would apply for large organizations with many

---

[34] Banfield, *op. cit.*, esp. pp. 126–158.
[35] Perrow, *op. cit.* Thompson, *op. cit.*

different kinds of links, e.g., schools, police forces, and welfare agencies in a large city. One study suggests that the above hypotheses are correct. The investigator studied interorganizational relations among welfare organizations in 52 cities. He found that as soon as one moved into cities over 500,000, the workers were very likely to say that their agency had written rules and regulations guiding interactions with other agencies. As one moved to smaller cities, the proportion saying their agencies had written rules shrunk.[36] If one can make the assumption that in larger cities there are more organizations and larger ones than in small cities, the data would be consistent with our hypothesis. Preliminary evidence also suggests that as one moves to larger cities, directories of agencies become increasingly more valued by members of various welfare agencies.

## Type of Organizational Structure

A group of recent writers on organizational analysis have come to the conclusion that there are a variety of types of bureaucratic organizations ranging from the Weberian monocratic to the human relations and they are differentially effective for various goals. If one accepts this formulation, the question arises as to how the structure of an organization affects the type of linkage it permits. Some speculate that there is pressure for consistency between the internal structure of the organizations and their linking mechanisms.[37] Thus, the rationalistic organizations would be most consistent with linkage structures which were formalistic while human relations structures would be most consistent with structures which were primary-group oriented. We would hypothesize that linkages between two rationalistic organizations are most likely to be formalistic while linkages between two human relations structures are most likely to exhibit primary-group-type characteristics.[38] The case

---

[36] Johns and De Marche, *Community Organization and Agency Responsibility, op. cit.* E. Thomas, "Role Conceptions and Organizational Size," *American Sociological Review,* 24, 1959, pp. 30–37.

[37] Clifton D. Hollister, "School as a Bureaucratic Organization," in Litwak and Meyer, *Relationship between School and Community Coordinating Procedures, op. cit.,* Chapter 18, pp. 453–491; also *Bureaucratic Structure and School-Parent Communication in 18 Detroit Elementary Schools,* Ph.D. Thesis, University of Michigan, 1966. Litwak and Meyer, "Balance Theory . . ." *op. cit.*

[38] Josefina Figueira McDonough's study of 17 Agricultural Agencies provides empirical evidence on this point. Unpublished project memorandum, January 1969.

of linkage between organizations with different structures might have linkages which are somewhat in-between in formality.[39] In addition, it should be understood, as Ferman points out in his analysis of job training programs, that differences in organizational structure can be as much a basis for conflict as differences in goals.[40]

Several writers, as already noted, have looked at the same phenomenon from another point of view. They have tried to indicate how types of outer environments might affect the internal structure of the organization. Thus they point out that where an organization has to deal with a changing and heterogeneous environment, one will have a collegial-type bureaucracy, e.g., decentralized decision making with departments split on functional lines such as the General Electric model.[41] In this paper we develop only one side of the possible feedback, i.e., how the structure affects the linkage mechanism. However, we are convinced that there are reverse effects as well and will briefly talk about them in the last section of this paper. We will not develop the properties of organizational structure in this paper but in general assume (as suggested by organizational theorists above) that they will be highly related to the type of task (i.e., standardized or non-standardized).

## Amount of Organizational Resources

Aiken and Hage as well as Levine and White point out that organizations frequently link themselves with others to gain resources. However, we would make an additional point that it is the organizations with "extra" resources which are often best able to link with others. Thus, in a recent experiment a select number of schools in the Detroit system were given extra funds. Those schools had much greater community participation rates than schools without such funds.[42] The two sets of schools (those with and those without) had the same imperatives for community linkages; they differed only in the resources they had. Amount of resources does not itself predict the degree of formality of

---

[39] Litwak and Meyer, "Balance Theory of Coordination..." *op. cit.* Mott, *Anatomy of a Coordinating Council, op. cit.*, pp. 75–104.

[40] Louis Ferman, *Job Development for the Hard-to-employ* (Ann Arbor, Michigan: Institute of Labor Relations, The University of Michigan, June 1968).

[41] Thompson, *op. cit.*

[42] Litwak and Meyer, *Relationship Between School-Community ... op. cit.*

the linkages but, like interdependence, is a minimal condition for inter-organizational linkages.

## Multiple Factor Assessment of Formality and Informality of Interorganizational Linkages

Thus far we have looked at conditions under which formality in linkages is most effective. Although there are exceptions for any one hypothesis, simultaneous consideration of several factors should make such exceptions rare. More important, such an orientation highlights a more subtle classification of linking mechanisms beyond those discussed. We shall present our multifactor set of hypotheses in a tabular form. Because it is our intention to introduce several more considerations than originally elaborated by the Litwak and Hylton paper, we shall present this initial multifactor table in more simplified form than the original one. Since states of interdependence or amount of organizational resources say little about the form or coordination, we shall not include them in the table aside from making the assumption *that all organizations considered in the table have a partial state of interdependence and sufficient resources to maintain interorganizational links.* The factors considered include the degree of organizational awareness, standardization of elements being communicated, and the number and size of organizations involved. All of these relate to aspects of formality and have overlapping functions. For instance, a large number of organizations always requires modes of coordination external to the organization itself, and also requires special personnel and formalized agenda: or as another example, "non-standardization" puts a special stress on face-to-face relations and trust relations rather than on a priori rules and specialized personnel, while "organizational awareness" puts special stress on permanent rather than ad hoc forms of coordination as well as specialized personnel.

Table 1 shows the forces resulting in formalistic rules (cell 1) as the most effective of interorganizational linkages. We would anticipate this in situations involving high organizational awareness, many organizations, and standardized matter to be coordinated (i.e., cell 1). For instance, if one examines library exchanges, there are many libraries (theoretically all in the world could belong), the item being exchanged is standardized (e.g., book title and author), there is clearly

157

TABLE 1.  HYPOTHESES ON THE DEGREE OF FORMALITY OF
INTERORGANIZATIONAL LINKAGES (ASSUMING PARTIAL STATES OF
INTERDEPENDENCE AND SUFFICIENT RESOURCES)

| Number and Size of Organizations | High Organizational Awareness | | Low Organizational Awareness | |
|---|---|---|---|---|
| | High Standardization | Low Standardization | High Standardization | Low Standardization |
| Many and/ or Large Organizations | 1. *Rules:* Library exchange rules; city wide agency directories; cost of living clauses in union-management contracts, fair price laws; automatic stabilizers suggested by economist. | 3. *Coordinating Agency:* Federal Regulatory Agency, Courts, Community Council, Business Associations, permanent arbitrators. | 5. *Unrecognized Public Rules:* Adam Smith's "invisible hand" price mechanism, eligibility requirements in welfare departments, entrance requirements in colleges. | 7. *Ad Hoc Commissions or Conferences.* Ad Hoc Government Commission on Riots, Violence, etc. Ad hoc Citizen's Fact Finding Committees on Union-Management disputes. Ad Hoc Alliance of Businesses to help in hiring hard to employ, Ad Hoc Alliance of race organizations. |
| Few and Small Organizations | 2. *Internal Org. Rules:* Agency mimeographed directory for their staff. Organizational agreements to keep common business hours. | 4. *Direct Staff Conferences:* Joint staff meetings, grievance committees in union-management relations, case conferences in social work agencies. | 6. *Ad Hoc Personal Rules:* Individual worker keeps his own address book of regularly used numbers, ad hoc luncheon meetings to arrange business matters such as price of goods. | 8. *Personal Friendships:* Exchange of stock market tips by friends at the country club, meeting of business leader friends at each other's homes to decide on community policy, referral of clients to agency where friendship insures the clients' admittance. |

an awareness of interdependence in that most libraries belong to the exchange and know it.

By contrast, cell number 8 has the opposite elements. There is low organizational awareness, low standardization, few organizations involved and very small ones, and the item transmitted is nonuniform or has low standardization. In such a situation the most effective coordination takes place under the guise of friendship. This would be the kind of situation which Rubin and Stinchcombe describe where a small group of investors form a partnership to make a new product involving a large number of contingencies. Here, friendship would be an effective mode of coordination given the above structural conditions. From such considerations derives the observation concerning the amount of business transacted in the country club and other social settings as well as Hunter's observation that basic policy matters are frequently decided in the homes of a "friendship clique." [43]

All other cells in Table 1 deal with situations where pressure for coordination is not consistent. Thus the reader can see that in cell 3 we predict that the most effective device will be a formal organization. Here, formal organization is necessary because the number of organizations to be coordinated is large and each is aware of its interdependence. But they all lack one element (high standardization) which permits the ultimate in rationalistic coordination-rules. As a consequence, the coordination mechanisms will be on a lower point of the continuum of formality coordination than rules.

Cell 5 parallels cell 1. We are now dealing, however, with organizations which do not officially recognize that they are interdependent. The classic case of coordination by rules where people are not aware of it would be the "invisible hand" theory of price mechanisms as the basis for coordinating business firms' relations to each other. Prices can be completely standardized, and Adam Smith argued that no organization should have any knowledge of its interdependence with others. Another case of coordination by rules, but where organizations are not officially aware, is enrollment in college when fixed by standard criteria, e.g., scores on Graduate Record Examinations and high school grades. Depending on what level any college within a state fixes the standard, the other colleges will have more or less applicants. Similar points can be made about state and county welfare organizations. Eligibility for clientele can be set down by specific rules and, depending on how it is

---

[43] Hunter, *op. cit.*

set down, the states and counties can encourage or discourage migration of welfare clients from one part of the country to another.

Cell 7 parallels cell 3, referring to many organizations and low standardization. The only difference between them is official organizational awareness. Under such circumstances the most effective coordination is an ad hoc commission or conference. This coordinating mechanism is between a formal organization and a voluntary organization as far as formality is concerned. The ad hoc coordinating apparatus has no permanent personnel or equipment, thus types of expertise and commitment may vary from one organization to another. Thus, one might have ad hoc commissions set up for fact finding (e.g., a fact finding committee under the Taft-Hartley Law to provide a basis for settlement of a threatened strike).

In cell 2 are all the attributes necessary for coordination by rules (high awareness and standardization) except that very few organizations are involved. Rules might in fact exist, but because so few organizations are involved the most effective procedure would be to let each organization abide by its *own* rules. There would be no need to have a city-wide published directory. Rather, a typed or mimeographed list of names and addresses which is run off by the agency for its employees would suffice.

In cell 4 we have high awareness but low standardization and few organizations. The low standardization suggests a face-to-face contact and the small number involved suggests direct staff meetings as being most effective. Thus, a family agency might have a day set aside for a visiting consulting psychiatrist. Buell's description of coordination on hard-core families fits this model.[44] If we consider doctors as small business concerns, an internist requesting a surgeon for consultation would be a good case in point.

Cell 6 parallels cell 2, including few organizations and highly standardized events, except that agencies are not aware of their interdependence. Under these circumstances the most effective form of coordination is to have each worker compile his own list of agencies which he carries around in his address book. This situation might also result in ad hoc conferences between agency heads in the setting of fees for clients which they exchange. For instance, when dealing with rehabilitation, a welfare

---

[44] Bradley Buell, *Structure and Substance in Interagency Joint Planning and Collaborative Practices* (New York: Community Research Associates, 1963). Paper presented to National Institute on Service for Handicapped Children and Youth, March 12, 1963, Chicago.

agency might have to speak about fee fixing with the hospital, occupational therapist, or family therapeutic agencies. Where they feel that there is no virtue in organizational awareness then an ad hoc meeting for each case may be effective.

There are two features of this table which we would want the reader to consider. First, there is the beginning of a theory which suggests the conditions under which various degrees of formal coordination might be most suitable. Secondly, the scheme provides a classification mechanism by which behaviors which ordinarily might not be considered to belong together can be argued to in fact have the same structure, e.g., regulatory agencies and budget committees of community chests.

There are, however, two important qualifications. First, there are many other structural features of these mechanisms besides the degree of formality, e.g., their stress on conflict or adjudication, the degree of autonomy given to the linkage device, etc. Second, our analysis has proceeded on the assumption that elements in the environment (e.g., number of organizations, standardization of task, etc.) affect the linkage mechanisms but that there is no feedback. In fact, there may be a feedback relationship but we shall develop this point only partially in this paper.

## CONDITIONS UNDER WHICH ADJUDICATIVE AND COMMUNICATIVE LINKAGES ARE MOST EFFECTIVE

We now wish to turn our attention to a different aspect of linkages—the degree to which they contain adjudicative or communication structures. There are two major assumptions about the interdependence which characterizes confederated alliances. On the one hand, there is the assumption that the organizations in the confederated network are involved in a competitive constant sum-type situation. The more one organization gets, the less for the others. This is typified by people who derive their analysis from management-union relations, problems in social class, political party competition, and international relations. On the other hand and in sharp contrast are those whose work originated in social planning and social work.[45]

---

[45] Alfred S. Kahn, *Planning Community Services for Children in Trouble* (New York: Columbia University Press, 1963).

Thus, in business it is often assumed that two concerns compete with each other for a fixed market and try to drive each other out completely. However, if this is impossible, it is to their advantage to cooperate. In union-management relations the conflict is not so sharp, but both *are* competing for the lion's share of the profits. In political party conflict there is sometimes a close approximation to a zero sum game in that the party which wins an election might win all the offices.[46]

By contrast, in social planning it is often pointed out that by co-operation each organization can gain above what it could on its own. Thus, each library loses little and stands to gain much by some mechanism of book exchange and microfilm services. In social work it was pointed out years ago that various medical, welfare, family, and school agencies might gain immeasurably when each deals with the same family and coordinates their advice. This idea eventually resulted in a social service exchange. Business concerns also might benefit from some organization which will represent their common interest, e.g., a lobby to keep out competitive foreign goods, reduce taxes in a given industry, fight a common union, support common research designed to lower costs of productivity for all companies in the industries.

One can, as Thomas suggests,[47] think of at least two major types of interdependence—facilitative and competitive. Our central hypothesis is that competitive interdependence requires adjudicative functions. The key point about competitive interdependence is that cooperation occurs under conditions of mistrust or threat. Ideally, the organizations involved would like to eliminate the other. This is an underlying threat despite their mutually avowed cooperation. As a consequence, any difference which might arise is always bound to be disputed. It is for this reason we hypothesize that to be effective there must always be some way of settling disputes.

By contrast, facilitative interdependence means that each organization can gain from cooperating with the other. If differences arise, each calls for further clarification on the assumption that differences can only be a consequence of errors in communication. Therefore communication techniques are stressed. And communication techniques include machinery such as computers, telegraph and telephones which permit high volume and quick flow of information. Thus the social service exchange,

---

[46] Dahl, *op. cit.*, Chapter 1 on Great Britain.
[47] Edwin J. Thomas, "Effects of Facilitative Role Interdependence on Group Functioning," *Human Relations,* 19 (1957) 347–366.

which sought to keep track of which organizations were involved with which clients, might ideally invest in a computer setup.

Thus, our major hypothesis is that where organizations are involved in competitive interdependence the most effective linkage will incorporate adjudication procedures. But when organizations are joined around facilitative interdependence the effective linkage procedures are those that stress communication techniques. Of course, where there is a mix of facilitation and competition the most effective linkages might well contain both adjudication and communication mechanisms.[48]

## Adjudicative Linkages

We now introduce two more tables: Table 2 deals with adjudicative linkages. Table 3 deals with communicative links.

Table 2 shows when adjudication will take place by use of rules, when by organization, when by primary-group-type relations, when publicly and when privately.

Thus to pick up on our prior analysis, adjudicative processes will be most effectively handled by a formal linkage where there are many organizations, when they are aware of their interdependence, and where the contact is over very uniform events. Thus, for example, we have union-management cost of living escalation clauses in written contracts (cell 1 in Table 2). Also, there are a priori written rules which both sides have agreed to which automatically raise or lower wages. By contrast, the most effective linkage would be direct face to face negotiations where few organizations are involved, where they have low levels of organizational awareness of interdependence, and the element to be communicated is unstandardized (cell 8 in Table 2). Thus leaders of two hostile ethnic organizations might meet informally—without official consent of their membership—in order to deal with a common problem, e.g., faulty city services or the invasion of a third ethnic group which both dislike. In wartime often one side or the other wishes to initiate peace negotiations while at the same time not undermine the fighting morale of their armies. At such times they might have "unofficial" contacts which are characterized by being face-to-face and involving large elements of trust. Where there is low standardization but large numbers

---

[48] Banfield, *op. cit.* pp. 307–341.

TABLE 2. HYPOTHESES ON DEGREE OF FORMALITY OF ADJUDICATIVE INTERORGANIZATIONAL LINKAGES (ASSUMING STATES OF COMPETITIVE PARTIAL INTERDEPENDENCE AND SUFFICIENT RESOURCES)

| Number and Size of Organizations | High Organizational Awareness | | Low Organizational Awareness | |
|---|---|---|---|---|
| | High Standardization | Low Standardization | High Standardization | Low Standardization |
| Many and/or Large Organizations | 1. *Adjudicatory Public Rules:* Union-management cost of living clauses in written contract, fair price laws, minimum wage laws. (Non-violent) | 3. *Adjudicatory Agency·* Regulatory agencies, courts, budget committee of community chest, permanent arbitration staff. (Low public violence) | 5. *Adjudicatory Non-Recognized Public Rules:* Adam Smith's "invisible hand" price mechanism, bank rules against investing in Negro business enterprises. (Some public violence) | 7. *Adjudicating Ad Hoc Agency:* Ad Hoc government panels to arbitrate major strikes, ad hoc alliance (committee) of race relations organizations to settle internal disputes. Large Union-management strike negotiating committees (both groups combined). (Moderate public violence) |
| Few and Small Organizations | 2. *Adjudicatory Organizational Rules:* Private organizational rules to shut down when competitor is struck by common enemy (e.g., newspaper strike), organizational rules on mutual domains as concerns clients. (Non-violent) | 4. *Adjudicating Inter-Staff Committees:* Union-management local department grievance committees, regular staff conference between agencies to work out competing domains. (Low personalized violence) | 6. *Adjudicatory Personal Rules:* Individuals within organization have a set of personal rules which they follow for determining whether a client should go into their organization or that of a competitor. (Some personal violence) | 8. *Adjudication by Friends:* Friends or people one personally trusts meet in "smoke-filled" rooms to settle disputes between two organizations. (Moderate personalized violence) |

of organizations and high levels of awareness of interdependence, then we hypothesize that the most effective adjudicative linkage is an adjudicative agency (cell 2, Table 2). Illustrative of such adjudicative agencies would be public regulatory agencies, budget committees of community chest programs who have to decide which agencies are to get funds, and courts deciding disputes between two or more firms. Since many agencies are involved, generally a large staff rather than a single individual would be most effective. And since the events to be adjudicated cannot be completely standardized, an agency rather than a set of written rules is most effective.

If few organizations are involved, if standardization is low, but groups are aware of interdependence, an adjudicative device permitting face-to-face confrontation between two or more organizations will be effective. This is so because the issues are nonstandardized, cannot be settled by rules, and the few agencies involved can unravel their problem directly with one another. Union-management grievance committees in local departments of an industrial plant illustrate this point (cell 4, Table 2).

This discussion has not dealt with two important aspects of coordination; violence and autonomy. We examine now the dimensions depicted in Table 2 relating to the form of violence used in adjudicating. The question of autonomy of the linkage procedure will be developed in the following section. It is sometimes thought that organizations involved in competition are unlikely to cooperate, but will only fight. Evans and Aiken and Hage [49] point out that agencies with common goals are not likely to cooperate because they would naturally be competitive. We differ on two grounds. First, competition does not prohibit coordination where groups are aware of their interdependence. Second, those with common goals are often not in competition.[50]

Brody explored the hypothesis that increased conflict would lead to breaks in contacts between large social groups.[51] Contrary to his expectations, he found the greater the potential conflict, the greater the interaction. He explained this by pointing out that where people are

---

[49] Evans, *op. cit.* Aiken and Hage, *op. cit.*

[50] The reader must remember our strategy of first presenting single hypotheses to which there may be many exceptions and then presenting the multi-factor hypotheses (tabular form) to which there may be few exceptions. It is these complex hypotheses which justify our analysis.

[51] Richard A. Brody, "Some Systematic Effects of the Spread of Nuclear Weapons Technology: A Study Through Simulation of Multi-Nuclear Future," *Journal of Conflict Resolution,* 7 (December 1963), pp. 663–763.

aware of their interdependence, then increased competition forces them into closer cooperation. Competition forces them away from each other only when they see the threat aspect of their relation but not the interdependence. We would further speculate that extreme forms of *violence* are not consistent with a confederation of organizations. Violence will either destroy the organizations or will make them quickly aware of their interdependence which will reduce violence. To illustrate, assume that two or more nations armed with nuclear weapons are in partial states of interdependence. They might, through rash misjudgement, utilize the weapons and destroy each other or they might engage in increasingly violent forms of diplomacy, or even conventional war, to a point where there is danger of nuclear war. Once their very existence is threatened they are likely to become aware of their interdependence and begin to utilize less violent means. Brody's experimental simulation studies on nuclear proliferation are consistent with these speculations. Union-management relations leading to strikes also often have this rhythm. In order to handle conceptually extreme forms of violence we must turn to the problem of how confederations break up, or deal with the fact that extreme violence leads to heightened dependency awareness, which leads in turn to a reduction in violence.

With this in mind we hypothesize that moderate violence is better than either non-violent or extremely violent means in situations where low awareness is desired. There are two reasons for this. First, moderate forms of violence engender enough hostility to prevent organizations from seeing their actual dependence on one another. Second, they make it easy to delineate external targets. This, in turn, permits the building of internal organizational cohesion.[52] In this connection, the shift of many Negro organizations from a concentration on achieving civil rights through established legal norms, to a current emphasis on militant black power is a case in point.[53] Black power groups feel that it is necessary to create independent black organizations. As a step in this direction they regard it as necessary publicly to persuade the black community that it is not dependent upon whites. In our language, they seek to lower the awareness of interdependence. Further, they seek to do this through moderately violent tactics (civil disobedience, sit-ins, boycotts, etc.). And they often use moderate violence as a device for delineating an explicit

---

[52] Lewis Coser, *The Functions of Social Conflict* (The Free Press of Glencoe, 1956), pp. 87–110.

[53] Lewis Killian and Charles Grigg. *Racial Crisis in America* (Prentice-Hall, 1964).

enemy and this is useful for building their internal organizational structures.

Labor unions seeking to prepare a fearful membership for the possibility of a long strike often have used the same tactics—sought to lower levels of awareness and to use moderate forms of violence. The central point of these illustrations is that in many instances an organization might see low levels of awareness as useful for preserving a confederation, and under these circumstances moderate violence is an effective mode of linkage.

Violence has been related to yet another theme by students of conflict resolution, namely that conflict will be more severe the less the contending organizations share in common. Thus, if there are no commonly shared rules or values, then conflict is much more likely to take a violent form,[54] especially in cases of organizations with completely polarized interests. To accommodate this consideration into our analysis it is necessary to take into account the number of areas in which organizations are linked, and whether the interaction between them is competitive or facilitative.

We would expect that where many areas—all competitive—were involved the potential for violent conflict would be great, while a more controlled adjudication would be the case in instances involving fewer and less competitive areas. Because competition in many different areas is a complex and non-standardization event, we think that the above hypothesis can be captured in our scheme by substituting standardization for number of areas of contact. More important, we would speculate that when competition takes place in a non-standardized area it is harder to put specific content boundaries on it. As a consequence competition tends to involve *other* aspects of life, to polarize, and to produce violence. For example, Dahl and his colleagues have pointed out the bitter conflict that occurred when political parties polarized around ideologies of social class, race, or religion.[55] Sometimes groups find it advantageous to maintain a polarized state, and when they do moderate violence in linkage mechanisms are the most effective. The reason for this lies in the fact that a moderate form of violence will engender enough hostility so that organizations will not stress those areas where they do have overlapping interests, and this will prevent de-

---

[54] Dahl, *op. cit.*

[55] *Ibid.* Robin Williams, *Strangers Next Door* (Englewood Cliffs, N.J.: Prentice-Hall, 1964).

polarization. Again, black power and labor movements are illustrative.

For example, the black power movement encourages further polarization by stressing black business, black educators, black curriculums, and black aesthetics. They justify this on the grounds that the ideal state of de-polarization (desegregation) is impossible in the current society. Under these circumstances, the blacks are likely to do better if they move to a rigid polarization because it would increase their own organizational strengths. Hence, insofar as polarization is correlated with non-standardization this analysis can be captured in Table 2.

There is a final aspect of violence suggested by this conceptual scheme, and that is the distinction between public and private forms of violence. The first usually refers to social movements, acts of social protest, or revolutions, while the latter more frequently refers to subterranean deviant behavior. Our prior analysis of formal versus informal interorganizational linkages bears on this problem, in the sense that public forms of violence would lead to formal modes of linkages and private violence to informal ones.

To summarize: adjudication through the use of moderate forms of violence is likely to be most effective when organizations seek to maintain both low levels of awareness and polarization. Cell 7 in Table 2 represents this situation. We make the additional point that organizations linked in competitive interdependence are likely to find adjudicative rather than communication linkages most effective.

## Communication Linkages

We turn our attention now to facilitative forms of coordination, as depicted in Table 3.

Here we find that awareness of interdependence, type of organizational structure, and number of types of organizations suggest some hypotheses about the linkage structures which will facilitate communication. There are at least two types of communication problems which can arise. One is the problem of disseminating available and needed information as quickly as possible. The second involves doing research or otherwise acquiring needed information. As to the first, there are at least four phenomena pointed to by communication research as having an effect on the speed and accuracy with which a message is com-

TABLE 3.  HYPOTHESES ON DEGREE OF FORMALITY OF
COMMUNICATIVE INTERORGANIZATIONAL LINKAGES (ASSUMING
STATES OF FACILITATIVE PARTIAL INTERDEPENDENCE AND
SUFFICIENT RESOURCES)

| Number and Size of Organizations | High Organizational Awareness | | Low Organizational Awareness | |
|---|---|---|---|---|
| | High Standardization | Low Standardization | High Standardization | Low Standardization |
| Many and/or Large Organizations | 1. *Public Communication Rules:* City directory of agencies, library exchange rules, mass media. (Low initiative, low intensity, low focused expertise, high scope). | 3. *Communication Agency:* Research centers servicing several organizations (e.g., Educational Research Labs), information centers (e.g., Eric educational abstracts). (Low initiative but high intensity, scope, and focus). | 5. *Ad Hoc Communication rules:* Ad hoc endorsement committee which provides written list of legitimate charities. (High initiative, moderate intensity and focus, high scope). | 7. *Ad Hoc Conferences or Alliances:* Ad hoc White House conference of Children's Agencies, ad hoc disaster center during tornado, ad hoc Alliance of race relations organizations to pass housing legislation. (High initiative high intensity and focus, high scope) |
| Few and Small Organizations | 2. *Organizational Communication Rules:* Individual Agency directories. Use of form letters or agency printed instructions on communication. (Low initiative, low intensity, low focus, low scope) | 4. *Joint Staff Communication:* Joint staff meetings, interlocking boards of directors. (Low initiative, high intensity and focus, low scope) | 6. *Personal-Professional Communication Rules:* Each individual in organization works out his own standard rule of contacting other agency, e.g., personal telephone listing. (High initiative, moderate intensity and focus, low scope) | 8. *Personalized Friendship as a Communication Device:* Hunter's description of power elite, social workers who are close friends coordinate between their agencies via their friendships, etc. (High initiative, tive, intensity and focus, low scope) |

municated.[56] First is selective listening in that persons like to listen to information which fits preconceived ideas. Second is selective interpretation; when exposed to a message they do not like, many people either distort its meaning or selectively forget the part they don't like. It has also been noted that the more complex the message, the more individuals should be in a face-to-face situation so as to make use of instant feedback. Thus, the mass media may not be useful for sending complex messages. Finally, it is sometimes necessary to send a message to many organizations, sometimes to only a few. Therefore, it is important to know how much scope a particular linkage permits.

Different linkage mechanisms permit each of these problems to be handled.[57] To overcome the problem of selective listening, it is necessary to have linkages which give the initiative to the organization sending the message rather than the target. For instance, social work agencies trying to reach hostile delinquent gangs send a professional into the field to try to make friends with delinquent gangs. This gives more initiative to the agency as compared to appealing to the gangs through the mass media. Analogously, during the war one industry would often send an expediter to stay with the supplier organization. This provided much greater initiative than if they sent letters. Still another illustration is where one firm puts one of its members on the board of directors of its supplier to insure that its voice will be heard.

To overcome the problem of selective retention, it is generally thought that the person carrying the message must have a primary group type relation with the target. The assumption is that to change a person who is opposed requires a relationship of trust, continuous face-to-face contact so the message can be reinforced, and contact in all areas of life to prevent the message from becoming segmentalized. Again it can be pointed out that certain linkages permit more primary group contact than others. Thus most of the means by which organizations exchange staff, mentioned above, permit more primary group intensity than the mass media. It is clear that just having a face-to-face confrontation is not sufficient to develop intense primary group feeling. For example, prison guards have close contact with prisoners, officers with enlisted men, teachers with students, but rather than primary group intensity

---

[56] H. H. Hyman and P. B. Sheatsley. "Some Reasons Why Information Campaigns Fail," *Public Opinion Quarterly,* XI (Fall 1947) 412–423 J. T. Klapper, "What We Know About the Effects of Mass Communication: the Brink of Hope," *Public Opinion Quarterly,* XXI (Winter 1957–58) 453–71.

[57] Litwak and Meyer, "Balance Theory . . ." *op. cit.*

one might have mistrust or indifference. It is clear that various linkages have differential bases for evolving primary group intensity. Similarly, it has already been pointed out that different media have differential capacity for passing on complex information. Having an expert in face-to-face contact with the target group is better than sending complex information through mass media. Finally, it would be noted that all other things being equal (e.g., simple noncontroversial message,) the mass media can reach the most people in the quickest time.

Where does this analysis leave us? First, it suggests that we might consider dividing organizations into those which are friendly to each other and those which are indifferent or hostile. In one sense we have already done this by making the distinction between facilitative and competitive interdependence. However, even within the facilitative group it is easy to argue that the organizations with low awareness are indifferent or hostile to coordination. Rather than introduce a new category of organizations, e.g., those hostile and those not, we shall make a simplifying assumption. We will assume that in all cases where organizations lack awareness of each other they are either hostile or indifferent. As a consequence, in all such cases for one organization to reach the other it must have mechanisms which permit great initiative. In addition a moderate degree of primary group intensity may be necessary to overcome organizational indifference. Also, wherever an event is not standardized there will be maximal opportunity for selective perception. Thus for non-standardized events considerable primary group instensity is necessary for the most effective communication because the complexity of the situation permits many alternative interpretations. For the same reason, linkages which permit focused expertise would be most effective when dealing with non-standardized events. To really differentiate between focused expertise and primary group intensity it would be necessary to re-introduce the type of organizational structure as well as consider the standardization of the event. Where organization structures are human relations (therapeutic, collegial, treatment, or democratic) then primary group intensity is an essential part of their milieu. For this reason alone, any mechanism which sought to link them to other organizations would operate most effectively if it too had primary group intensity. By contrast, in a rationalistic bureaucracy (rules oriented or custodial) primary group intensity is not a key element. In such a situation where there is a non-standardized event, linkages which permit focused expertise but not primary group intensity would be most effective. Finally, when many organizations are involved the most effective linkages are those which permit wide scope (e.g., mass media, computers, etc.). What should be noted is that there is often a contradiction between the demands for wide scope and those for primary group intensity or focused expertise. The latter require face-to-face confrontation. Unless one has a tremendous number of people to devote to the linkage procedure this severely limits scope. To bring these various strands together we would hypothesize that in situations where there is little standardization, few organizations, and low degrees of organizational awareness the most effective communications linkage procedures are those which have high initiative, high intensity, high focused expertise and low scope (cell 8 in Table 3). This might be illustrated by the executive (high expertise) of one company making a golfing engagement (high initiative, low scope) with his friend (high intensity) who is an executive of another company to point out how the two companies might cooperate on a given business deal to raise their profits. On the other hand, where the message to be transmitted is standardized, and the number of organizations large, and the organizations are aware of their interdependence, then the most effective procedures are those which require little initiative, can speedily cover many organizations, stress one way expertise and are impersonal (e.g., sending out a form letter in a mass mailing or mass media on time of meeting, agenda, and items to be discussed; Table 3, cell 1). The types of linkage procedures which fit these various combinations as well as the logic of their development has been presented elsewhere [58] and the interested reader can pursue the matter. At this point it is only necessary for the reader to examine Table 3 to see our hypothesis on which type of linkages (aside from the extreme cells of 1 and 8 which we have covered above) would be most effective. Thus in cell 2 (few organizations are involved, they are aware of their interdependence and the event is standardized) the agencies can most effectively communicate through a personnel letter or telephone (using low initiative, low focus, low intensity, low scope). For cell 3 (which is a situation of high awareness, many organizations and low standardization) the most effective linkage will be a separate group of communication specialists (using low initiative, high intensity, high focus, high scope). There are many organizations so the linkage needs a specialized staff, since the lack of standardization prevents the use of time saving rules. In cell number 4 (high awareness, low standardization and few organizations) we hypothesize low initiative, high intensity, high focus, low scope (e.g., interagency staff meet-

---

[58] *Ibid.*

ings will be most effective). Here, unlike cell 3, there are sufficiently few contacts so that specialized personnel are not needed. All of these situations are ones of high awareness where linking procedures can be passive because agencies specifically assign people to the job of communicating with other organizations. However, in cell 5 (where there are many agencies and a standardized event is being communicated) there is no official organizational awareness. In order for coordination to take place one of the agencies or individuals within the agencies must take the initiative. One consequence might be an ad hoc set of rules set up by organizations on a temporary basis. Thus, two unions from different federations might agree on an ad hoc basis to honor each other's picket line. In cell 6 (a standardized event, few agencies involved and no official awareness of interdependence) initiative for contact falls on the individual worker. Because neither his agency nor the other is aware, he has to develop a moderate degree of primary group intensity so as to persuade individuals in other agencies to cooperate. And since the event is standardized, little in the way of focused expertise is needed. This communication mechanism resembles a "professionalized friend." By this we mean somebody with whom one has continual but highly limited contacts and is willing to exchange small work-related favors. There is no deep friendship here. In cell 7 we again have a situation where there is no agency awareness of interdependence. However, since there are actual states of interdependence the agencies have to take the initiative in getting together periodically, e.g., ad hoc conferences. We hypothesize the conference linkage here because there are many organizations dealing with non-standardized events. So they need some focused expertise—face-to-face contact—as well as having to deal with many people. In addition, because there is little official awareness plus a lack of standardization some primary group intensity would be needed. For example, agency personnel would have to know and trust each other.

To summarize, when dealing with facilitative communications, the linkages must be assessed in terms of their ability to provide the agencies involved with initiative, intensity, face-to-face expertise, and scope. In general, for the situation of standardization, many organizations, high level of awareness, and rationalistic organizations, the most effective linkage mechanisms would have low initiative, low intensity, low focus expertise and high scope. The opposite type of linkage would be effective where there is low awareness, few organizations, low standardization and human relations types of organizations.

## AUTONOMOUS VERSUS DEPENDENT LINKAGES

An implicit, but nonetheless key distinction in the discussion thus far, involves linkages which have autonomous power as compared with those which are dependent on the member organization. For example, in competitive interdependence, one might find labor arbitrators whose decisions are legally binding, community chests which control the budgets of member agencies, and regulatory agencies whose decisions have the force of law. These are illustrative of autonomous linkages. By way of contrast, a union-management committee set up to negotiate a contract may have no autonomous enforcement powers. Before the decision can be legally binding, it must be ratified by the union members. Similarly, lawyers for two contending business firms might work out an agreement, but before it can become binding it may have to be reviewed by the two boards of directors. Or, a president can appoint a fact-finding committee to look into a dispute between two organizations, but for it to become binding it needs ratification by the respective organizations.

The same point can be made with regard to facilitative interdependence. Thus it was pointed out that under many conditions where information is lacking and the costs of necessary research are great, a coordinating council may undertake complete responsibility for the research.[59] We pointed out in social work the social service exchange as a linking organization with the sole responsibility for gathering relevant information, maintaining records, and providing information. More generally newspapers, journals, and university post-graduate seminars may have these autonomous functions. In contrast to these autonomous information-gathering groups, there are those which are dependent on the members for whom they work. Thus, among universities a staff member might make a discovery which would be circulated among the members of other universities. Similarly, human relations organizations might finance a joint meeting to which they send members, but the decision as to what action to take is still the agency's.

Given the fact that linkage is sometimes autonomous and sometimes dependent on the agencies involved, the question arises as to what conditions suggest autonomy for the linkage mechanism.

First, let us take a situation of competitive interdependence. In competitive situations an organization is least likely to surrender autonomy to situations where it feels its very existence might be threatened.

---

[59] B. R. Clark, "Interorganizational Patterns . . ." *op. cit.*

174

This sense of threat is most likely to occur where organizations are not aware of interdependence but only of conflict. To illustrate, where two business firms are in a state of competitive partial interdependence (i.e., they are affected by each other's prices but can't drive each other out of business) and are aware of it, they are more likely to accept a third party arbitration than are two firms in exactly the same situation who think they can drive each other out of business. Again, granted the competitiveness of the situation, an organization would be more likely to surrender its autonomy in situations where there was an impartial expert, because expertise is highly correlated with standardization of tasks. Finally, an organization is likely to surrender autonomy where powerful third party interests (not directly competitive) insist that disputes be settled by some autonomous agency. Thus, union-management organizations in conflict might accept a binding arbitration from the government if the community interest were overwhelming and they had a facilitative interdependence with the government agency. In general third party interests enter where the organizations are very large or where conflict will affect the public.

Yet another reason for autonomous knowledge gathering is the need for an impartial gathering and dissemination of information. Thus when there is any suspicion that results may be colored by vested interests, the demand may be made for an impartial, independent data-gathering process. The recognition of the legitimacy of such demands as well as the willingness to support such an autonomous fact finding agency will be most likely carried on where organizations have a high awareness of their facilitative interdependence or where some third party demands it.

Let us now address ourselves to the question of autonomy and effectiveness. One major observation is that the more autonomous the coordinating agency the more the confederation approaches a centralized authority characterized by intraorganizational structures. It should, as a consequence, have many of the same virtues and defects. One characteristic of a highly centralized authority as compared to a decentralized one is that it is most effective when it is dealing with a standardized event or task. At this point we advance the hypothesis that autonomous coordination will be most effective where the events to be coordinated are standardized.

We would further speculate that where it is important to develop and maintain a sense of organizational cohesion or survival, it will be ineffective to grant decision making to a coordinating mechanism. Thus in the earlier remarks concerning the black power movement, it was suggested that the stress on polarization between organizations was part of the strategy for building up organizational integrity within the confederation. Following similar logic, if the black power movement is to maintain polarization it will find non-autonomous coordinating mechanisms most effective. As noted above, demands for depolarization in situations of partial interdependence are highly correlated with demands for low organizational awareness. This leads us to our second major hypothesis concerning autonomy: autonomous coordination will be least effective under conditions of low awareness.

Finally, autonomous coordination will be most effective where large numbers of organizations are involved. The reasoning behind this follows the same logic used in the discussion of numbers of organizations and formality. Thus if rules are used for coordination, they have to be public so that other organizations can see them. If separate agents are used for coordination, they must stand outside any particular organization and be publicly so identified to be effective. Insofar as *external* and *public* are two important aspects of a definition of autonomous coordination we would speculate that autonomous linkages will be effective where many organizations are to be coordinated. In addition, many organizations and large organizations are most likely to be associated with third party groups which insist on autonomous coordinating agencies. Insofar as this is correct, autonomous coordinating devices would be most effective where many and large organizations are being coordinated, otherwise the confederation would be involved in conflict with powerful third parties.

As indicated above, stated singly these hypotheses may have many exceptions. The importance of our analysis is the simultaneous consideration of all the variables involved. Thus, autonomous linkage processes will be most effective in situations where organizational polarization or survival are not requirements (high awareness of interdependence), where there are impartial experts and standardized forms of knowledge (high standardization), and where a powerful third party is pressing for autonomous coordination (many organizations).

For simplicity's sake we have presented these three conditions (i.e., polarization, third party, experts) as though they were always correlated with our basic dimensions as well as with each other. In fact they are not, and this leads to very interesting consequences.

For instance, the Federal Communication Commission represents the public in the area of assignment of television channels. As such, the FCC is an agency which represents a powerful third party interest which insists on autonomy. This means that as a coordinating agency amongst television organizations it should have considerable autonomy. However, it is also true that some of the decisions made by the FCC (e.g., who amongst several competing organizations has the right to a given channel in a given city) may involve a television organization's survival. This should mean that granting autonomy to the coordinating agency (FCC) would not be effective. Often there is no impartial expertise, and in fact we deal with matters that involve conflict between basic values as well as guess work as to what the facts of the case might be. This should occur in situations where autonomy to the coordinating agency is not effective. The consequence of these cross pressures for and against autonomy of the coordinating body leads to interesting results. Some of it is covered by Banfield when he speaks about mixed social and central decision making process.[60] Gary Rhodes [61] points out with regard to regulatory agencies that such cross pressures enable one to anticipate when contending organizations seek to use back door political pressure, when they seek to use interminable delaying tactics, and when they seek through pressure on the president to appoint their own representative on the FCC. The point is that all of these are responses to a situation where one criterion (powerful third party interest) suggests autonomy of enforcement on the part of the coordinating agency, while the other two criteria suggest the opposite. In this chapter we will not go into the many possible forms of coordination which emerge under all types of pressures. Rather, we will assume the correlation between standardization, awareness, and number of organizations mentioned above.

Our thinking on when autonomy will be most and least effective is summarized in Table 4.

Cell 1 of Table 4 suggests a situation most effectively handled by an autonomous coordinating procedure. This is where there are impartial experts, standardized elements are being communicated, where organizations do not view their survival as in danger, where there are many organizations, pressure for externality, and a good chance that powerful third party forces would press for independence in fact finding or enforcement of arbitration. It will be noted that devices such as agency directories and cost of living clauses in union-management contracts tend to be autonomous of their creators—once they are put into effect.

---

[60] Banfield, *op. cit.*
[61] Gary Rhodes, seminar presentation, Winter 1968.

TABLE 4.   HYPOTHESES ON DEGREE OF AUTONOMY OF INTERORGANIZATIONAL LINKAGES (ASSUMING PARTIAL STATES OF INTERDEPENDENCE AND SUFFICIENT RESOURCES)

| Number and Size of Organizations | NON-SURVIVAL—DEPOLARIZATION (High Organizational Awareness) | | SURVIVAL—POLARIZATION (Low Organizational Awareness) | |
|---|---|---|---|---|
| | IMPARTIAL EXPERT (High Standardization) | NO EXPERT (Low Standardization) | IMPARTIAL EXPERT (High Standardization) | NO EXPERT (Low Standardization) |
| THIRD PARTY INTERVENTION<br><br>(Many and/or Large Organizations) | 1. *High Autonomy Rules:* City wide agency directories, cost of living clauses. | 3. *Autonomous Coordinating Organizations:* Research centers, regulatory agencies, budget committees of community chest, permanent arbitrators. | 5. *Time Limited (Low) Autonomous Rules:* Ad hoc endorsement agencies. | 7. *Low Autonomous Coordinating Groups:* Strike negotiation committees for large industries, Ad hoc Conference on Children. |
| NO THIRD PARTY INTERVENTION<br><br>(Few and Small Organizations) | 2. *Semi-Autonomous Organizational Rules:* Organizational directories or rules on accepting clients. | 4. *Semi-Autonomous Staff Meetings:* Local plant grievance committees, regular case consultation between agency staff dealing with hard core families. | 6. *Low Autonomy Personal Rules:* Each individual in organization makes his own decision on coordination, e.g., personal telephone numbers. | 8. *Very Low Autonomy:* Agreements between personal friends have no official standing with organization unless it can be sold to the organization. |

178

By contrast in Cell 8 we have a situation where a non-autonomous procedure would be most effective. There are no impartial experts (low standardization), and therefore all points of view to represent each organization must have a right to be heard. There is also a feeling that organizational survival might be at stake, due to pressures toward polarization, the absence of intervening powerful third parties, and the absence of demands for externality.

In cell 3 are autonomous coordinating agencies. This is hypothesized to be an effective device here because since the organizations involved are aware of their interdependence, neither survival nor polarization is at issue. In addition, there are many organizations which indicates that there is public pressure to give autonomy of enforcement to fact finding, but there is low standardization so there is no impartial expertise. This means organizations will not settle for rules but want the privilege of at least arguing their case. Typical of this situation would be permanent arbitrators between large industry and large unions. Survival issues are usually explicitly excluded from arbitration. Also, after the contract has been written, union and management are aware of their interdependence. And because of the size and number of groups involved there are powerful public forces which argue for some quick way of settling disputes—other than publicly disruptive strikes. This situation would contrast with cell 7 where there is low awareness of interdependence. This is the situation just prior to union-management agreement on a contract. At this point in time each views the other as a powerful threat to its survival and as a consequence is willing to engage in conflict to defend itself. The negotiating groups have no final power. What they decide upon must eventually be ratified by the members of their respective organizations. The lack of standardization prevents the use of impartial outside experts, and this is often indexed by the fact that the economic experts of each side come up with diametrically opposed answers. In addition, there are pressures for settlement on the part of a powerful third party. The remainder of the table can be interpreted similarly.

## AUTHORITY STRUCTURE WITHIN THE LINKAGE PROCEDUCE

We pointed out that it is unlikely that confederated organizations can survive radical asymmetry. However, around the norms of reciprocity there might be modest forms of asymmetry. Thus in the community chest programs there are various groups that have fixed markets to whom they can appeal. In a strong Catholic or Jewish community, the respective nonsecular agencies could raise considerable amounts of money without the help of community chest programs. However, unlike the American Cancer Society, they frequently provide services which are closely tied to local institutions.

In contrast, there may be other agencies in the same community chest program who could raise virtually nothing on their own. It would be our hypothesis that when modest forms of asymmetry hold, the least dependent agencies will play a larger role in the linkage procedures. Thus many years ago the Catholic agencies refused to join any community chest drive unless planned parenthood organizations were excluded. Jewish agencies would not participate unless they could run their own separate drive. Red Cross would not participate unless distinctive Red Cross applications were included in the drive, etc.

## SYSTEMS OF CONFEDERATIONS

In concluding this discussion on types of coordinating devices, we should like to discuss briefly the problems of networks of coordination systems. This is similar to what Evans refers to as organizational sets.[62] Levine and White point out the need to consider interdependence that is sequentially linked versus that which is not.[63] We have no "theory of sets" but merely point out several types and suggest some of their characteristics. Rothman, in his research on race relations organizations, points to one type of network. This is a set of organizations, all with the same general goal, frequently coordinating by doing the same thing with different populations.[64] Thus race relations organizations may be involved in a drive to pass an open housing bill. The Negro organizations appeal to their clientele, the Jewish to their clientele, the Protestant to theirs, and the Catholics to theirs. In addition, Rothman's data suggest that each of these groups has a narrow set of interests which causes closer internal cooperation. Hence, Jewish agencies have specific Jewish interests aside from the general problems of open housing, Negro agencies have specific Negro problems, etc. As a consequence, the total system

---

[62] Evans, *op. cit.*
[63] Levine and White, *op. cit.*

resembles a series of clusters tied together by some super-coordinating group.

In sharp contrast to this organizational network is that described by Kahn in his analysis of children's services.[65] He points out that agencies here are linked sequentially to each other, e.g., police and schools tend to be intake agencies, courts tend to be evaluation and diagnostic agencies, and finally probation and treatment agencies provide the therapy.

Such differences in the network of coordination are important. For instance, giving aid to one agency in a sequential network may be of little help to the total set. Quite the contrary, it may lead to a breakdown of the system. For example, providing the police with more funds may radically increase the number of children who are found in need of aid. This in turn may overload the courts and treatment homes, causing long delays in court and the transformation of treatment homes into custodial centers. This differs from a homogeneous network where contributions to any part will help the whole. In a sequential system, to overcome defects in other organizations, the focal organization might (1) alter its own rate of productivity (sometimes police do not bring a child to the court until he has committed three offenses), (2) take on the functions of the faltering institutions (police sometimes make their own diagnosis and try to send the child to a treatment home bypassing the court entirely), (3) join in an effort to produce more funds for the other agency, or (4) seek technological breakthroughs which enable the other agency to handle more tasks with the same resources.

It is of interest that when Kahn speaks about the need for improved coordination between child agencies, he is really speaking about developing standardized accountability procedures which will increase the number of children handled. Under current procedures, they are either not brought in or, if they are brought in, are dropped out of the system through poor accountability records. Given the fact that the entire system lacks resources, increasing the number of cases will probably lead to a breakdown of the system. Now it might be argued that such a breakdown might be a basis for appealing for more resources. Even here we would argue that what is necessary is for all elements in this sequential chain to get together and collectively raise funds.

One other way in which the sequential system differs from a homo-

---

[64] Rothman, personal conversation. April 1968.
[65] Kahn, *op. cit.*

geneous system (the race relations example) is that it may be more difficult for all members of the chain to appreciate their interdependence. By contrast, the members of the homogeneous system, because of common function, find it much easier to see their interdependence. Several writers tend to advance a different notion. For example, both Evans and Aiken and Hage argue that the more similar in goals agencies are, the more competitive they are and therefore the less likely they are to interact. As we already mentioned, such an analysis forgets that competitive firms may also be interdependent, i.e., competitively interdependent. Where they are aware of this, they may interact intensely. Many business firms in the same field have business associations to avoid cutthroat competition. Also, it is a mistake to assume that organizations with similar goals do not have common interests. All steel manufacturers have a common desire to promote legislation which will show that steel is more useful than competitive metals or plastics, and a desire to cooperate when dealing with a common union so labor costs are kept down. The idea that commonness in functions means competition (which means avoidance of linkages) is wrong on two counts. First, competition does not necessarily lead to avoidance of linkages but often to their encouragement. Second, commonness of goals does not necessarily mean competition.

This partial analysis of homogeneous and sequential networks is presented merely as evidence of the need to elaborate such a scheme in all its details and ramifications.

## SOME STILL-TO-BE-RESOLVED PROBLEMS: DISTANCE MAINTAINING MECHANISMS AND THE "FEEDBACK" ROLE OF THE LINKAGES

Throughout this chapter we have made the point that the maintenance of partial interdependence is the key to a confederation of organizations. The entire analysis sought to suggest the most effective linkages for various situations. Implicit in our analysis is that these are also the mechanisms which maintain the proper social distance between organizations. We propose that insufficient social distance will be maintained between confederated organizations in those situations which call for very formal modes of coordination, where in fact very informal ones are used. For instance, formal modes of coordination are most effective in situations where the activity to be coordinated is standardized, where there are many organizations in the network, and where they are aware of their interdependence. If organizations are in fact using informal modes of coordination such as personal friendship, we would suggest that the organizations will be too close, fostering favoritism, nepotism, etc. in lack of social distance.

On the other hand, the organizations may drift too far apart when the opposite conditions exist (Cell 8 in our tables) and linkages are maintained through formal rules. In this case ineffectiveness is often associated with red tape and bureaucratic inflexibility. Sieder provides a good illustration of organizations which are too closely linked.[66] She points out that a close friendship between personnel of two organizations in a network leads to the systematic exclusion of other members of the network. As a consequence the full resources of the network are not used, and ineffectiveness is associated with having agencies which are too close. She also provides illustrations of the opposite problem, by pointing out that a social worker seeking to place a handicapped child in a camp found that the rules and regulations excluded many groups of children. Here the suggestion is that more informal coordination rather than rules and regulations would have maximized the effectiveness of the network.

We suggested at the beginning that one difference between interorganizational and intraorganizational structures is that the former must give equal attention to maintaining as well as closing distance while the latter concentrates more on closing distance. Now we can more precisely state this matter. Because a confederation must maintain partial states of interdependence, while a single organization seeks complete interdependence for its internal units, the former will have greater concern than the latter in distance maintenance mechanisms.

There is yet another point which can be derived from Sieder's illustrations. The linkage procedure might produce a feedback relationship which changes the conditions of the situation, such as the number of organizations involved and their level of awareness. We have also pointed out that violent forms of competition in situations of actual states of partial interdependence may lead to raising the levels of awareness. Thus race riots, price wars, and actual wars might make the contending parties aware of their interdependence in a way they were not prior to the violence. In addition, it can be pointed out that much of the work on cost benefit analysis or other attempts at developing accounting

---

[66] Sieder, *op. cit.*

schemes are generally bases for introducing standardization which permits the use of rules (i.e., mathematical formulas) which in turn make organizations more aware of their interdependence. The development of potential feedback is a matter which can probably not be settled without more empirical data than has been collected up to now.

At this point we conclude by saying that if our hypotheses are correct—where a linkage is ineffective for a given cell—we will find either too great or too little social distance. If there is feedback we would hypothesize that there will be a change in the conditions of the cell—number of organizations, level of awareness, and level of standardization.

It is also clear that our analysis has been formalistic and we have not tried to say that some substantive areas are more important than others. For instance, are economic links between organizations more important than political, religious, or wider cultural ones? There has been a long history of controversy over these issues and we can add little aside from saying whichever theory one adopts, our analysis will suggest the interorganizational framework. Empirically, this means that for any given analysis, one of the jobs the investigator must undertake is the assessment in which area linkages are most central.

# SUMMARY AND CONCLUSIONS

We began this chapter by speaking about the distinctive character of interorganizational relations as compared to intraorganizational ones. They have distinct differences in structure: (1) amount of centralized authority, and (2) the need to maintain distance between units as well as have cooperation. In addition, they are designed to handle different problems. A confederation is optimal for maintaining legitimated conflict or pluralistic values or means which are partially in conflict. A single organization always seeks a way to concentrate on a single goal or order multiple goals by a priority system so that conflict is eliminated.

We next moved to a discussion of when formal and when primary group linkages might be most effective. The factors thought to be central were partial states of interdependence, levels of organizational awareness, standardization of the unit being exchanged, number and size of the organizations, type of organizations and level of resource. It was pointed out that formalistic linkages were ideal when dealing with a standardized event, many organizations, and high levels of awareness. In contrast, personal friendships tend to be ideal when dealing with few organizations, unstandardized events, and low levels or organizational awareness. It was also argued that interorganizational relations could be specified in terms of competitive or facilitative interdependence, and suggested that linkages which stressed communication would be most effective for facilitative coordination while those stressing adjudication would be most effective for competitive interdependence. It was further hypothesized that formal modes of adjudication would be most effective in situations involving many organizations, high levels of awareness, and high standardization. Informed modes of adjudication were thought to be most effective in the opposite circumstances. It was also argued that non-violent modes of public adjudication would be most effective in the former instance while more violent modes of private adjudication would be most effective in the latter circumstances. With regard to communication, it was pointed out that linking mechanisms which stressed initiative, intensity of focus and low scope would be most effective in situations of few organizations, low awareness of interdependence and non-standardization. On the other hand, passive, impersonal, high scope mechanisms would be ideal in situations where there were many organizations, high awareness, and standardized events.

We next turned our attention to the amount of autonomy granted the linkage mechanism itself. For instance, did it have the right to make and enforce decisions? It was hypothesized that linkages which stressed autonomy of decisions and enforcement would be most effective where survival or depolarization was not at stake, where impartial experts were available, and where there were powerful third parties demanding quick decisions. We argued these conditions were in turn related to high levels of awareness, high standardization, and many organizations.

Members of the confederation might also have differential authority over the linkage procedure. We suggested that linkage procedures with differential authority among member agencies would be most effective where asymmetrical interdependence occurred. However, extreme forms of assymmetry could produce a breakdown in the confederation.

Next we pointed out that relations between organizations might be further affected by the structure of their network. Here we suggested that organizations linked in a sequential fashion might experience different pressures than those linked in a homogeneous or pooled network. The former might well have a harder time developing an awareness of their interdependence, and providing more resources to only one member is as likely to break up the system as to help it. Any given member might have to assume new functions as a means of redressing a flaw in another member organization.

Finally, we concluded by pointing out areas for future exploration. Specifically, where mismatching of organizations occurs ineffectual performance in coordination is predicted. This might arise as a result of too much or too little social distance between organizations, or because of a change in levels of awareness, standardization, numbers of organizations, or other key variables easily affected by feed-back.

Perhaps we have raised more questions in the reader's mind than we have answered. However, interorganizational analysis has been neglected by sociologists even in the face of the fact that this is the time when such questions should be raised. The following chapter pursues the problem of inter-organizational membership taking as its point of departure classical laissez-faire economics.

---

* We would like to acknowledge especially the contribution of Jim Ajemian, Josefina Figueira McDonough, Gary Hamilton, and Gary Rhodes, who as members of the Interorganizational Project had extensive comments though they do not necessarily agree with our conclusions. In addition, Spencer Colliver, William Hutchison, and John Longres provided some ideas in the course of a graduate seminar. We should also like to acknowledge the Social and Rehabilitative Services, Department of Health, Education and Welfare, Project Number 425, for providing financial support. This is the first paper of the Interorganizational Project.

# VIII
## RIGGING THE MARKET FOR PUBLIC GOODS

*Norton E. Long*

THE REASON I WANT TO EXPLORE RIGGING THE MARKET FOR PUBLIC goods is that one of the most important transformations of the post-war world has been the movement towards direct intervention as a strategy to change the outcomes of interorganizational behavior. Planning *is* an attempt to influence interorganizational behavior. Indeed, successful planning asks how one actually gets into organizations to affect not only their incentive systems but also their definitions of the situation.

Rigging the market is normally considered reprehensible since it amounts to substitution of an intended outcome for the unintended result of market forces. It is analogous to loading the dice. What is interesting about rigging the market, as a conception, is that it provides a socially significant model of how an intended result might be achieved. If there are individual and organizational actors accepting the discipline of a market, then rigging that market can direct their behavior to the attainment of a desired objective without having to persuade them of its desirability or having to instruct them as to their specific roles in its attainment. Rigging the market thus becomes within the limits of its feasibility and, for the range of objects which it can attain, a potentially useful device for the implementation of planning.

A market is a model setting forth the behavior of individuals and organizations under a set of assumptions. Given those assumptions, and the relevant properties with which individuals and organizations are endowed, there is logic to their behavior. Feeding certain data into the model produces a logically entailed outcome. If the model is sufficiently similar to real life situations, we have for those situations an instrument that can generate warranted expectations and, at least in principle, suggest intervention strategies to produce desired results. It appears that there *are* real life situations to which the model is sufficiently isomorphic for it to have predictive power. Insofar as a rigged market can generate socially desired expectations, the discovery and refinement of its appropriate models and the conditions for their real life isomorphism is a piece of useful and usable social technology. Further, the model suggests alterations in real life situations to produce a better fit between the model and reality, hence increasing the power of its logic to generate warranted expectations.

The market concept like much of classical economics has suffered from a tendency to collapse models and to confuse them with realities to which they may not conform. This has happened partially because of the mistaken supposition that the market was an empirically induced generalization, and the equally fallacious idea that markets have characteristics of natural law. However, as a model that claims only to have an internal logic that can process data so as to generate specific logical entailments, the market doesn't need either empirical or natural law grounding. Its relevance to real life is similar to that of an algebraic formula; if it applies, it is useful. If it applies with a considerable degree of generality and predictive accuracy, it is a powerful tool. Since the classical economics model was conceived to have socially desirable results, it was awarded natural law status, as a result of which socially beneficent behavior would "naturally" occur, assuming, of course, the absence of ignorant or malevolent intervention with a benevolent "natural" social process. What might have been a beneficent game that people could be induced to play became instead a metaphysical ethic or an equally metaphysical notion of science. This has obscured the true usefulness and the limitations of the usefulness of a logical model.

The model of the market undoubtedly arises from insight into a pattern perceived in real life situations. What a model does is to strip the rich ambiguity of the real life situation down to a few variables that produce logical entailment and are conceived to interact in a calculable way. If, for the purposes in hand, the model fits sufficiently so as to produce useful expectations, it serves its purpose like an algebraic formula. The market model is not only descriptive in that it has application to real life situations, but is prescriptive in the sense that if the logical entailment of the model is deemed desirable, it makes sense to try to get real life to conform to the model. This is the sense in which classical economics is a normative theory and the sense in which a positive programme for laissez-faire makes sense despite the contradiction. Because we can understand the coercive logic of the market model, we have an explanation as to how a range of interpersonal and interorganizational behavior can acquire a logic, and therefore a power, of its own.

Now, goods are in some sense different in the public sector than in the controlling private sector. One of the things we have been discovering, and our friends behind the iron curtain are discovering, is the extraordinary value of a market system for achieving self assignment of role and achieving commonality of incentives and definitions of situations. During World War II, we struggled with a command economy and with the problems of coordination by fiat that the people who believed in simplistic problems of the individual organization loved to talk about. In the War Production Board people thought that if they could state an objective they could then issue orders, developing a nice chain all the way down from a notion of requirements to meet war and civilian needs to the actions of individual and institutional actors all the way down the chain. We found during the war that this was hopelessly impossible. The paper flow was immense, the confusion became compounded, and the problem of getting action and reaction was way beyond any kind of central nervous system we could set up.

The attraction of the market model stems from the paucity of available tools for dealing with interorganizational behavior. It provides us with one set of conditions under which we have some confidence that we can have fairly well warranted expectations. It is possible that it has other virtues; perhaps vices too. Thus, when during World War II the War Production Board sought to secure the manufacture of fractional horse power motors, it tried to program the desired end result in detail. It found, as in other cases, enormous difficulties due to lack of knowledge, lack of feedback, and scheduling problems. However, when it set specifications and a profitable price for the desired end item, the market was capable of starting a complex cueing and response system by which self assignment of role occurred and a more or less automatic feedback system, geared to the production of the desired end item, was activated. Where before a cumbersome flow of paper was necessary with detailed readjustments requiring central direction, the market system eliminated the need for what became a hopelessly overloaded central communication and decision making bottleneck. The Board tapped an ongoing social system, in being, that could be used for its purposes, and thus escaped the costs of creating an ad hoc one.

There are other than information features to a market system of interorganizational behavior. It seems to combine solutions to the problem of legitimate commands and appropriate incentives. For example, during World War II it was a subject of debate as to whether the labor force should be put in uniform and assigned like troops. The decision was that it would be less costly in terms of friction, if not in terms of equity, to use a rigged labor market so as to channel labor to favored organizations. Some market enthusiasts went so far, Milton Friedman reputedly, as to advocate that field commander bid against each other for scarce tanks, planes and guns. In this case, the putative virtues of the market concept were unpersuasive.

Further, the Office of Price Administration was bedevilled by a requirement that it not interfere with historic profit margins. In practice, this meant the disappearance of low end items from stocks. The market was rigged, but not by or to the desires of the O.P.A., and because it was compelled to achieve its objectives by coercion rather than profit incentive manipulation, its task was made doubly difficult. It had to depend on a stick with no carrot and it could not use the customary accepted market system of behavior. Like any set of customary behaviors, there is a legitimacy to orders that are not seen as coercive commands but as cues activating a habitual response pattern.

The attraction of the market as an instrumentality for the achievement of social purposes was given a notable lift by the postwar performance of western countries and Japan. As Andrew Shonfield remarks in his *Modern Capitalism,* scarcely anyone going into World War II believed the existing system capable of a tolerable performance. By the fifties, dogmatic socialism was moribund. Only the United States had failed to attain the highest growth rate in its history. The bloom of the brilliant postwar performance has faded in the late sixties, but dogmatic socialism has not revived to replace modern mixed enterprise capitalism. Whether inability to deal effectively with international monetary problems and the recurring urge to protectionism and economic nationalism will spell an end to the promising post World War II developments is far from clear.

Post World War II has been characterized by the gradual development of planning. Countries representing such diverse cultural backdrops as England and France have embarked in the new venture of planning. Despite claims to economic orthodoxy, West Germany has had far from a classically free economy. The United States, despite distaste for the term "welfare state" and a self-imposed sluggish growth rate under Eisenhower, has made its peace with a macro-Keynesian policy of maintaining high level employment—a policy that has been tempered by fear of inflation and unwillingness to accept interventionist strategies that very low unemployment might require. The French, until student riots and strikes shook their economy, gave every appearance, despite Gaullist eccentricities, of a sophisticated capacity to plan. The conspiracy to plan that produced the famous *industrie consorte* was in some ways a classic example of rigging the market.

What the French were able to do was to arrive at agreement among officials of key government departments on a firm course of action. Given the importance of French government in finance and industry, such a determination could reduce considerably the uncertainty as to future outcomes. With the government willing and able to commit itself to a course of action, its planners had real bargaining power with which to induce leading private enterprises to disclose their intentions and make firm commitments. Commitments by the government and a major sector of industry transform the expectations on which rational behavior depends. This is a version of the "prisoner" problem in economics: If every one on a street paints his house, everyone gains; if you are the only one, you've wasted your time and paint. The government and its co-conspirators in industry, by creating firm expectations as to each other's course of action, rig the market, and by removing uncertainty the conditions of rational behavior are altered. It becomes possible to utilize resources at a rate that would otherwise be too dangerous in an unrigged market.

Because a market does exist, and market-like behavior is to be expected of participants, it is possible to use the mechanism of the market to attain intended results. While initially the market was celebrated as a mechanism through which the pursuit of individual interests was synthesized into systematically functional outcomes, confidence in the systemic beneficence of the unintended outcomes of an uncontrolled market has waned. But the utility of the market as a means of achieving concerted action is increasingly recognized. So much is this the case that a new technique has come into use, that of a *public* market to achieve a *public* purpose. The military and the space agency have pioneered a device which is getting increasing attention as a tool that might have application in other fields. Some educational radicals, impressed with the inflexibility of educational bureaucracies, have advocated the creation of a publicly supported market for education as a way of introducing responsiveness and innovation into a moribund field.

In the public sector there are some very serious problems about how to achieve coordination because there is nothing comparable to the market. People treat it as if the hierarchy—the top echelons of government—provide the analog to the market with the brain of the President, or of his cabinet, or the governor, or the mayor, providing the basis for achieving institutional coordination. In fact, we are finding that this is increasingly not the case. I would suggest that one reason why rigging the market for public goods has become quite salient in terms of very important social concerns is that we have, up until recently, depended very heavily on the private market to achieve nearly everything that was achieved of importance in this society. The *job* has been the main predictor of anyone's social status, and the *job* has been the main way in which you shape people up. The market has been the way in which you assign people roles and housing, and allocate the use of territorial space. The market processes, of course, do not allow much concern with such externalities as air and water pollution, and the other ills that are by-products of densely settled industrial societies.

While some of the enthusiasm for the public market stems from attachment to private enterprise and enthusiasm for private profit, a good bit of it springs from a belief that we are better capable of coordinating the activities of a set of private enterprises toward a public objective through a publicly controlled market than through the ordinary processes of governmental action. It is true that one attraction of the public market-private enterprise combination lies in its capacity to generate sufficient political support to maintain a program. However, this capacity is also needed for the maintenance of any conventionally administered public program, perhaps even more so for the coordination of programs conducted by separate public agencies. The critical issue is not whether political support should be required for public programs. What is at issue are the consequences of the kind of support which is mobilized and the effectiveness of the structures through which it is delivered. It is clear that the mixed public-private of urban renewal, despite federal rhetorical commitment to the housing of the poor, had outcomes that were quite perverse. This probably occurred despite the good intentions of Washington and those of the other actors involved in the process. Urban renewal had and probably still has a logic that is powerful and adverse to the ends of the rhetoric of commitment to the poor. Whether this logic is inevitable within the compulsions of the general system or subject to transformation within that general framework is an unanswered and largely unexplored question.

One may remark on two aspects of the urban renewal experience: First, it had a logic that led to consequences of a systemic sort that were unintended; to wit, the drastic reduction of low cost housing available to the poor. Second, the rhetorical commitment to the poor was unaccompanied by knowledge of the means by which these intentions could be translated into an effective action program. The public markets created by the Department of Defense and N.A.S.A. do not, in some magical way, make possible the attainment of societal goals. What they do make possible is the mobilization of relevant cognitive competence and the initiation of an effective search procedure for the development of goal definition and goal attainment. Appropriate interorganizational motivation is critical for this process. Why, when, and whether a publicly supported market is superior to in-house capabilities must depend on the variant logics that determine organizational outcomes. It would appear that one of the most difficult problems for an in-house governmental effort is that of combining a plurality of competing entities with a device for rigging their competition in such a way as to serve an overall purpose.

How much this difficulty stems from an inability of centrally placed actors and institutions to rig the "market" of institutions by manipulating incentives is an interesting question. It should be as possible for an agency of government to manipulate the incentives of other agencies as for the same agency to manipulate the incentives of private enterprises. However, whereas Congress and the President often give an agency directive power in a field, this power is rarely of such a nature as to resemble that of the Defence and Space Agency's capacity to influence the profit calculations of companies. Directive power over an agency frequently seems a threat to its autonomy rather than an increase in its business. Indeed, since in many cases directive power is given without funds to be transferred to the directed agency, it amounts to an uncompensated loss of previous powers of self direction. At best it may seem from the directed agency's point of view a politically expedient means of hanging on to the substance of one's business while waiting to regain one's freedom from external control.

There would seem to be no inherent impossibility of government agencies behaving in much the same fashion as private enterprises which are seeking to sell their services in the private market. In fact, the Bureau of Labor Statistics and the Census are classic examples of agencies which, in addition to the funds appropriated to them, derive important revenues from the sale of their services to other government departments. These two agencies quite literally compete for business, and do so to a great extent on the basis of the cost and quality of their wares. While there is doubtless some politics in the determination of who gets what and whose business, much of what transpires seems similar to the competition in the private market. In contrast to the competition of the Bureau of Labor Statistics and the Census is the competition of the Bureau of Reclamation and the Army Corps of Engineers for the business of damming developing watersheds. This competition, however, is not so much based on costs and engineering performance as on competing ideologies and constituencies. It represents not so much competition between enterprisers seeking to sell similar products to the same customers, but rather a competition, to divert resources to different uses and to convince customers of the desirability of those ends. While this process is on a continuum with that of the Bureau of Labor Statistics and the Census, it represents a more formal political competition. The Census and the B.L.S. represent alternative means to much the same ends. The Bureau of Reclamation and the Corps of Engineers, however, represent alternative ends for quite different customers and with limited resources. The success of one not only deprives its rival of the business but deprives its rival's customers as well.

The rivalries within the government for scarce resources are indeed a form of competition but they are not for the most part competition within a market. They resemble the competition of diverse industries for scarce resources rather than the competition within an industry. At a more general level, of course, just as industries are competitors for scarce resources in capital, labor, and other areas, these markets function to allocate resources between industries that are not competitive in their product line. So, too, diverse government activities are competitors for the scarce resources allocated by the political process. If the political process functioned in the fashion of the ideal capital market, resources would be allocated in accordance with the comparative political return of the competing agencies. The political process is, of course, subject to as many or more imperfections as the capital markets. The means of measuring political return and comparing rates of return are vastly more imprecise than those of the private markets.

But the political process does, in a way, resemble the capital markets. The scrutiny (such as it is and with its biases and imperfections) is a scrutiny of the political return of particular activities and agencies. The overall outcome of the interaction of government activities is unintended as is the classic market's. Indeed, where the classic market has at least a specific model whose logic is supposed to lead to individually and collectively unintended systematically beneficent outcomes, the political analogue is lacking. Not, of course, that establishment liberals do not hint at some such result where appropriate electoral, party, and other competitive conditions are deemed to exist, but these hints have never been reduced to the form of a logical, let alone a testable model. In fact, Lowi refers to Schattschneider's account of the old time tariff hearings as examples par excellence of logrolling in which even individual rationality had no basis in any calculation of the individual consequences of systemic outcomes. In all likelihood, systemic outcomes were uncalculated if not incalculable. One may wonder if this may not be the crux of the matter. The tariff logroll of yore has been replaced by an executive process. And the grounds of this executive process seem to be the development of theory, a capacity to calculate the systemically dysfunctional outcomes of the older process and to conceive an alternative process whose logic seemed more likely to lead to more systemically functional outcomes.

Keynesian economics made it possible for certain purposes to sum the outcomes of the diverse activities of government and estimate the import of this unintended outcome for the economic system as a whole. The ability to do this in a sense transformed, at least intellectually, a process that resembled a force of nature into a purposeful human activity. Since the collective outcome of individual agency activities now had calculable consequences for states of the economic system, it became possible to exercise rational choice with respect to that collective outcome. One now had a reason beyond the dubious slogans of economy and efficiency for budgetary management. Beyond this, actors in various agencies with diverse and seemingly unrelated purposes could employ an intellectual apparatus that could make clear at least one dimension of policy with a potential for shared common concern and the intellectual tools to move this concern from the rhetoric of good intentions to a rational calculus with policy consequences and corrective feedback. Oddly, the attainment of macro-system ends might be more readily achieved through the operation of Keynesian economics than through the rational and individual activities of separate agencies involved in the fiscal calculus.

The appropriations committees of the House and Senate, as Wildavsky points out, proceed by incremental steps. Agencies first get themselves in the budget and then gradually up their appropriation. Rarely do the committees, except in wartime, dramatically move an agency's appropriation up or down. There is a kind of fair shares and almost, in a business sense, a historic share of the market which agencies possess, attempt to maintain, and from time to time try to improve. The committees behave like banks or investors with the agencies proving their worth as political business investments. In Vincent Ostrom's sense, there is a public enterprise system. Congress invests and from time to time ups its investment in particular cases. Infrequently losses are recognized and cuts are made. It is noteworthy that investing in a promising business to a prudent extent formulates the governmental task quite differently than an approach that attempted to define problems and to seek their appropriate solutions. It would seem patently absurd to build half bridges. No such absurdity on the face of it attends a limited investment in a politically promising government activity. However, such an approach requires a failure to conceptualize the problem and the means to its solution. It permits a politics of good intentions that in practice frequently means a rationing of such problem solution as is provided to favored parties or, in many cases, the production of varying brands of political patent medicines that at best have values as placebos and in any event are intentionally or unintentionally fraudulent and stultifying.

Since the rationing system of government is made up of bodies who cannot know much about the agencies and the programs they fund, the incremental system, like inching out on thin ice, may seem to make some sense. It may be regarded as a kind of limited risk trial under conditions of rather primitive uncertainty. What the system does most clearly imply is the lack of any responsible judgement of program and program objectives. We are rarely consciously guilty of building half bridges. The physical appearance of asininity is too apparent. But the analogues of half built bridges abound in government. Agencies are prepared to take a half loaf rather than no loaf. If the bridge they originally intended building is unbuildable, they may find a lesser stream or use the funds in some other worthy way. As public goods become an ever larger part of the consumption of an affluent society, the agencies that purvey them increase in significance. The functioning of the market for public goods becomes of major importance. Unlike the market theory of the classical economists, there is little theory to justify belief in the systemic functionality or beneficence of the public market. Its imperfections are too apparent.

Of late in a variety of areas there has been mounting dissatisfaction with the piecemeal activities of the congeries of diverse agencies and agency activities that abound in various problem areas. Notably, this has been the case in poverty and juvenile delinquency. The model cities program of H.U.D. is at least a rhetorical recognition of the need to transcend past policies. Federal efforts to cajole and coerce some degree of regional and metropolitan planning and plan implemention are further recognition of the imperfections of the present governmental market and the need to rig its working to some public purpose that insures an outcome that is systemically functional and beneficent. However, the intention to transform the ineffective patterns of institutional action that characterize the welfare field is not self-executing. Rhetorical commitment need not be insincere to be ineffectual. One suspects that the cognitive problem has not been solved by those who would rig the market in welfare. The problems are more complex than those of macro economics and, in any event, we have no theory with implications for a coordinated intervention strategy to alter system states in welfare such as Keynesian economics provides.

As in the economy, the governmental system is characterized by a multiplicity of agencies and activities that have an historical explanation and vested survival interests. Unlike the economy, there is little or no analytic rationale of the systemic consequences of the system of government activities. Indeed, as Galbraith points out, while we have the tools to think to some purpose about the rate of growth of our gross national product, we have given little thought to its composition and not too much that has been helpful to its distribution. The state of theory for the economy, however, is far more promising than for the polity where its need has scarcely commanded effective recognition. Neither the composition of the mix of government activities nor their collective and largely unintended and unknown impact has received much attention. Like the economy, the collective outcome of government activities resembles the forces of nature to which men adapt but which they do not purposefully control. The situation is better in the economy since there we have analytic theory setting forth the conditions under which individual self-regarding activities can be expected to produce desirable results. This analytic scheme produces at least in principle the possibility of a purposive societal choice of the market as a device for achieving its objectives. The presumed contrast of government and the economy presents one as well nigh naturally socially responsible and the other as requiring at least to a degree the contrivance of its responsibility.

The lawyers' principle of sovereignty gives government a specious appearance of unity and perhaps unified purpose. The reality, as we know, in metropolitan areas can be a competitive jungle of organizations whose actions are uncoordinated by any conscious overall purpose. What is now generally recognized to be true of metropolitan areas is only somewhat less true of national, state, and local governments. The formal unity of the government embraces an ecology of agencies and activities. The ecology has, through history, developed systemic modes of behavior that are functional to its survival and the survival of some of its members. It is not a humanly controlled instrument for the purposeful accomplishment of conscious human purposes. In its totality it is a natural force. Even in its components, individuals and agencies are often powerless to pursue goals other than those dictated by their own survival needs. Organizations are often condemned for following maintenance strategies as opposed to programmatic goals. Few would blame businesses for regarding the avoidance of bankruptcy as a prime objective. A greater and equally unrealistic demand of selflessness is made of public enterprises. The pervasive powerlessness to pursue goals that go much beyond survival and organization maintenance results in many agencies being radically incapable of achieving their ostensible purposes. A system is created in which actors and agencies are powerful for limited purposes only. The system is very powerful in its overall unintended outcomes, but, for the most part, no one has either the power or the responsibility to deal with many of the seemingly most important human problems. Witness the belated recognition of some twelve million Americans verging on starvation whose plight is ostensibly a high priority concern in our official ethics and rhetoric but in actuality the empowered responsibility of no one.

Individual governmental agency activities, like individual business activities, may be rational from the point of view of a particular organizational actor, but there is no necessary connection between the individually rational activities and a societally rational outcome. Except in the model of classical economics, there is little reason to expect that such a coincidence could be other than fortuitous. However, the historically developed ecology must be to a degree systemically functional in its capacity to endure. This fact, to the extent that it is a fact, says very little about how effectively scarce resources are being used to serve human purposes. An ecology may persist over time and still be characterized by gross waste and inefficiency as measured in terms of its production of desired and feasible outcomes. As Keynesian economics has facilitated both an appreciation of system states and intervention strategies relevant to them, public policy has developed some capacity to manipulate the interorganizational field to attain desired results. We are further along in our capacity to envision desired system states in economics than in politics. To be sure, much of the backwardness of political theorizing results from its disconnection from a direct concern with the social and economic outcomes of political action. This un-concern, when not merely naïve, represents the Marxian notion of the meaninglessness and sham of bourgeois democracy.

How to rig the markets for public and private goods to achieve im-portant social objectives is a matter of increasingly critical importance. As the activities of government become more and more profoundly con-sequential for most of us, the degree to which they and those of the economy represent the uncontrolled, undirected play of the natural forces of interorganizational fields becomes serious and dangerous. Only the willed product of men is ethically significant, and only the willed product of men is corrigible in such a way as to create the pos-sibility of self-correcting, cumulative knowledge. The outcomes of the interaction of the interorganizational field in the public area are less theoretically understood than in the private sector. We frequently arm agencies with directive powers and a mandate to do something without any clear idea of the steps by which it is to be brought about. The intervening variables between good intentions and their realization re-main unknown and all too often are treated as if they could be magically dispensed with.

Herman Miller in a fine book tells us that our social revolution is twenty years old. But during this period the disparity between Negro and white income has been on the increase. And we have this extraor-dinary phenomenon—extraordinary for Americans but rather com-mon for Africans, South Americans, and Asiatics—of the presence of increasingly large segments of the population which are outside the of-ficially recognized economy, and which are growing in very sizeable numbers. So much so, that Mitchell Ginsburg, the Commissioner of Welfare in New York City, will tell you that we have a relief population in the City of New York that is greater today than it was in the very depths of the depression. And I suspect that it is not only greater ab-solutely but greater relatively. And yet there is not the slightest under-standing as to how this has come about. In fact, Congress has been very careful to see that one doesn't spend too much money to research it, although Congress is obviously and savagely irritated by its being a fact. This isn't a fact unique to New York; it's a fact you can find all over.

The problem is exacerbated by the fact that where professions derive their prestige from the clients they deal with, there is bound to be a constant shift away from the poor. Without an alteration of incentive systems one can expect to see attempts to discard the poor. Of course, there are occasional instances of ideological hangovers from the Judaic-Christian tradition, or from Marxism, or from any of the other compulsive theologies which obsess the SDS. Others seem willing to intervene in the existing "natural" market because they don't want the town burned down and suspect that an American version of South Africa might be somewhat less gentile than South Africa. So, for a variety of reasons, people are becoming increasingly concerned with how to rig the market for public goods so that poor people will be treated as if they weren't poor. This seems almost like a contradiction in terms, but this is really what is at stake, in the same sense as "how does one empower the powerless?"

The more difficult problem is how to interfere with these systems without *radically* altering the division of income. Certainly a most serious concern is the problem of redistribution. How does one get those things to the poor which will most significantly alleviate their poverty? This is even harder to do if they are going to remain poor, because by definition poor people don't have as much as rich people.

For short periods of time, perhaps the answer to the problems of the poor *is* the Peace Corps, the SDS, and a variety of other ideologies. But there is serious doubt about their staying power, particularly in view of Rosengren's analysis of organizational change over time.

In this connection, one interesting question that's being raised about dealing with the poor (so that you can still have them as poor) is how to turn the poor into a profitable opportunity and commodity for industry. In short, it is becoming increasingly clear that one way problems can be dealt with is through the creation of a public market for the organization of private power for the solution of public problems.

Recently the Secretary of Agriculture came to the belated public recognition that there were some twelve million near starving people in the United States. Some perspicacious soul pointed out how easy it would be to solve the matter. It would only cost some billion of dollars. Doubtless the cost estimate was based on what it would take to do the job with high protein fish flour. Here are the elements: twelve million people, a billion dollars, fish flour. All that seems lacking is the will. A disembodied will without leverage on the interorganizational field to produce a meaningful logic means typically a rhetoric of frustrated good intentions and the growth of cynicism.

200

The sociological fraternity has been informed by Martin Lipset of Harvard of the fact of norms in conflict in the system: the so-called "achievement" norm, and the so-called "equality" norm. And this bedevils the problem of goods allocation, because we say equal citizens should be equally treated, and on the other hand we say that differential achievers should have differential incomes. And if you increase the amount of the society's product (that is, public goods distributed through the public sector), you then have the very tough problem of how to recognize and deal with unequal achievement among formally equal citizens. We have, as you well know, solved this problem after a fashion in the smorgasbord of suburbia and the central city. In the old days, before we had porky Black people, raising embarrassing questions about the equality norm, you could have good neighborhoods and bad neighborhoods in cities, and college preparatory schools and dumping grounds for others in the same city. But it is now more and more difficult to get the bland assumption of the appropriateness of the unequal distribution of unequal public goods among equal citizens. We *are* committed to these two norms—achievement and equality—and they have very important consequences for how you handle the problem of public goods allocation, and what kinds of public goods you actually produce.

The planning arm of the State of Connecticut has made three projections of the future land use patterns of the state. One of these might be called a "let nature take its course" projection. The planners had interviewed citizens, realtors, and local public officials. What they all envisioned as heart's desire was five acre lot homesites and replicas of 18th century towns. It was easy for the planners to show that the attempt to realize these individual desires would produce a collective mess, destructive of open space and extremely costly in utility lines and extended journeys to work. The planners were able to come up with two alternative projections, one polynucleated, the other linear in the pattern of settlement with immense advantages in the preservation of open space and the reduction of utility line and journey to work costs. These findings have been published and widely disseminated through the state as educational materials. There has been little disagreement with the validity of the planners' findings. However, the planners' reliance on the coercive power of their projections has proved overly optimistic, if not naïve. Agreement with the projections has provided no realistic basis for choosing among them. Particularly it has not specified a means-ends chain that might be activated by an act of choice.

The State of Connecticut might have chosen among the projections and sought to realize its choice by intervening in the interorganizational field, that is, by attempting to rig the market in the desired direction. Having analyzed the logic of the unrigged market that was leading to the undesirable "nature take its course" projection, the state would have to take stock of its own capacity to alter that logic. State investment in highways, utilities, education, recreation, conservation, and health and welfare could have considerable impact on the pattern of land use decisions. This impact could be used to influence the market. To do this, however, the State would have to be able to coordinate the activities of its own departments in a common effort to achieve the desired objective. The State needs to be able to rig the action of its own departments or its plans must remain little more than pious exhortations.

The example of the land use pattern of the State of Connecticut is a useful example of a system state whose attainment requires the cooperation of a multitude of individual and organizational actors. Even more than the difficulties confronting the War Production Board, it presents the problem of how to initiate means-ends chains that will produce behaviors functional to the production of the desired system state. Agreement with the desirability of the projected land use pattern produces no necessary knowledge of or agreement about the individually relevant means to its attainment. As in the case of the War Production Board, the least costly, most effective strategy is intervention which uses the system in being as a going accepted behavioral calculus of individuals and organizations but loads the calculus in such a way as to produce the desired result. Using the market as a model for control and as a means of preserving the advantages of initiative in self-assignment of role, it may turn out that public policy may well wish to improve the fit of the local interorganizational field to the normative market model. The reason for this may well be not so much as, with the classical economist, to remove public control over system states but, quite the contrary, to increase the possibilities of its effective exercise.

Another example of the utility of the market as a device in the public sphere is its capacity to enhance bureaucratic responsiveness to clients whose roles may be changed to that of customers. It is not only behind the iron curtain that concern is expressed with bureaucratic rigidity, unresponsiveness to consumer needs and desires, with attendant waste, inefficiency and political costs to the regime. The whole welfare delivery system in many parts of the United States is coming under similar scrutiny. The powerlessness of the clients (customers) is not only dys-

202

functional for them but is coming to be regarded as dysfunctional for the production of desired system states. Effective customers may be a necessary variable for the achievement of planned system states that are generally desired. While it may be true, as has been remarked, that the American system of welfare resembles the feeding of sparrows through horses, it can still be doubted that most Americans would vote for this system if they so understood it. At a less invidiously conceived level than welfare, (that of education,) concern, as previously noted, is increasing with the lack of productivity and the self-centered immobility of educational bureaucracies. While Adam Smith's praise of the market may sound like a call for an academic popularity contest more likely to produce student flattering vaudeville than serious education, it is not without merit. Surely it might have been an improvement over the Oxford of his day.

It's especially true in a "mandarin" society where we *really* stratify in terms of education, that the educational system becomes the most important means of role assignment in which it is treated as legitimating. I suppose what all of the shooting is about in education is that the Blacks have re-discovered Plato and Plato's *Republic,* and they have suddenly recognized that the schoolmen claim, either from divinity or the I.Q. test, the correct method of determining who are the men of gold, who are the men of silver, and who are the men of brass. That claim really is open to some serious kinds of questions. In fact, you might say that education is our equivalent of the Hindu caste system, which was so sacred that it couldn't be a matter of politics. Now that it *has* become a matter of politics, people no longer accept I.Q. as the sacral determinant of role allocation through the educational system.

So, if you were to look at the American system of stratification, you would see that the charmed circle of our stratification system is education, with education leading to jobs and matrimony, jobs and matrimony leading to income, and income (provided you're not discriminated against) leading to housing. Then you have a magnificent explanatory device leading to suburbia and the metropolitan area. Obviously, one of the things that you clearly have to have if there is an equality norm among citizens, but an inequality norm among consumers, is a rhetoric rendering inequity acceptable. Hence, while we will all be equal citizens, the country clubs of suburbia must be open only to those who have enough money to buy the housing. That, I take it, is what Marx meant by bourgeois democracy being a fraud. And if you go to these country clubs, then you go to "superior" educational establishments, which will then admit you to "superior" colleges, which will admit you to "superior" graduate schools or to "superior" corporations, in the sense that Galbraith talks about them in *The Industrial State*. And this will achieve a legitimized role assignment which will make some of the people relatively happy.

The conception of the market as applied to education does not have to lead to a mindless, glandular popularity contest or the free-for-all of the South American university. It does require consideration of how to empower customers in a desired fashion and how to organize markets for the production of publicly desired educational products. Unfortunately, unlike the Defense and Space Agencies, H.E.W. has far less conception of goals and means for goal attainment. However, it should not be impossible to develop instruments for the determining of student possession of minimal skills in reading, writing and arithmetic relevant to their effective use in a job context. If industry and government agree on the critical significance of the certified possession of these skills for employment and career, we would have the means to rig the educational market towards the attainment of a desired system state. Public funds and personnel departments would seek those educational institutions scoring high on the desired dimensions. Students, once the employment correlation was made clear and high, might be expected to transfer their patronage to the extent they could to the effective institutions. Parents and concerned taxpayers would have a yardstick to judge institutional performance. Performance measures could show the cost at system levels in terms of goal attainment of educational slippage wherever it occurred. Concern with distribution of educational resources could be transformed from sentimental affect to cognitive understanding of measurable consequences.

Rigging the market for public goods turns out to be a device for transforming the public ecology of activities into a rational, controlled instrumentality for the achievement of consciously held and critically understood social purposes. It is a device, in principle at least, for utilizing such theory as we have that explains the interaction of interorganizational fields under model conditions for the attainment of normative ends.

# IX

## THE SOCIAL ECONOMICS OF MEMBERSHIP

*William R. Rosengren*

It is clear from much in the preceeding chapters that organizations and members carry values which are bargained for, negotiated, and sometimes exchanged. They may, in some sense, be characterized respectively as producers and consumers, as purveyors and purchasers, as brokers and investors. As a result, transactions between them have much the same character as economies.[1]

One fact which immediately disadvantages the member in such a market place is that the organization's economy is somewhat more stable and durable than is the economy of the person. This is true partially because the organization can exert more coercive power than the client can and this fact tends to be translated by the organization into the presumption that its values and products are more reasonable, more honorable, more legal, and technologically more plausible than are those of the client. Hence, the organization's economy is larger and tends toward monopoly, while the member is disadvantaged unless there is a *collectivized* member group—such as the labor movement— by which client values can be presented in a less unstable form.[2]

---

[1] The use of an economic perspective is hardly new: Neil Chamberlain, *A General Theory of Economic Process* (New York: Harper, 1955); George C. Homans, *Social Behavior: Its Elementary Forms* (New York: Harcourt, World & Brace, 1961); Peter Blau, *Exchange and Power and Social Life* (New York: John Wiley, 1964).

[2] The likelihood of this occurring is increased through the operation of the cohort phenomenon in school and universities. A discussion related to this point is found

205

But this does not often occur for many reasons, not the least of which is the fact that clients are in other ways socially powerless to increase their own value without trafficking with an organization. That is to say many clients are ill, infirm, very young, impoverished, undereducated, discriminated against, legally constrained and otherwise unable to mobilize the resources of others on their behalf and on their terms.

In addition, the values carried by most clients are far more "convertible" than are those of most organizations. Hence, the institutional economy is more enabled to take what it wishes from the client while offering only a specific kind of exchange. This has to do not only with the weaknesses of the client indicated above, but also with the fact that the quasi-member usually has only highly diffuse legal recourse, while himself appearing before an organization which has achieved a considerable degree of legal entrenchment beyond which it can hardly be pushed. Compulsory education and specific curriculums in public schools, psychiatric commitment laws, and discharge against medical advice come to mind immediately as examples of this relationship.[3]

Also, because of the fact that the organization is in a more favorable position for defining the situation, it delivers goods that are thought to be socially valuable—and therefore necessary. And this is one reason which underlies the drift toward professional dominance. Hence, under normal circumstances of the market, the client cannot make ends meet—cannot balance his economy—without an exchange with an organization. Now, simple logic would tell us that the reverse should also be the case; that in a true economy the organization ought not to be able to manage without clients. But we know that this need not be so, because we speak of and know of goal displacement, goal deflection, and instances of "paper" organizations which in fact *have* no clients. This derives from the simple fact that organizations can acquire or create values which can be exchanged with *other* organizations as well as with individual clients. Thus, the organization is in a position to traffic in two markets while the client is limited to only one.

---

in Stanton Wheeler, "The Structure of Formally Organized Socialization Settings," in *Socialization After Childhood*. Orville G. Brim, Jr., and Stanton Wheeler, Eds. (New York: John Wiley, 1966), pp. 51–116. Of course the current so-called student revolution can be easily understood as an effort to reduce the asymmetry between students and the educational officialdom.

[3] This tendency toward "powerless clients" is cogently described in Warren C. Haggstrom, "The Power of the Poor," *Mental Health of the Poor,* Frank Riessman, Jerome Cohen, and Arthur Pearl, Eds. (New York: The Free Press, 1964), pp. 205–223.

However true that might be, the fact of the matter is that organizations offer services for consumption thought to be either desirable or essential, while clients carry values somewhat less golden and only somewhat necessary to the system. Charles Perrow has gone far in specifying just what it is that the client may contribute to the economy of voluntary associations. It is also appropriate to examine what objects of worth can be extracted *from* the client as well as what he might receive in return.

In addition to name, manpower, and monetary resources which can be bestowed upon the organization by the client, the organization can differentially distribute these same values—and more—among their clientele. As to distributing the same, the imprint of a "superior" college degree is not gained cheaply nor it is without further bargaining power once acquired, as Long has pointed out. But more to the point of these remarks is that the most delicate bargain is struck when the client retains some degree of autonomy of action and the organization holds in abeyance its dominance, while at the same time delivering the valuable service. The limiting case, of course, is in the prison or the psychiatric hospital wherein devices such as trusteeships, or home-visits, or patient government are found. Here, the "steel fist in the velvet glove" is hidden in the cash register to extract payment if the bargain turns sour.[4]

Somewhat more complex arrangements, however, are found in organizations such as schools and universities. In these, as Talcott Parsons has pointed out, anonymous collectivized decisions may withdraw the organization's value from the client, even though the member may have thrown all that he possessed into the agreement. Much the same occurs in some elite psychiatric hospitals and in some welfare agencies. In the first instance, the rhetoric of staff conference may lead to a reduction of the patient's status (i.e., extract *more* while giving *less*). In the second case an administrative or legal decision may exclude the client from any bargaining position whatsoever.[5]

Such examples—and the currency involved—fade off into what occurs in voluntary associations. A prime value these places have to offer is comraderie—social contact and interaction. This is perhaps the most golden and basic metal for it has been repeatedly shown to be part of

---

[4] Blau and Scott have labelled this kind of contingent autonomy, "pseudo-democracy." Peter M. Blau and W. Richard Scott, *Formal Organizations* (San Francisco: Chandler Publishing Co., 1962), pp. 186–192.

[5] Carl Gersuny has discussed a related process in his, "Serviture and Expropriation as Dimensions of Clienthood," paper presented at the Annual Meetings of the Eastern Sociological Society, New York, April, 1969 (mimeographed).

the exchange of social life. It is brought into a very free-wheeling market, however, in voluntary associations, where failure on the part of a member to offer up the proper "interpersonal" coin may result in a total closing of his account. This also represents, in some sense, the most even point of bargaining between member and organization because trading is essentially in *kind*.[6]

However that might be, the problem in voluntary associations is further exacerbated by the fact that the coin of this realm is inherently unstable. Unlike the tender of most organizations, it is seldom very clear just what is being exchanged, or what the value of the units actually is. And it is equally unclear why one bargain leads to great profit while others result in liquidation. But this, again, is a limiting case.

The general hospital, at the other end of the continuum, is equally limiting but of some interest nonetheless. Here, the value of interpersonal money is less, but it is still present in the system, and is sometimes called the informal organization. This accounts for the fact that some doctors think that some patients are "crocks" while others are not.[7]

The interpersonal market, as well as the rules for its negotiation, gets more complex in such organizations as universities, elite psychiatric hospitals, and some welfare agencies which have only moderately precise economies. All of us in the academy are familiar with the elaborate rules of etiquette, and gestures of programmed grading by which a student's personality is not allowed to effect the grade awarded. Psychiatrists and social workers have a very elaborate rhetoric of instruction as to how one might work out his own feelings toward patients in order that the appropriate exchange can be made. And one function of the confessional box—intended or not—is to prohibit the introduction of extraneous values into the unequal exchange of sin for grace. Perhaps the psychoanalyst's couch and the turned back of the listener also symbolizes an effort to stem the tide of "foreign" currency into this marketplace. But as in international exchange, foreign currency does occasionally flood the organizational market and hence renders it something less than fully stable. One importance of this fact is that if the organization, by intent or not, attempts to transfer false or devalued goods to the member, the member may then use this untoward manip-

---

[6] Analogous, of course, is the study of social interaction from the symbolic interactionist point of view.

[7] The term "crock" implies that the physician feels that the patient is demanding more than the doctor is willing to give.

ulation of the market in order to extort the organization. Students sometimes employ this tactic with teachers, and I am fairly sure that it happens elsewhere too.

Thus to mention just two values, the organization may distribute
autonomy and social interaction to the member. The curious fact, however, is that the more of *either* the organization throws into the client-
institution market, the more tenuous becomes its hold on its own reserves. This is analagous to the de-centralization and multi-product
problem in manufacturing and marketing: the critical policy decision is
to know just how far one can go in this direction before there is loss of
control over the operation, and hence loss of value. Hence, the more
open schools, psychiatric hospitals, or welfare agencies become, the
greater is the danger that the organizations' value reserves will be given
away freely without the extraction of payment from the member.[8]

But organizations may also offer members the values of power and
authority, in an extrinsic sense. Here the client is particularly disadvantaged in the exchange because he normally has little of either to
throw into the balance. The organization may give legal authority in the
form of what is currently thought to be wisdom, a prestigious imprint,
a license, or even a mandate. It goes without saying that values of these
kinds may have derived earlier in history from family, kin, peer group,
or apprenticeship. But those processes were quite different because they
were more in the nature of gift-giving rather than economic exchange.
That is, the recipient of values in those systems seldom received them
until the prior owners had no more use for them, usually because of
age, death, or ritual status reduction. In modern societies, however,
organizations attempt to *add* to the total societal wealth store without
themselves losing too much in the deal. What was once a matter of
transferring the family jewels has now become Keynesian social-eco-
nomics.

However that might be, most clients have little power or authority
with which to bargain. Indeed, this is precisely what they have come
to the organization to obtain. Hence they must lose much in order to
acquire these goods. Again, limiting cases come to mind: the professional schools of law and medicine, the military, and ecclesiastical
schools where one gives his future career—indeed his self—in order to
garner power and authority. He also receives, as a dividend, a form

---

[8] This represents an instance of a breakdown in the division of labor between
organizations and their clients—similar to the lack of distinction between producers
and consumers discussed by Parsons and Perrow.

of guaranteed future comradeship in the form of "guild" membership, and this need not be bargained for elsewhere at a later time.

Now at the other end of the continuum are organizations such as psychiatric hospitals, prisons, and low-paying jobs which don't give power and authority to the client, but take them from him. But then, of course, the member is likely to give little in return for having been exploited: no loyalty, no commitment. He may even try, where he can, to slip counterfeit into the register—alienation, rebellion, and sabotage.[9]

The first type-cases are bullish markets in the sense that their values are enhanced by virtue of the fact that the paying organization pays also to the degree that its extra-organizational linkages are valuable. These may then become a source of later enrichment as far as clients are concerned. For as Long has pointed out, attendance at a prestigious school leads to a job in a good corporation, to membership in a nice country-club, and of course to dollar wealth. The member must make a risky and large initial investment, but there might be a multi-portfolio payoff.

The second cases are more bearish. Prisons and other such places are members of market sets which include organizations such as police departments, parole divisions, lawyers, state hospitals and other such places which later on give little but extract much. In short, entrance into this market is likely to result in a future credit rating of dubious quality.

All of this, of course, relates to the fact that since the organization holds the larger credit balance it is able to enforce the initial assessment of the client's worth as far as tradeability to other organizations is concerned: "once an ex-con, always and ex-con" and similar labels are part of the lexicon of interpersonal exchange.[10] And stigmata, like Confederate bills, are not negotiable, except to social antique collectors who may display their worn out currency, thereby gaining some small revenue. I am thinking, for example, of de-classe social dumping grounds of one kind or another where the organization is the custodian of cast-off curiousities. I recall in this connection, for example, paying a visit to a state penitentiary some years ago. The warden took me directly to the gas chamber in order to show off the sexagenarian wife killer who had proudly spent the last half century cleaning up that wicked place.

---

[9] Theodore Caplow predicts outcomes such as these in organizations too highly stratified, minimal interaction between members, and involving low valience for the lower level members. See his, *Principles of Organization* (New York: Harcourt, Brace and World, 1964).

[10] The importance of prior organizational processing for the social typing of clients is demonstrated in Elaine Cumming, *Systems of Social Regulation* (New York: Atherton Press, 1968).

Mixed cases, however, are more complex in regard to how the first exchange may effect later profits and losses.

At stake, initially, are the finely graded prestige rankings amongst schools, colleges, military academies and other places which are neither clear sterling nor tin. Hence, wise clients try to assess the place before entering into an agreement. We don't know how many such wise clients there are, although the presence of counseling experts, referral agents, and applicant testing corporations suggests that there is a large profit to be gained by trafficking in flexible and unvalued currency and indicates that the number is large.

That is, potential entrants into such a confused market must turn to *other* organizations so that their values as incoming members might be properly assessed. Also, they would be wise to consume some of the *products* of other organizations—books on college rankings, guidance counsellors, etc.—in order to set a negotiating value upon the final group of organizations to which they might turn with their portfolio of certified skills and values.

If one persists with the economic-symbiotic model, it is hardly surprising to find that the referral agencies and agents somehow manage to serve both the *client* and the *organization* at the same time, thereby resembling "assay" offices amid the new digs, in which values are in fact determined. For example, doctors treat patients and also work in hospitals; testing services assess students and then tell the universities what the results mean; practicing clinical psychologists usually have an affiliation with a psychiatric hospital to which organizationally "valuable" clients are routed.

Where the value of the coinage is unstable—as it is in most organizations—the problem arises as to what the client is worth once he leaves. This may have a snowball effect on both the client and the organization in the following ways: as a result of some of the forces which have already been mentioned, a worthless input is likely more often than not to result in a not very valuable output. And a shoddy product tends to reflect negatively upon the system which produced it. Hence, one has the cycle of the worthy and prestigious organization becoming more so, and the brass organization tending toward tin. The first, of course, may attribute its increasing worth to its own inherent value, failing to acknowledge the fact (therefore seldom grateful to it) that it was able to produce so much because its raw materials were so rich. We often see this in prestige colleges and universities. This is organizationally useful as well as self-aggrandizing because the departed clients, in the form of alumni, usually bestow gifts of gratitude upon their benefactor.

Organizational worthlessness, on the other hand, is usually accounted for by pointing to a base product and the poor raw material that was available, failing to own up to the fact that low *organizational* input is not unrelated to low client output. In the case of universities, for example, the students have their *own* ideas about how all of this came about, and this is reflected in the fact that modest and middle range colleges have a dreadful time extracting endowment funds from their graduates. A history of successful athletic teams sometimes helps in this regard.

Some elite psychiatric hospitals report high success, often neglecting to report that most of their patients were not schizophrenic; military academies can ennoble themselves because of the later heroism and high rank of their graduates, often without mentioning the fact that the cadets were zealots before they were plebes. The trick, of course, is to devise ceremonies and legends such as plebe year and hazing, so as to convince the new member that he was indeed worthless at the beginning.[11] Therefore, any change that occurs, as a result of organizational processing, is bound to be defined as an improvement. This is a good way to extract at least some degree of gratitude at the end.

Long has pointed out that an important fact of exchange life is that organizations acquire the prestige and value of their clients, as well as the other way around. This is also true of such individual staff members as doctors, lawyers, professors, and others. Doctors are attracted to ill people with baffling diseases; lawyers have an affinity for individuals with shocking legal entanglements; professors like "good" students. Now it is also true that doctors, lawyers and professors come to their place of occupation as products of greater or lesser worth of earlier processing and work organizations. Hence, their individual value reserve and accumulation contributes or detracts from the organization through which they travel. It also has an impact upon the kinds of client values which the organization will be able to attract.

As initially valuable staff members join a valuable organization, there is a resultant increase in its bargaining position with respect to worthy

---

[11] Much of this is implicit in Sanford M. Dornbusch, "The Military Academy as an Assimilating Institution," *Social Forces* 33, (1955), pp. 316–321; see also William R. Rosengren, "The Rhetoric of Value Transfer in Organizations," *Sociological Inquiry* (in press).

clients. In fact, the addition of a single highly valuable staff member may result in the acquisition of a very large number of highly valuable clients. At the same time, one person who seriously disables the organizational economy may drive away a large number of very worthwhile clients with much to trade. Hence, an overly-tough prison guard may provoke to violence an inmate on the road to rehabilitation. (or a soft guard might turn a compliant prisoner into a troublemaker, depending upon what the value system there happens to be). One scholar of national repute may attract a really competent group of students (and lots of money as well), while a single bad teacher may drive students away in droves.

Incidentally, administrators of middle-range universities which are on the make know all about this and will even dip into short reserves to make just such a gamble on a famous name. And the documentations of vitae and credentials set this magnificent pari-mutuel system into motion at least once a year.[12]

It is also true that not only does the client acquire the values of the organization, but the staff member does, too. One can only recall the reported fact that George Simmel was a genius unrecognized in his own country, largely because he taught for so many years at universities thought to serve brass students. In fact, the translations of Albion Small, emanating from the University of Chicago, were largely responsible for his current regard. To some extent the same is true to Max Weber, resurrected from near oblivion by the value of Parsons, and Henderson and Parsons.

These, of course, are only examples of treasures rediscovered from the dungeons of low organizational value. No one knows how many professionals of value are entrapped in the back drawer because of the low value of their clients and their organizations.

There is a further peculiarity in the exchange relationships between members and organizations that has to do with the fact that the values carried by organizations tend to increase with time, while the glitter of client-members tends to tarnish after a while. (This, I take it, is one way of interpreting Weber's contention about the self-perpetuating nature of bureaucracy.) And generally speaking, the lower is the value retained in the client, the more freely is it negotiated and more cheaply is it bought by the organization. Finally, there are some organizations

---

[12] See Theodore Caplow and Reece J. McGee, *The Academic Marketplace* (New York: Basic Books, 1958).

in which the exchange is completely asymmetrical and in which near total value is extracted from the client and given over permanently to the organization's coffers. The client, in turn, is rendered totally impoverished. Again, the most limiting case dramatizes this: Nazi concentration camps, where not only psychic worth but the physical body is reconstituted as organizational value. Sometimes, as in the above case, the extraction of final value from the member is accomplished very quickly and with impunity.

In other organizations the process occurs more slowly and may never actually reach the final stage of account closing, as in nursing homes where the bearer of minimal client value is stored, and custodial state hospitals where much the same low level economy prevails. Hence, there are points of diminishing return beyond which the values embodied in the client are so minimal as to prevent a very great organizational investment—client input, organizational input, and organizational output are at a mere subsistence level.[13]

This issue of diminishing value leads to a number of serious resource allocation problems in societies driven both by norms of exchange and norms of humanism. There is great pressure from within the system itself to expend a high degree of organizational resources, even though it may be suspected in advance that the clients on whom such resources are expended are likely to yield a very low return indeed. This, of course, is the problem of the economics of welfare and perhaps of bankruptcy. And as Norton Long has pointed out, our society has not yet discovered a workable formula by which a profit can be turned on clients with minimal value, while at the same time enhancing the value of the member. In the field of medicine, for example, serious and quite literal economic questions are raised about the cost involved in maintaining the life of a quadraplegic, the severly mentally retarded, or the individual with end-state kidney disease. Very much the same dilemmas are faced with respect to the abject poor in relation to social welfare programs, and also with regard to those in the sub-basements of the educational market place.

In the case of health, for example, the argument often turns to the fact that an investment equal to that needed to extract a small value return from five quadraplegics, when used in a program of emergency coronary services would yield a very large return, invested as it would

---

[13] Many have remarked upon the dreary lack of activity characterizing life in custodial psychriatric hospitals and prisons.

then be among a very large number of members. Hence, organizational economies, with respect to their response to clients' bids for a bullish market, very frequently hinge upon the "unit" versus the "batch" decision which went far to transform modern industry after the invention of inter-changeable parts.[14] The analog, of course, is to be found in programmed learning technologies in schools, the assembly-line character of some hospitals, the "pipeline" concept in education which results in the uniform production of droves of new Ph.D.s, and other organizations where the emphasis is upon turning out a mass and uniform product.

A major problem encountered in batch production of clients, however, inheres in the fact that this kind of system requires a large investment, an available resource reserve, as well as a technology which is difficult to turn to other purposes. This is in the same sense that a tailor can sew either suits or overcoats, but it is somewhat difficult to turn an automobile factory into a crockery plant. And anyone who has ever worked in a steel mill knows that an assembly line is hard to stop once it gets a start, and is difficult to set in motion once it has ground to a halt.

Both of these facts mean that batch systems are likely to continue producing what might in fact turn out to be a poor product, or even to continue extracting value from their members while transmitting a poor coin to them in return. This has been known to occur in general hospitals, in psychiatric hospitals, and of course in educational institutions.

Parenthetically, the large resource reserves required to set a batch production system into operation mean that the organization has to engage in exchanges with systems in its environment which may, at critical moments, lead to a liquidation of the entire enterprise. We see this, for example, in the unstable market position of batch systems of higher education in which the reserve fund is constituted of federal research grants and training grants which might be withdrawn at the next budget hearings. Of course, the private university may be in a not very much better position because its "angel" might suddenly be transformed into a bill collector, and of course the client picks up the tab in the form of tuition increases. These, in turn, are often mysteriously converted into higher faculty salaries, and the cycle begins once again.

I think that this problem is connected with the issue of dubious trust

---

[14] See Joan Woodward, *Industrial Organization: Theory and Practice* (London: Oxford University Press, 1965).

215

that was examined by Bidwell, and the patterns of professional dominance analyzed by Freidson. In nearly every strictly economic exchange of which we know, both parties to the bargain-in-the-making would wish to have some real gesture of good will—some assurance that the bargain will be met in full. Hence, the department store will seldom take a sofa off the sales floor until the customer has come up with a down payment. These are usually nonrefundable as in the case of applicants' fees to graduate schools.

It is important to keep in mind the fact that this margin buying is usually asymmetrical; the down payment demanded of the customer is usually of greater value (and more easily converted into other values) than is the token gesture on the part of the seller. The store can turn the cash down payment to other value producing purposes, while the customer cannot even sit on his sofa. Of course, it is easy to see that these same processes go on in the relations between clients and service organizations.

The patient seeks some indicator of the competence of the medical practitioner. And if the practitioner is a member of a dominant profession, the client's down payment is a generalized willingness to acquiesce to the wishes, commands, and ministration of the physican. But the physician need only to point to his certification document hanging on the wall. In fact, in relation to the dominant professions, the client has very little recourse, even in the most critical situations. And if the bargain *really* turns bad—if the patient dies—even his survivors have few avenues of redress open to them. And as Friedson has pointed out, nearly all occupations and organizations try to move in the direction of dominance. It is simply the economically rational thing to do because it enhances one's bargaining position.

In addition, the organizational representatives usually demand a *first* investment on the part of the client which commits the client prior to the time when the organization actually enters the agreement. Applicants to graduate schools reject other investment alternatives while the university's options remain open. Sometimes the patients of military dentists must sign disclaimers which absolve the organization of responsibility should the wrong tooth be extracted, and so on. So the client—being more or less uninformed—is forced back to the simple tactic of trust while the organization increasingly demands a larger and larger down payment *in advance*.

In the kinds of cases described by Bidwell, where trust is most central and organizational dominance is "soft," a number of interesting things

216

can come about. First, the student tries, insofar as he can, to gather as much prior information as he can about the trustworthiness of the university: the reputation of its faculty, the percentage of recent graduates having gone on to graduate study, the mean annual income of recent graduates, and the like. The parents, who are in reality the reserve fund of the student, are also interested in these things and more: the quality of the food served, the stringency of dormitory visitation rules, the zeal with which antidrinking and marijuana regulations are enforced.

Both the student and the university, to be sure, put their best foot forward on *two* occasions; when the bargain is first struck during Freshman Week and later when the deal is consummated on Baccalaureate Sunday. What transpires in the interim may have more the character of a bazaar. Much the same, I suspect, occurs in the negotiations for trust and dominance in other organizations.

There is yet another "economic" matter that arises in the relation between clients and organizations—between goods and their producers—and that is the question of durability. Having made an investment, the client and his cohorts are interested in knowing whether the value he has bargained for is likely to wear out soon: is his education really current?; is his job-retraining pertinent to modern industry?; will his psychological transformation turn to bad paper before he has turned a profit on it?; and so on. For somewhat different reasons, the organization is also interested in the durability of its product.

Durability is probably less of a value in a rapidly changing society than in a more stable one. The productive effort gone into automobiles, for example, seems much greater in periods of relative economic scarcity than at times when the market is very good. I suspect that much the same is true of service organizations. The concept of a "classical" education was certainly thought to be a highly durable product at one time, and clients whose own value reserves lent themselves to processing for durability in this sense were probably rewarded *more* on the basis of *less* of an investment on their part than other clients. We find the obverse of this in the case of educational programs designed to meet a more current and perhaps transitory extrinsic market: medical sociology comes to mind as an example, and today the question of durability is a very real one.

Product durability, of course, relates to the extent to which the organization provides some kind of warranty or guarantee concerning the values it exchanges with its quasi-members. Again using the physical product analogy, I recall having had a suit hand-tailored in a foreign country a few years ago. Upon taking possession of the goods, the tailor asked me when I expected to return to his country. My reply was that it was not likely that I would ever return. But he said, "Well, if you should ever come back, please bring the suit so that I can make good anything that needs to be done." I've never had that experience with the highway discount stores where some of my clothes come from.

Durable values in the service sense, of course, tend to be exchanged in high resource organizations and with high resource clients. Take the medical school, the seminary, or the law as examples. Here, the graduate vows *his* durability in the form of professional commitment. The organization vows *its* durability in the form of guild protection, licensing, and the imprint of legality, as well as some assurance that the graduate shall have a source of clienteles throughout his future career. For one good way to insure durability is to see to it that the product is both dominant and scarce. The parallel of this with the high cost of medical care and the built-in scarcity of doctors is quite obvious. This, again is one limiting case.

Low resource organizations—prisons and some psychiatric hospitals —represent the contrasting limiting type. Here, durability as a value hardly exists at all.

At this juncture I want to turn to one additional consideration which relies very heavily on Parson's insight that clients of organizations in some ways resemble the subjects of research enterprises. I should like to expand on that parallel, frame it once again in social economic terms, and take the position that all service organizations are in some sense experimental in nature. The guarantees which they provide with their goods are not iron-clad. After having explored this avenue, I shall conclude by exploiting Weber's observation that "science" tends to be self-correcting, and by this means set forth what I would regard as a principal societal function performed by large scale organizations today.

The essentials of the argument are as follows: since *no* organization has a completely viable technology, its exchanges with clients are to some degree experimental. Experimental activities acquire some of the characteristics of a scientific endeaver. Scientists try to correct and per-fect whatever it is they do—to do things more effectively or to do different things that attain a higher level of effectiveness. But since these processes occur against the backdrop of social economic exchange, the result can be a very odd mix indeed.

As Lefton has pointed out, at the initial coming together of member and organization, the organization makes a real effort to determine just how stable its client materials are and to elect the most plausible means of delivering a service to him that will carry the appropriate durability. The client, for his part, tries to make a similar kind of assessment as to the credibility of the organization's promise-to-pay. Hence, a "contract" is made which in fact may be faulted at a later time: it may turn out that during the course of the transfer of values, either the client or the organization may acquire some additional information about the other that reveals that the original contract, as agreed upon, was a poor one. The client may decide that he agreed to give too much for too little; the organization may make a similar judgment, or decide that the original values brought by the client were too meager, and so on.

We are all familiar with these processes in the product market place: automobile salesmen and building contractors are very knowledgeable in this area. Customers continually return with the complaint that thus-and-so wasn't completed or was completed improperly. Organizations, on their side, often contend that the customer gave them a bad trade-in, failed to make payment when due, and so forth. In extreme cases, sometimes with the intervention of a third party, the old contract may be voided and a new one made. The probability of the issuance of a new contract favoring additive rewards to the client is enhanced when the organization has made a large initial investment and the client a small one—and more markedly so where it is a buyer's market. Contrariwise, the probability that the new contract will be on the side of the organization is heightened where the reverse is the case—where the client has thrown much into the bargain and the organization rather less. For example, one *may* be able to get an air conditioning unit installed in one's new car, free of additional charge, but only if the dealer's showroom is glutted with cars and you've given him only a vague promise to buy. In periods of high societal growth value this possibility exists more frequently than many can imagine, so it's rather surprising that many customers don't take advantage of this fact.

Much the same occurs in service organizations. First, let us assume that most professionals try to do the very best job for the client of which they feel themselves capable. Given that assumption, as they gain more knowledge about their clients during the exchange process, they may often feel obliged to break the original bargain and make a new contract.

Take hospitals as a type-case: a patient may enter surgery upon the advice of his general practitioner in order to have a hernia corrected. During the course of surgery the doctor might discover some other malady, heretofore unknown. And if this new difficulty is thought to be operable, chances are very good that the contract will be drastically altered while the patient is still under anaesthesia. The doctor might, of course, consult first with some of the patient's original co-signers—husband, wife, etc.—in order to gain some validity for changing the rules of the game unbeknownst to the other party. But even if the doctor frankly informs the patient of the desirability of a new contract, it is unlikely that the patient will not agree to it. This is one additional function of professional dominance and client trust in organizations.

This is not only a limiting case, but it's a pure case as well wherein the new contract presumably is of equal value to both the client and the organization. The patient gets a larger increment of health than he had bargained for, while the medical profession has performed its self-correcting function properly, and perhaps even provided a valuable learning experience for interns and medical students. The fee may or may not be larger.

More asymetrical examples instantly come to mind: in the prison, for example, a convicted felon may have agreed to a plea of guilty under the informal agreement that he would stand a fine chance of parole in a couple of years. But *he* might violate the conditions of the contract while in jail, so of course the penal authorities go on to enforce the stipulations in the small print. More poignant, however, are those instances in which the medical or psychiatric staff of the prison (mustering whatever professional dominance they can) determine that the inmate is "not ready" for discharge, and hence void the original agreement in its entirety. In more extreme cases, extrinsic forces such as governors, legislative commissions, and the law might simply throw the old values out the window and rig a completely new market. For instance, I recall an incoming State Commissioner of Paroles pronouncing that during his term in office it would be just about impossible for a Negro or a prisoner with a tattoo to get a parole!

Mixed types, of course, are somewhat more complex. In universities, for example, we have invented conditional admission status in order that professors can change values quite arbitrarily. This may work either to the advantage or the disadvantage of the student—flunked out or awarded a fellowship. The first tends to be more frequent when there are too many students; the latter when there are too few. The very same forces, it should be said, are at work on individual staff members, too.

In psychiatric hospitals—elite ones especially—the renegotiation of contract is most confused indeed. It is difficult to assess the client's original worth in the first place, so it is hard to come to an agreement as to the conditions of value transfer. And as hospitalization continues, values shift almost daily. This may have something to do with the rich patient sub-culture remarked upon so frequently in these kinds of places.

By and large, the organization as against the client is advantaged in the matter of contract re-write. Organizations which contain dominant professions are even more so. And this may help to explain further why it is that most occupations seek for the dominance of which Freidson speaks; the organization simply obtains an edge on its self-correcting functions.

One fact which relates to what has been said is that the organization is able to redefine values and make them stick, while the individual client is not. In short, institutions can define what ought and ought not to be worth offering to clients. And since they can mobilize more resources than can the client, they can limit the service choices available to potential clients and members. Further, because this is a collectivized business, in servicing *people* (these individuals being the constituent personifications of the social system) organizations in fact service society, and thereby create social structure.

It is important, now, to consider just what is meant by servicing in the generic sense. I want to emphasize this point rather heavily: *the delivery of a service constitutes a correction of a perceived defect in values carried by clients.*

In this sense, prisons punish and sometimes correct gross deviations from norms. Hospitals try to correct imperfections in the human body; schools and universities attempt to fill lacunae in both knowledge and social commitment. Some psychiatric hospitals make an effort to perfect one's skills in interpersonal relationships. More radical psychiatric enterprises try to bring the client back into the world of consensually validated reality. Churches—somewhat less so now than in the past—are called in the service of the soul—widely acknowledged to be in need of servicing.

An additional conjecture of some importance is that the delivery of corrective services such as these are of imputed value not only on technical grounds but on moralistic grounds as well: stupidity is not

221

only technically unnecessary, it is downright wrong. Illness is not only correctable, it also undercuts the social structure. Hallucinations induced by LSD are not only deviations, they are threatening to the social fabric. Lack of religious involvement not only devalues one, it undercuts primary group relations.

The same has been shown to be true for product transactions between businesses and customers. For as Veblen pointed out long ago, wealthy consumers are widely acknowledged to be not only economically astute, but somehow more virtuous. The relation of this to the "Protestant ethic and the spirit of capitalism" is so obvious as to require no further comment.

One remaining question: just because these same functions are now provided by complex organizations and no longer by family, kin, peer group, and situs, does this mean that the entire social fabric has remained fundamentally unaltered? The answer must of course be an emphatic *no*.

What has changed is the basis, and the source of conceptions, of the "good," the "plausible," the "valuable," as well as the processes by which goodness, plausibility, and values are distributed among people. These, I take it, can all be subsumed under the concept of the division of labor and are what social structure is all about.

Due largely to some of the social forces discussed in this book—rigging the market, trust, domination, exchange, differential resources, etc.—social economics in general—goodness, plausibility, and value have become the property of complex organizations.